Voices of Practice

VOICES OF PRACTICE

Narrative Scholarship from the Margins

Sean Michael Morris, Lucy Rai, and Karen Littleton

Hybrid Pedagogy Inc.

Washington, DC

Contents

Foreword

Maha Bali

"[M]arginality [is] much more than a site of deprivation; in fact...it is also the site of radical possibility, a space of resistance. It was this marginality... as a central location for the production of a counter-hegemonic discourse that is not just found in words but in habits of being and the way one lives. As such, I was not speaking of a marginality one wishes to lose – to give up or sur-render as part of moving into the center – but rather of a site one stays in, clings to even, because it nourishes one's capacity to resist. It offers to one the possibility of radical perspective from which to see and create, to imag-ine alternatives, new worlds" ~ bell hooks (1990, p. 149-150).

I like to play solitaire sometimes to relax. My grandma taught me as a kid, and it's nice to have that little part of her with me into adulthood. There's something about the routine, but not routineness of it, physi-cally holding the cards, the light decision making, that helps empty my mind a bit when it's been going full speed. Or double speed as was the case since the pandemic hit, which for some reason made me start play-ing solitaire sometimes. I often play it on the couch somewhere, and my daughter often sits on the other side and plays along if she is in the mood. The other day, she decided to play solitaire on her own. I was sit-ting far away, but when I passed by to watch her playing, I noticed that she was playing solitaire upside down, you know, as if someone else was the main player, and she was on the sidelines helping out? I laughed so hard at the time (she's still a little mad at me for laughing at her expense), but when I thought about it, I realized something important. She had learned to play solitaire as a secondary, not main player, and solitaire, from her perspective, looked this way: upside down. It never occurred to her to reverse it now that she was the primary player. My laughing at her stems from my privilege of having been the primary player for a long time. I didn't see it from her perspective. I found it odd, quaint, amusing.

But now I realize that this is what it means to be on the margins and to internalize that perspective. And in reality, that's not a bad thing, though people in the centers, those who dominate, want us to think that our goal should be to become "like them", to lose that marginal perspective.

The other day, I was emailing back and forth with someone I'd met online and whose job title I didn't know. I had given a Hyflex workshop for faculty at her institution, after she had met me at an online conference, and I was asking her to write a letter supporting an award I was applying for. Her letter was incredible, but what shocked me was discovering her title "Dean of Online Learning," an administrative position at her institution. I told her I was amazed because she was so open and friendly and caring, and we don't often associate those characteristics with administrators, unfortunately (I want to admit this is me stereotyping, of course, because I know many kind administrators). She told me how she was a first generation college student and marginal in so many ways, but took the decision to take on admin roles in her institution. I thought about how all the ways she was marginal, all her experiences and her history, probably helped shape the kind of person she is today. Holding on to that is possibly what makes her a more compassionate administrator than those who have had a life of privilege. Or who would rather leave their marginality behind as they gain power and become closer to the center.

I'm one of those people who is semi-privileged. I learned later the term intersectionality. I am a woman in my part of the world, with all the oppression this brings on, who studied a STEM field, with all the gendered challenges there, but I also grew up relatively financially privileged, with well-educated parents. I am an Egyptian working at an American institution, so I know my "place" as a postcolonial and am reminded of it every day, in the inequalities created by the hybridity of my bicultural institution, and my need to assert all the Westernized parts of myself in order to succeed there, and more as an academic in the world, but never quite reach everything. To always aim to challenge academic gatekeeping, but never truly dismantle it. The master's tools, of course.

I'm a faculty developer, currently an associate professor of practice, an alt-ac (alternative academic), who remembers being a staff member at the Center for Learning and Teaching, given responsibility for advising faculty members with years of teaching experience, but having no authority or power to do so. I have much more power now, as a PhD holder, as a professor (albeit non-tenure-track, only teaching one course a semester). I will never forget being told "Yes, but what about the real faculty?", something my first boss used to ask whenever I gave my viewpoint on something as an academic who teaches. She was my mentor and she meant well. I don't think she meant I wasn't "real" as much as that I was radical in my views about pedagogy.

Gaining power in position, I still maintained a kind of peripherality in my perspectives, which I held onto with a passion that would not budge "because the institution wanted me to" talk about outcomes or rubrics or plagiarism detection or learning management systems / virtual learning environments. I would have none of it. I fed on my own dissent. And everyone would know it. Of course I wasn't like the "real" faculty. I was way ahead of them. Well, not really. But I was different from many of them. I gained confidence when I got my PhD. People suddenly considered me more credible. I swear I was saying these things for years, and then once I was awarded a PhD, suddenly, I was more credible. It was baffling. I say all this, and I am quite vocal, but sometimes I do things that I think might get me into trouble and I don't talk about them too loudly in my institution. Only on Twitter and my blog and in front of the world.

Although, in reality, when you get close to people and you whisper to them about how you never really follow the calendar or order on your syllabus, you realize that many others don't either. They just don't talk about it out loud. Even when I used Twitter and my blog and all my public scholarship to spread my views, to find communities who think like me, to help me grow in the direction I wanted, even after I became invited for keynotes and invited to contribute to book chapters, and expert panels and advisory boards, and what have you... I always wondered if they chose me as a "token international" or "token global South" person. I never knew where exactly I belonged, in my own institution, and in my online spaces. So I kind of went and co-created my own, like Virtually Connecting, and Equity Unbound, and worked with others on developing a practice of Intentionally Equitable Hospitality (Bali, Caines, Hogue, Dewaard & Friedrich, 2019) that strives to ensure our spaces are hospitable to those furthest from justice, that they have a say in what kind of table they want to work on and whom they want to invite to it, under which terms.

Still, despite all kinds of microaggressions I have faced at my institution (especially by older males when I was early in my career), and despite systemic inequalities I try to fight in whatever capacity I can (as a member of the American Association of University Professors, a senate member, writing publicly or locally, in conversations, in my own classes and workshops), I still love being in academia, fighting for the rights of students, white collar staff, blue collar workers, and even sometimes faculty when they've been harmed. I still believe that education matters and can make a difference in the world. We know this when students contact us years later to check on us or tell us how we've impacted their lives. I knew it when during the coronavirus pandemic, faculty who had worked with my center for years felt calmer than most people, felt somewhat more prepared for this moment, and rolled up their sleeves to help out.

Marginality can be visible and invisible. Class background. Sexuality. Chronic or temporary disability when you're communicating online. Those at the centers can never see what it looks like to be on the margins, because the world looks different from the margins. Like when my daughter saw solitaire upside down.

This unique perspective, especially on suffering and in-betweenness, is why we need to have voices from the margins in our textbooks, teaching our classrooms, managing our educational institutions and representing us in media and in government. This is why Kamala Harris matters so much to girls, black women, Asians and immigrants in America. Because cognitively understanding systemic inequalities does not prepare you to truly understand the experiences of being marginal/ized.

Margins are a site of struggle and resistance. And bringing voices from the margins together and centering them, diverse as each one of them is, has been one of the most eye-opening learning experiences I have ever had, and requires a tremendous amount of epistemic listening because it is not what we are used to reading daily, and it challenges our perspective on the world.

I still don't always know where I belong, as some authors in this volume will tell you. I started to see how my "imposter syndrome" is a result of interpersonal oppression intermingled with institutional and systemic oppression, and that we internalize this oppression to an extent that can be harmful. But it also makes us who we are, and gives us a unique perspective that is worth holding onto.

References

Bali, M., Caines, A., Hogue, R.J., DeWaard, H.J., & Friedrich, C. (2019). Intentionally Equitable Hospitality in Hybrid Video Dialogue: The context of virtually connecting. *eLearn*, 2019.

Bessette, L. S. (2020, Nov 2). The staff are not ok. *Chronicle of Higher Education.*

hooks, b. (1990). Choosing the margin as a space of radical openness. Yearning: Race, gender, and cultural politics. *Between the Lines.* pp. 145-53

Prusko, P. & Kilgore, W. (2020, Dec 1). Burned out: Stories of compassion fatigue. *Educause Review.*

Introduction

Sean Michael Morris, Lucy Rai, and Karen Littleton

This volume is about personal stories, episodes from the lives of educators which have in some way shaped their practice. More specifically, it is about educators with roots in professional practice prior to entering academia. Throughout this volume authors ask themselves how professional and personal stories have shaped them as educators and scholars? How can reflections on such stories deepen our understanding of teaching and learning?

The origins of this book grew from serendipitous conversations between Karen Littleton (Professor of Education at The Open University), Lucy Rai, (Director of PRAXIS, the scholarship and innovation centre for the Faculty of Wellbeing, Education and Language Studies) and Sean Michael Morris (Instructor at the University of Colorado Denver and founder/director of Digital Pedagogy Lab). During these conversations we were troubled by several shared reflections on the relationships between professional practice, scholarship, the status of knowledge and how it is conveyed and valued. With diverse backgrounds in social work, education and creative writing, we shared a deep belief in the value of stories of human experience, in creativity and in disrupting institutionalised norms of what 'counts' as scholarly writing. From this grew an ambition to collate a collection which would give a voice to scholars who were quietly drawing on extensive reflections from their professional practice to inform their teaching and scholarly research, but perhaps not being able to meet institutional targets or influence international discourses. We wanted to honour and authenticate these experiences as valued scholarship, scholarship which often struggles to surface within traditional academic publishing.

Voices of Practice values practitioner stories as important, and under-valued, scholarly tools. Institutionally, the scholarship of teaching and learning can be situated as of secondary significance to research. Ravecca and Dauphenee (2018) propose that scholar-narratives have the potential to disrupt 'fortress writing' which privileges traditional hierarchical scholarship research and the power relations associated with it. They suggest that narratives represent 'invitations to engage in scholarship, where the aim is not to prove us right and debunk other positions but to open the scholarly terrain to different sorts of questions that are not dependent on solidifying and defending a "position. (Ravecca and Dauphenee 2018, p127). Disrupting this tendency to solidify and defend is potent, as it enables the co-creation of permeable and expansive 'dia-logic spaces' (Wegerif, 2019) characterised by: diversity and plurality; fluidity and provisionality—as well as curiosity, questioning and creativ-ity. Our hope is that the miscellany of voices and perspectives, in inter-play throughout this book, will resource new dialogic spaces and seed inquiries powerfully rooted in professional 'funds of knowledge' (see Moll, 2019, p. 131). By raising up and valuing these diverse voices (and the allied funds of knowledge) we can transform our institutions as epis-temic communities; our fields of inquiry and also "people's 'self-defin-ition, self-expression, and self-understanding" (see Esteban-Guitart and Moll, 2014: p. 37).

This volume thus challenges the notion that knowledge arising from empirical research is, by default, of greater value than scholarly reflec-tions by practitioners on their own stories. It applies a concept of critical pedagogy which Dominguez, drawing on bell hooks (2000) and Friere (2015), suggests 'explores in detail the everyday personal, affective, embodied, relational, livingloving aspects of critical pedagogical praxis' (2019, p.19).

The volume is divided into three sections, each responding to the voices of the authors and the stories they tell. The organisation of the collec-tion, in other words, circulated around the writers rather than the other way around.

Reflections on Identity

This volume seeks to put identity and voice at the centre of our conver-sation about scholarship, and so we open with stories—narratives from the margins—that set a stage for a collection that paints a backdrop for academe not traditionally exposed. These stories demonstrate the ways in which narrative scholarship is a vulnerable, political scholarship, one that reminds us about the human and humane behind the academic. In these chapters, authors reveal truths behind cultures of exclusion and inclusion, experiences of belonging and not-belonging, advocacy and going it alone. These reflections on identity set the stage for much of the work done by the chapters which follow.

Pathways to Academe

Just as many of the voices in this collection have found themselves pondering the how, what, and whether of being a scholar, challenging in their own ways the definition of "scholar" and the sphere(s) in which that term applies, so have they etched their own unique paths into the scholarly life. Academe is a landscape well-guarded and gated, kept from non-traditional scholars and practitioners by expectations set around the prestige of publishing, the advanced degree—and, more subtly, the postures of scholarship which are in nature like a secret handshake, signals for a closed society that meets in plain sight. In these chapters, authors detail their beginnings, the paths they have chosen to follow, or which they have been given no choice but to trail blaze.

Scholarship and Practice

Once inside academe, how does the the marginal scholar "fit in"? What opportunities are given for utilizing the skills learned in their fields within the more theoretical landscapes of traditional scholarly discourse? Here we see a deeply affective narrative of the balancing act of being both a practitioner and an academic, of making one's way simultaneously inside and outside of the university. In these chapters, authors discover their voices—voices informed by trying to fit in, by learning to code switch, or by recognizing the performativity of life and career inside the ivory tower. These chapters close the collection with implicit questions about the way forward for scholar-practitioners in academe.

***

This is a book that has arisen from processes of sustained collective reflection and deep interiority, as much as professional practice and action in the world. Engagement with it thus requires, of you the reader, a willingness to 'meet (this) intensity with intensity' and to dismantle the protection of assumption, projection and authority (see Winterson, 1995 p.10). It demands a willingness to un-know and to listen—with openness and absorbed attentiveness – to the cacophony of voices that resonate throughout the book. Let these voices bring you to an intersubjective place of encounter and allow them to astonish, disquiet and disrupt. Our hope is that much of the writing in this book jars. The jarring should prompt us to question: the ways in which scholarly thinking is communicated and given valence; the stories that we hear and value; the ways in which ideas are shared and the diversity of identities that find a voice.

References

Dominguez, C. (2019). Each and everyday, love us free: Critical pedagogy as a living-loving praxis. *International Journal of Critical Pedagogy*, Vol. 10 (1).

Esteban-Guitart, M., and Moll, L. C. (2014). Funds of identity: a new concept based on the funds of knowledge approach. *Cultural Psychology*, Vol. 20, 31–48. doi: 10.1177/1354067×13515934

Moll, L. (2019). Elaborating Funds of Knowledge: Community-oriented practices in international contexts. *Literacy Research: theory method and practice*, Vol. 68 (1), pp. 130-138. doi: 10.1177/2381336919870805

Ravecca, P. and Dauphinee, E. (2018). Narrative and the Possibilities for Scholarship. *International Political Sociology*, Vol 12(2), pp. 125–138. doi: 10.1093/ips/olx029.

Wegerif, R. (2019). Towards a dialogic theory of education for the Internet Age. T*he Routledge International Handbook of Research on Dialogic Education*. London: Routledge.

Winterson, J. (1995). *Art Objects: Essays on Ecstasy and Effrontery*. New York: Vintage International.

PART I

Reflections on Identity

We open with stories—narratives from the margins—that set a stage for a collection that paints a backdrop for academe not traditionally exposed. These stories demonstrate the ways in which narrative scholarship is a vulnerable, political scholarship, one that reminds us about the human and humane behind the academic. In these chapters, authors reveal truths behind cultures of exclusion and inclusion, experiences of belonging and not-belonging, advocacy and going it alone.

But I Teach Now

Anne Butterworth

I'm a nurse...

This is what I say when I meet people.

I don't say I'm a lecturer.

I don't say I'm a researcher.

Sometimes I add, *...but I teach now...*

The lanyard knitting jumble on my shelf at home illustrates my multiple identities. Jack of all trades, master of none? A traitor to some; an imposter or interloper to others.

Have I lost my way? One foot in both camps, not fully accepted by either.

Am I spread too thinly and doomed to fail? Or am I the cat that's got the cream?

My main job titles over the last few years tell me I am an academic, who also practices clinically. So why do I not feel like a real academic?

I'm a Nurse...

My identity as a nurse is well-rooted and cannot be disentangled from me. How I think, behave, feel reflects the knowledge, attitudes and values of my profession; and my experiences caring for patients and relatives. A nurse can spot another nurse at 20 paces, we give ourselves away. Communication nuances—medical language, levels of knowledge and nods of understanding. We can try and hide it, but invariably we're found out.

...but I teach now...

Teaching has always been part of my role as a nurse—through mentoring students and junior colleagues. It is an expected, integral part of practice, but seemingly an irritation to some. For me, the look of wonder and enlightenment in the eyes of those you have taught is a reward akin to the gratitude of a patient for care received. I can rationalise that teaching a number of healthcare students can exponentially impact on patient care, beyond my own individual capabilities to provide a good service. So why can I not leave practice alone?

Perhaps because clinical currency is a valuable commodity—a unique selling point within academic schools that have lost touch with practice-realities

But I know that students feed hungrily on my clinical stories; that narratives weave themselves through their interpretations and translations of their own emerging professional identity. They bring practice alive, make it meaningful and worthwhile, remind us why we are here. They trigger memories of shared experiences, enable connections between the theoretical and the practical. They promote professional values, and aspirations to make a difference and provide the best possible care. They highlight the human elements—patient and family experience; nurse experience. What happens when things go wrong, when we make mistakes (as we all will). For there is little within the text books to prepare you for this.

There is a reason why hearing first-hand experience is so powerful. Why ex-addicts make the best mentors for those working through their dependency problems. It's because the rawness and detail and emotion in retelling, no, reliving your relevant experiences makes you believable and people want to listen. You are then offered wisdom status and respect.

But this status is fragile and easily lost if the experience is not deemed to be relevant, or you are not seen to be believable.

Some of my colleagues who have not practised in a long while also tell stories; but there is always a concern that old tales become outdated anecdotes—interesting to hear, but not necessarily translatable to the rapidly changing healthcare landscape of today and tomorrow. I am wary of this and selfishly do not want to lose my practice wisdom status... and so I continue to nurse.

I don't say I'm a researcher.

When I apply this logic to my research role, I already know I have no standing in this arena. I joined the party late, prioritised practice and small scale audit projects, failed to engage with academic audiences and make myself known. With eminent colleagues all around me, I can only hope to slowly chip away and learn as much as I can. I have a lot of catching up to do.

It is hard to adjust back to junior status with years of senior practice behind you. And how strange it seems that academic roles are so very different despite the homogeneity of grading bands, titles and job descriptions. 'Lecturer' can mean mainly 'teacher' or mainly 'researcher' with their accompanying organisational positioning (researcher as more highly regarded). Indeed, in a previous 'teaching practice-focus' post, we worked entirely separately from those with a research-focus and were institutionally denied the right to research through unmanageable teaching workloads which did not acknowledge time for scholarly activity. Researchers were protected by their teaching-light contracts and did not have to witness their colleagues' marginalisation and exclusion. On the other hand, perhaps we were spared the competing stresses involved in a more evenly distributed teacher-researcher role, as in other HEIs.

Perhaps this experience is partly what motivated my PhD studies—to have what I couldn't previously have. Or simply the desire to become a legitimate academic—as a researcher, a more highly regarded member of the team; am I seeking to climb the academy class ladder? Nurse done good and becomes a doctor...

I don't think that's it. Well it's certainly not the main reason.

As a nurse, I still enjoy the new things I learn every shift. Just as I love telling stories, I love hearing them too, as wide-eyed as one of the students in my classroom. From patients, relatives, colleagues... and it reminds me why I'm there, with aspirations to make a difference.

Now imagine that I can transmit the first-hand experiences of patients and their families to a much wider audience. It's not just my experience now, being translated by my students to try and develop their individual practice, but multiple voices from practice harmonised together and heard on a greater scale with the aim of effecting broader change.

This may well be a romanticised view and a vast over-estimation of possible impact. But the transitions between my different roles of practitioner (micro), teacher (meso) and researcher (macro) have shown me that different levels of activity have the potential to not only improve at that individual level, but to cumulatively inform.

Just as practitioner wisdom provides currency in the classroom, it also oils the cogs of the research process. A foundational understanding of the field of practice can provide much needed insights in the planning of a research project—from idea inception (what needs researching?) through to what types of data could be obtained, and how (how could we know/find out?). Researchers must make relationships with others in order to conduct research, perhaps not dissimilar to the therapeutic relationships made in practice. You need to connect to others to find out things about them—the process is called assessment within clinical practice, and data collection within research, but their intents are the same.

My own preferred methodology, ethnography, relies on making connections 'in the field' in order to make sense of the 'everyday' experiences of others. 'Living' amongst them (through participant observation), clearly requires acceptance, but a level of cultural knowledge can help to ease the way. Practitioner wisdom might then act as my passport, helping me to negotiate access through the fortressed borders of healthcare research. Might it also act as membership ID when recruiting research participants ('ah, we can trust you, you're one of us?'). Time will tell...

The Urgency of Practice

Today I have really started to understand the potential devastating impact of Covid19, and my loyalty is swung immediately back to nursing. Family members, friends and colleagues look to me as a clinician—to give them answers, to translate, to predict. But I am as baffled as they are, obsessed with crumbs of information emerging from whatever media I can consume. I want to say bugger off to my studies and my teaching job at the minute. I want to roll up my sleeves, wash my hands for 20 seconds, put on PPE and get stuck in. What am I waiting for?

...Because I can't. I made my choice and I'm committed to other things. Things I know I do really believe in, things I really want to succeed at. But over the course of a few weeks the world has changed...is changing. And I need to play my part, be useful.

Now I need to be a legitimate nurse, the adaptable citizen that contributes the correct skills at the correct time. I'm on a seesaw and the balance is tipping the other way.

Here I go...

...and 'Ouch!'

I have banged my head against the restraining walls of my academic life—but can't they see what's important right now? I need them to let me go... my professional governing body (the NMC) has put the call out... Your country needs you...

Practice... that's what's important now. Students of healthcare are being recalled back into practice, 'all hands on deck' to help the sinking HMS NHS. The teaching and research can wait (since I don't have the skills to research Covid19 cures).

...and so I campaign until I'm released. Some colleagues are supportive, and some are irritated with my choice and my persistence. I have a month. The hospital is still bleeding whilst my usual out of hours practice area is coping well—all primary care is telephone based now and not seeing patients face to face has freed up some slack in the system. Locums have no clinics to run, so pick up extra out of hours shifts. They are well staffed. They don't need me there. I'll help at the hospital.

...but... 'Ouch!'

I have banged my head against the protective walls of the NHS—but can't they see what's important right now? I need them to let me in! Why does it take so long, applications, HR processes, mandatory training... I have 24 years experience as a qualified nurse! But my clinical currency does not extend to acute hospital wards where this war is being raged. It's 20 years since I worked on a hospital ward, so of course they need to check my credentials. And so I follow the processes, with a gentle nudge here and there, and undertake the 'Covid skills for qualified nurses' training week.

Back as a novice (junior status again), alongside newly qualified student nurses and those returning to practice I refresh my knowledge of the trade. Once on the wards, I am gently guided by some experienced and battle-weary colleagues who accept my presence but cannot understand the choice I have made to return to practice. Patients are curious—I am a rare specimen, an oddity—and they feel the need to thank me for being there (though they never see my face beneath the blue mask and laboratory goggles). Yet it is I that gains the most from my return. I bear witness. I see. I hear. I feel. I share. I try to 'do'.

But I act with a different level of freedom than my nurse compadres. They have a fear of the new, the unknown …'I've never done that before...' They are socialised through initiative-inhibiting policies that reduce the risk of negligence and liability. This limits the art of their practice but also protects them through offering the security of clear boundaries. Where gaps occur in competency and skill in my field of vision, I can offer a bridge—experience as an advanced practitioner and a teacher has given me a different view of the unknown. Rather than fear it, I embrace it as learning opportunity. I can quickly judge potential risks and mitigate these as needed, adapting practice to meet the presenting need. So this is how I help during my pandemic NHS leave. At micro level, but using both my clinical and academic skills—a hybrid, an adaptable practitioner.

As researcher, I observe.

As teacher, I facilitate.

As practitioner, I do.

As human, I feel.

I need to be all these things.

My journey is not from practitioner to academic. There is no end-point destination here. Yes, I am spread too thinly at times (expert at none!). My multiple identities make me an oddity and I am not a fully-fledged member of any one group. I know this compromises me—I cannot reach the dizzying heights of either clinical or academic expertise because I am flitting between disciplines. My ego will just have to accept that. Instead of feeling inferior in either arena, I will try and hold my head high, knowing that I offer something different—the expertise of generalism and the ability to transition and translate between different worlds. Academics are increasingly having to 'justify' their art through not only research-excellence frameworks, but through teaching-excellence and impact agendas. Maybe there will therefore be a greater need for those who can cross borders between practice and academia. A place where I can belong.

An Incomplete History of My Teaching Body

Arley Cruthers

My summer pandemic semester was very successful, except that I lost feeling in the left side of my face. Tingling spread from my temple, down across my cheekbones, across to my jawline. A static in the message. But though it didn't get better it also didn't get worse; I could still smile and raise my arm above my head, so my doctor chalked it up to stress.

The semester had been a flurry of parenting and grading and lesson planning and playing "Johnny, Johnny, Yes Papa" for the millionth time because I just needed to get one more paper graded and webinars and conferences and committees and extra projects and why did I say yes to that and how did I think I had time for that and iced coffee. I spent my teaching life saying words like 'grace' and 'patience' and 'community' and 'care.' I typed those words at 5:30 am alone in my living room: the side of my face tingling, distracting me as I tried to tell a student that I was sorry to hear they weren't feeling well, and of course, take the time you need with the assignment.

Me: I pared down my course to emphasize slowness and reflection and care. I designed it to ensure that all students had access and choice and agency.

Also me: And I didn't take a day off in 5 months to do it.

Teaching fully online, my body has never existed less in the minds of my students, and yet here it was: inserting itself into the conversation, refusing to be ignored.

***

When I started teaching, my difference was written all across my body. Students could hear the cadence of my crutches as I walked down the hall. When I wrote on the board, they hung off my forearms, clanging against the chalk ledge and jolting daydreamers awake. I literally wore my disability on my sleeves.

It was not possible for me to be a floating head, a disembodied voice projecting knowledge. I was a body first and foremost: a walking (crutching?) Laurel and Hardy routine. I knocked over coffee, left chalk handprints all over my black pants, tripped, fell, and picked myself back up again. This physicality found its way into my pedagogy. My first foray into experiential learning came because I couldn't stand up long enough to lecture.

I couldn't forget my body, and in doing so I seemed to remind students of their own. My office hours were full of students grappling with their own physicality: everything from weight gain to broken bones to sexual assault. Maybe my disability humanized me. Maybe they simply thought that a woman who knocks her coffee over more days than not was in no position to judge them. Whatever the reason, my disability appeared to be a way into my students' lives, and I was grateful for their trust.

In fact, teaching was perhaps the one place outside of the wheelchair sport community where my disability was an opportunity to build connection, not to stand out as a mark of difference. This visibility was not usually a gift. When you have a visible physical disability, you become a magnet for other people's stories. I walked on crutches, had one leg that pointed backwards, was over six feet tall, a Paralympian who could bench press 245 pounds. It was not possible to hide in a Midwestern college town. Mostly people just wanted to talk. They would stop me on the street to tell me that they'd broken their leg once in 1993 and they knew how I felt, or that they had an aunt with MS, or there was a girl in a wheelchair in their class — did I know her? — or that they had arthritis, schizophrenia, bipolar disorder. They would just blurt it out in the grocery store aisle, and I would be left holding this fragment of a story in my hands.

I did not know about pedagogy, but I knew that I was a place where students brought their stories. And I knew that my background as a wheelchair basketball coach made me think about writing in a physical way.

I planned my lessons the way I planned my practices. When students did in-class activities for fun in my classroom, their voices rang out. But then I'd get their final reports and the verbs would be dried out: all passive voice and airless nouns. Something got lost from my classroom to the page. Somehow, the confidence I had tried to build in them withered when exposed to genres.

I knew the feeling. When I graduated in 2009, I couldn't fit myself into a genre either. I was a Paralympian turned MFA student turned teacher turned coach. A Canadian in America. A disabled woman poised to have the hip replacement that might change her life. A wheelchair athlete leaving the career that sustained her for over a decade. How do you put that in job materials? How do you turn it into a pitch?

So, I came back to Canada. My surgery went wrong and I lost the ability to walk. After my second novel came out, my writing voice turned to dust. But I was still a quick writer, a collector of stories, a person who'd spent years trying to explain my sport to my academic friends and my academics to my sport friends. And so I turned myself into a communications and marketing manager for wheelchair sports. I could not write my own stories, but I could tell those of others. I could disappear into other voices for a while.

***

When I acquired a disability at age 11, I became grade-obsessed. I hated the slow, syrupy way that people would talk to me and I was mortally offended that the school assigned me an aide. I did not need help, I told anyone who would listen. I was a straight A student. I was a Very Smart Girl. Gifted and talented, in fact. I found a copy of a Grade 12 biology textbook called "Investigating Aquatic Ecosystems" and made a point of taking the book everywhere, noting that, uh, excuse me, would a girl who needed a teacher's aide be able to tell you the difference between freshwater and marine ecosystems?

Grades were objective, I thought. Grades did not discriminate. I graduated with one of the highest averages in the history of my school, winning full-ride scholarships to every school I applied to. It escaped my attention that my quest for perfection had not changed how people saw me. Everyone saw the wheelchair; no one saw the GPA.

Wheelchair basketball seemed to be the only society-sanctioned way that a disabled person could get respect, so I forged myself into the perfect supercrip. No one I knew used their disability as an 'excuse.' I didn't want to be one of 'those' disabled people. When I fractured my spine during exam season of my third year at the University of Victoria, I dragged myself to class. I wrote my final papers in a haze of Tramadol, but never thought to ask for an extension. I didn't need anyone's accommodations, thank-you-very-much. Paralympians don't need accommodations.

I kept going.

I pushed through and through and through.

I was comfortable with being uncomfortable.

During graduate school, my femoral head collapsed and a hip subluxation sent me to the emergency room; I went to my graduate seminar with the hospital bracelet still on my arm. I was in agony, and when the professor asked me to pass her some papers, I slid them down the table so I wouldn't have to stand. She complained to the department head that I'd "passed a piece of paper to her in a disrespectful manner," and I had to have a meeting with her. No professor or administrator had cared that I'd been in the hospital, that my femoral head had collapsed, that before I went to sleep I had to hook one foot over the other and tie them together so my hip didn't sublux while I slept. The minute my body didn't perform as expected, I'd been punished. That's just how academia was.

When I started teaching, my feeling was that if I could go to class after my femoral head subluxed, no one else had any excuse. I had strict attendance and extension policies. The more my body projected vulnerability, the tighter I held on to power. It doesn't matter if you tell students about your hip replacements if you won't give them an extension because they didn't contact you within the window of time you specified.

***

After graduate school, I left teaching and collected jobs: too many jobs. Previously, I'd excelled at playing wheelchair basketball, getting good grades, and writing novels. Those were all gone. My desire to prove myself remained. I worked at Paralympics, World Championships, Canada Games, Para-Pan Am Games. I did communications, marketing, public relations, crisis communications, major games communication. I loved wheelchair sports. I loved writing. I loved writing about wheelchair sports. My new job had all the adrenaline and stamina of my wheelchair basketball career, but I could do it from the bleachers.

I loved and loved and loved.

I worked and worked and worked.

I pushed through and through and through.

And eventually, I burnt out.

***

As I molded myself into a parasport communicator, I was also hard at work on another project: passing as able-bodied. I had surgery to revise the failed hip replacement, then did extensive gait retraining. I tried pilates, body sculpt, weight training, hiking. I flailed away to "shed and shred" workout videos. Every time I walked, I thought "heel, toe. Heel, toe" until one day, I could do it without thinking. My cane spent more and more time in the trunk of my car, and eventually collected cobwebs in my parents' basement. I even did two half marathons.

The half marathons felt like a success story, but they were really another form of burnout: a relentless carving of my body. But through those years, my limp became hardly noticeable. People stopped telling me stories. One day, I caught a glimpse of myself in a glass storefront. I saw an able-bodied person staring back. I still felt disabled, still had chronic pain, but it was secret now, submerged under my skin. In this new body, I returned to teaching.

***

Though the Paralympic movement is often framed as one that empowers disabled athletes, my former teammate Danielle Peers notes that Paralympism actually "perpetuate[s] the power relationships and social contexts that sustain disability" (Peers, 2012). In their discussion of supercrip representation in Paralympic sport, Silva and Howe note that "supercrip narratives may have a negative impact on the physical and social development of disabled individuals by reinforcing what could be termed "achievement syndrome"—the impaired are successful in spite of their disability." (2012). In fact, Ian Brittain and Aaron Beacom cite a study that was done after the London 2012 Paralympic Games by the charity Scope, which found that 22% of disabled people said that discrimination against them had actually worsened because people held them to the standard of Paralympians. (2016)

Just as seeing Paralympians 'overcome' their disabilities appeared to make the British public less sympathetic to disabled people who did not conform to this ideal, my Paralympic sport experience actually made it more difficult to empathize with the differences I encountered in my students. Both academia and Paralympic sport had taught me a model of humanity that was hierarchical, that those whose minds and bodies could not conform to the system deserved to be excluded from it, that you could only become excellent by besting other people.

When I returned to teaching, students had no idea about my history unless I told them. For the first year, I didn't say anything. I was aware of how much easier my life had gotten since people had begun to see me as able-bodied. Would I have been hired if I'd still walked using forearm crutches? It was hard to say. But I was precariously employed and basking in my newfound abled privilege. Besides, I was supposed to be teaching business writing, not sociology, not disability studies. My office hours were emptier. I could no longer rely on my body to do the job of projecting vulnerability, so I would have to think intentionally about how to create a classroom dynamic where students were comfortable sharing.

I began by creating a small assignment called Question of the Day, where I would post a question on the learning management system five days a week. The goal was to get students to do more low-stakes writing, to play with words. There were questions like "Do you believe in ghosts? Why or why not?" or "Tell me about a time when you did something brave." To encourage them to participate, I answered every question myself. I began to write about my chronic pain, my wheelchair sport career, my hip replacements. Slowly, my students responded in kind: with stories about their car accidents, their decision to remove their hijab or wear one again, their experiences surviving terrorism attacks or dealing with the death of a parent. And gradually, my office hours began to fill up with stories again.

In *Teaching to Transgress*, bell hooks writes "When education is the practice of freedom, students are not the only ones who are asked to share, to confess...When professors bring narratives of their experiences into classroom discussions it eliminates the possibility that we can function as all-knowing, silent interrogators." (p. 21). When I present as disabled, my body confesses. It shares that there is a story to me beyond my "all-knowing" academic persona. But my Question of the Day activity was virtual: a place where my body did not exist at all, and I got to write it into being. I still tightly controlled the image my students had of me.

Many of the stories I told during Question of the Day were the ones I used when I was a wheelchair basketball motivational speaker. I'd learned from wheelchair basketball that the only story about my disability that people were interested in was the one where I acquired a disability, got introduced to wheelchair sports, then won a Paralympic medal. Anything else was whining. So, the small moments of vulnerability I shared during Question of the Day perhaps encouraged students to trust me more, but they did not unsettle any hierarchies.

My academic career, coupled with my career as a Paralympian, had taught me that my body was something to be overcome. I believed in rigor, and by rigor I meant meanness with an academic face. I believed that every unkind thing I did to my body was honing me into a true academic, an elite athlete, someone who deserved to be at the front of the class or the top of the podium. So, my disability was therefore a site of pedagogical tension. My disabled body projected vulnerability, but my lived experience as a Paralympian made it hard to turn this vulnerability into a pedagogy of care.

***

I was lucky to attend Digital Pedagogy Lab in 2017, just as I'd spent a year softening my stances. I was ready for a shift in my pedagogy. In part, I'd been reading more about the pedagogy of writing instruction and I realized many of my stances weren't defensible. But I was also in the middle of a rough pregnancy. I constantly had to leave class to throw up. For the first time, I couldn't punish my body into submission. Once, I just stopped the class and said, "I'm sorry, I am pregnant and sick and you all will have to bring the energy today." And they did. It was one of the most productive class sessions I'd ever taught. That first true moment of vulnerability opened the door for more.

Creating a pedagogy of care required unlearning many of the lessons I'd absorbed about disability. It required thinking not just about my own body, but the systems that police our bodies, that exclude, marginalize and enact violence on some bodies. It required me to see grades not as objective, but as deeply subjective. It led me to ask my students more questions and to be open to the answers, even if those were uncomfortable. And it led me to see all of the assumptions wrapped up in the word 'rigor.' In *An Urgency of Teachers*, Jesse Stommel writes:

> It seems easier to far too many teachers to imagine that students do work the way machines do — that they can be scored according to objective metrics and neatly compared to one another. Schools, and the systems we've

invented to support them, condition us to believe that there are always others (objective experts or even algorithms) who can know better than us the value of our own work. I'm struck by the number of institutions that for all intents and purposes equate teaching with grading — that assume our job as teachers is to merely separate the wheat from the chaff. (2019, Kindle Locations 578-582)

Academia and Paralympic sport had combined to teach me that success was about conforming to a standard that had been set in advance. In most parasports, athletes are ranked by a classification system, which seeks to 'level the playing field' by assigning a number to each athlete based on the impact their disability has on their ability to compete. In wheelchair basketball, athletes are ranked from 1 (for most impairment) to 4.5 (for able-bodied or 'minimally disabled') and a team can only play 14 points at one time.

I had seen the problems with trying to sort people with wildly different disabilities and experiences with disability into static numerical categories, but it took an introduction to critical pedagogy to apply this logic to grading. I began to imagine a class where students could show their learning in multiple ways, where they could play a role in designing assignments and shaping the direction of the class, where the hierarchy between student and teacher was not to be reified, but reimagined.

For most of my teaching career, I'd puzzled over why my students' writing lost its vitality when they wrote reports and essays. But when I began designing with students, I learned that they were trying to leave their own voice behind and leap into the language of reports and memos. They could not imagine themselves being enough, so they had to put on a suit of business-ese. Now, I can design assignments that say your experience is welcome, your voice is welcome, your perspective is needed, you are enough.

***

"You are enough," I write to my students at midnight, my To Do list beside me up to 56 items.

"You are enough," I whisper to my daughter as I kiss her hair.

"You are enough," I tell my coworkers. "This job is hard. You're doing so well."

"My apologies for the delay in responding," I begin my emails. "Sorry for the hold up!" I rub my jaw, feeling the strange tingling. Pedagogies of care, I say. For whom, my body responds.

Am I practicing pedagogies of care or am I trying to be the Best Teacher Ever: doing away with grades for other people, but still chasing that gold star myself?

There is the unlearning, and then there is reimagining. I have done the former.

My body has shifted in and out of disability, I have shifted in and out of the academy, my pedagogy has shifted in relation to my students, but what hasn't shifted is my insistence that the only way forward is working hard: that with enough energy and effort, I can excel despite. Despite a body in pain, a pandemic, not enough childcare, not enough, not enough. Compassion is something I offer to other people.

In *Care Work: Dreaming Disability Justice*, Leah Lakshmi Piepzna-Samarasinha defines disability justice, in part, as "insist[ing] that we organize from our sick, disabled 'brokenbeautiful' (as Alexis Pauline Gumbs puts it) bodies' wisdom, need, desire." (2018, p. 21)

Sustainability is one of the tenets of disability justice:

> We pace ourselves, individually and collectively, to be sustained long term. We value the
> teachings of our lives and bodies. We understand that our embodied experience is
> a critical guide and reference pointing us towards justice and liberation. (p. 26)

My numb face: stress sanding away my body's edges. My white, cis disabled body existing in the academy doesn't liberate anyone. It doesn't challenge the system. It burns itself up for the chance to be included. Cripping my pedagogy is the only way forward.

Piepzna-Samarasinha again:

> This is about some of the ways we are attempting to dream ways to access care deeply, in a
> way where we are in control, joyful, building community, loved, giving and receiving,
> that doesn't burn anyone out or abuse or underpay anyone in the process. (p. 33)

***

This is an essay without an ending, written at 2 am. This is an essay sub-luxed, shifting, which makes sense because one of my ribs is subluxed right now. The muscles around it tug when I breathe deeply. This is an essay that tugs towards the body, that resists wrapping up neatly. This is enough, it begins to say. This is enough. You are enough.

References

Braye, S., Gibbons, T., & Dixon, K. (2013). Disability 'Rights' or 'Wrongs'? The Claims of the International Paralympic Committee, the London 2012 Paralympics and Disability Rights in the UK. *Sociological Research Online*, 18(3), 1–5. https://doi.org/10.5153/sro.3118

Brittain, I., & Beacom, A. (2016). Leveraging the London 2012 Para-lympic Games: What Legacy for Disabled People? *Journal of Sport and Social Issues*, 40(6), 499–521. https://doi.org/10.1177/0193723516655580

Cherney, J. L., Lindemann, K., & Hardin, M. (2015). *Research in Communication, Disability, and Sport. Communication & Sport*, 3(1), 8–26. https://doi.org/10.1177/2167479513514847

Silva, C. F., & Howe, P. D. (2012). The (In)validity of Supercrip Representation of Paralympian Athletes. *Journal of Sport and Social Issues*, 36(2), 174–194. https://doi.org/10.1177/0193723511433865

hooks, bell. (1994) *Teaching to transgress :education as the practice of freedom.* New York : Routledge,

Michalko, R. (2001). Blindness enters the classroom. *Disability & Society*, 16(3), 349-359.

Peers, D. (2012). Patients, athletes, freaks: Paralympism and the reproduction of disability. *Journal of Sport & Social Issues*, 36(3), 295-316. doi:10.1177/0193723512442201

Piepzna-Samarasinha, L. L. (2018). *Care Work: Dreaming Disability Justice.* Arsenal Pulp
Press. Kindle Edition.

Stommel, J. and Morris, S. M. (2019). *An Urgency of Teachers: the Work of Critical Digital Pedagogy.* (Kindle Locations 1992-1996). Hybrid Pedagogy Inc. Kindle Edition

Nostalgia and Identity

Sara Clayson

The starting point for this exploration of loss, nostalgia and identity as a teacher in Higher Education came from a moment of serendipity. When I first took this job, then based at one of the regional outposts of the Open University, I inherited my own office—my first room-of-one's-own—from my predecessor. She was taking early retirement and shedding a great deal of the stuff from her own teaching past so left behind a bookcase full of unwanted books. "Take whatever you want and dump the rest", she said with a dismissive wave of her arm before happily skipping out the door to her new life. One of those books was Claudia Mitchell and Sandra Weber's *Reinventing Ourselves as Teachers: Beyond Nostalgia* (1999). Although I couldn't immediately see a use for it, the title sounded interesting, so it got to stay on the shelf alongside my own collection moved in from the shared office along the corridor. Very shortly afterwards the university announced the closure of most of its regional bases and so started the traumatic process of watching beloved colleagues being made redundant, years of work being shredded and our branch of the university getting dismantled. I was one of the lucky ones—I got to keep my job—but my place in the university became almost entirely virtual, accessed from my spare bedroom at home. I became a 'designated homeworker'.

Mitchell and Weber's book got moved to a bookcase in my new 'workplace' at home, where it gathered dust for another year or so, and meanwhile I yearned for the old days—the routine of leaving the house and walking to the university office, daily collaboration with colleagues, the satisfaction and sense of purpose simply from being at work—and watched my professional identity disappear. My identity as someone who teaches at a university, as an academic with things to say, started to exist only in the past.

***

I'm with a student who I've been worrying about on and off since day one. I don't know what she looks like, I've never heard the sound of her voice, I know nothing about her apart from her name, address and date of birth. But I know that she's struggling. "I'm struggling," she tells me in her emails.

I say, "Have you got a mic, Kelly? Can you talk to me?"

A message pops up, Kelly Bennett is typing....

Kelly Bennett: No.

"OK, we can do this in the chat box."

Kelly Bennett: Thank you.

I miss my old office when my students would sit in a grubby arm-chair that I'd pulled in from the Staff Common Room, while I made them a cup of tea. Waiting for the kettle to boil, I'd take the opportunity to give my plants a drop of water. Perhaps I'd make a silly joke about the atrocious weather or the noise from the roadworks outside, and then I'd turn back to the arm-chair, mug in hand, and smile. We would talk, we would spread books and papers over the little coffee-table and, heads together, work through it. An hour later there would be another student back on track.

Now, I speak to my screen and she types into a little box.

"Can you tell me how far you've got with this assignment? Have you managed to read chapters 4 and 5?"

Kelly Bennett: Yes.

"OK. So, have you started writing up your notes for the assignment?"

Kelly Bennett: Yes.

"Good. So, what's preventing you from finishing it, do you think?"

Kelly Bennett: I'm struggling to put it together.

I do my best, try to be reassuring, try to clarify what she needs to do, try to give her confidence, "You can do this Kelly," I say. But I wonder if it is enough.

"How do you feel now Kelly? Has that helped?"

Kelly Bennett is typing....

Kelly Bennett: Thank you so much.

I've been hanging a lot on that little 'so'—it's all I've got to cling to. I hope she's going to be OK.

***

My resistance to virtual working—and to the wider changes in Higher Education—is certainly not uncommon amongst academics in twenty-first century universities. Research exploring the challenge to professional identity provoked by the increased use of technology to deliver teaching in universities has documented anxieties that mirror my own (Hanson, 2009; Smith, 2010; McNaughton and Billott, 2016). As centres of knowledge, universities have always been at the crux of the old and the new, acting as depositories for old knowledge and tasked with creating new knowledge. But the use of technology in teaching—so frequently referred to as 'innovation in teaching and learning'—makes many academics uneasy for a wide range of reasons, threatening their sense of themselves as teachers in the Academy. As McNaughton and Billott's study (2016) concluded, the academics they spoke to were "caught in a tension between preserver and innovator, they found it difficult to successfully integrate new and old professional narratives" (p. 655). What I am attempting to present here is an integration of old and new professional narratives by reflecting on them through the lens of nostalgia. In this way, nostalgia is offering a means to both preserve and innovate in my academic life and for my professional self to evolve in my virtual workplace. Nostalgia, it seems, can enable me to re-imagine and emphatically re-state myself as an academic who cares (Smith, 2010).

Working from home provokes an interesting collision of the professional and the personal. My office now houses bookcases on which texts on my professional practice and research interests sit next to my crafting books and classic novels. I frequently work with the cat asleep in her little bed at my feet, those feet wearing fluffy slippers. When I get tired looking at a screen, I nip into my garden and pull a few weeds. I cook a proper meal at lunch-time. For so many teachers, teaching is a vocation that speaks to their personal lives as much as their professional lives; I am used to taking a version of my personal self into professional contexts but I'm less secure hosting my professional self in my home. I feel more exposed, vulnerable and emotional. Dealing with difficult situations, which may simply have provoked frustration when I worked in an office, can now reduce me to tears. I cry, swear, jump with joy, and squeal with excitement far more openly than I did when surrounded by colleagues. Working from home is foregrounding the personal in my professional practice in new ways that I had not anticipated but which also allows a freer expression of emotional vulnerability and, in turn, acknowledgement of my feelings of nostalgia about the Open University. As Bonnett (2010) points out, while public expressions of nostalgia are vilified, seen as conservative and anti-progressive, private nostalgia and attachments to the past "speak not only of a shared humanity but also a shared vulnerability, an emotional range that includes love, loss and loyalty" (p. 6). Indeed, in the field of Psychology, it is widely acknowledged that nostalgia is good for us (Sedikides and Wildschut, 2017). Far from being an insidiously conservative emotion that is unhealthily inward-looking, nostalgia is a nurturing emotion that contributes to our resilience, our sense of self and our relationships.

My nostalgia for the OU starts with my experience of being an OU student. I've been lucky enough to have a wide range of student experiences—my first degree was at a polytechnic in the early nineties (a 'post-92' university by the time I graduated), a concrete monstrosity in a run-down area on the edge of the city. That building has recently been bull-dozed as part of the regeneration of the locality and the university has moved to premises closer to the city centre. I also studied at the grander 'Russell group' university of my home city, set on a romantically leafy campus through which students are still cycling, in duffle coats and long scarves, in the twenty-first century. But in-between those experiences, whilst working as a primary school teacher, I studied with the OU and as soon as I went along to my first tutorial, on a Saturday morning in a local Adult Education college, I felt at home. When, a few years later, I saw a job advertisement for tutoring posts at the OU, I jumped at the chance and so started a career in HE I could never have imagined.

***

It's a Tuesday evening in late-October in the early 2000s and I'm walking alone across an unfamiliar university campus trying to find the room where my first tutorial of the year will be taking place tonight. Most of the staff and students have already gone home so I'm seeking out the security guard to let me in.

"You with the OU?," he says with a grin when I knock on his door. "The tutor's not here yet but I'll take you to the room."

"I am the tutor," I laugh. This happens a lot. At 32, I am the average age of a typical OU student.

He unhooks his keys and locks the door behind him. "Well, they've already started to arrive, one of them was here an hour ago. They must be keen."

He takes me along endless corridors to our room—and walking through the empty buildings, with locked, darkened classrooms, always gives me a little thrill. That feeling I used to get when being in school at night—maybe for the Christmas disco or some other special event—being out of bounds somehow, somewhere you shouldn't be. It feels a little bit subversive, a little bit disruptive. We're hi-jacking other institutions' premises and using them to teach students who wouldn't have been allowed through the door otherwise. At the end of the corridor is our room for this evening and as I reach it I can see a couple of people are already awkwardly sitting at desks, urgently looking through their bags or flicking through the textbook, anything to avoid having to talk to the other. I'm trying to guess which of my students they are—we've already spoken a couple of times on the phone but this is the first time we'll have met properly.

"Hi," I say, walking into the classroom. "I'm Sara and I'm your tutor." They look up at me and then at each other, visibly relieved—I'm not what they expected. And it's started.

***

I feel nostalgic for the radicalism of the Open University and for the forward-thinking political climate that enabled it. We're not the only institution that has undergone worrying changes in the last couple of decades and the effects of managerial, neo-liberal, HE policies on academic identities has been well-documented (for example, Clarke, 2010). Yet, nostalgia itself has a radical potential, disrupting modernity by challenging progressive narratives (Bonnett, 2010). While the virtual world can seem to be relentlessly rushing forward, stopping to look back can remind us of what we want to take into the future.

Is it possible to take the radicalism of the OU—its desire to disrupt power structures and social hierarchies—into the future? That radicalism is rooted for me in the relationships I have with my students—they are people I want to get to know and care about. I want to see them do well, to have their lives enriched by learning, their horizons broadened and their opportunities to be increased. However, while I started this process of reflection longing for a face-to-face connection with both my colleagues and my students and while, then, I wholeheartedly agreed with Hanson's conclusions that "resisting e-learning is in fact an entirely rational act designed to strengthen a relationship based on 'being there' with the students" (p. 564), I am discovering that maintaining my core professional values does not have to mean a return to face-to-face contact or a physical office in a university building.

Moreover, if "nostalgia can be a site of creativity, danger and transgression" (Bonnett, 2010, page 10), then can we use it to critique received wisdoms about virtual working? We need to scrutinise how students behave in the virtual learning environment, how they use it to study and how they learn. Are students actually more passive when studying online? Are they really 'disembodied'? Are we? I have come to recognise that an important way in which online tuition can be subversive and disrupt the power dynamic is by giving students power over their learning environment.

***

It's my first online tutorial of 2019—this year, for the first time, I will only be teaching online. As it's the first session of the year, I have a large turn-out and the atmosphere is lively and buzzy. I'm excited too. I want to show my students how actively engaged I am, so that they have the confidence to actively engage. There's my photo in the corner of the screen, I switch on the webcam and wave 'hello'. Now I'm telling them about where I am and ask them to do the same. A couple of people say 'hello' over their mics—this is very promising. Usually no-one wants to speak. It feels like it's going to be a good session.

My way of managing online tutorials is to plan every second of them with military precision—they are tightly controlled operations with a printed off list of instructions next to my keyboard detailing exactly what I need to say and which button I need to press at every stage of the evening. I can't wing it, there's no room for spontaneity or improvisation. But about half-way through the session I realise that something is happening that I didn't plan for. In encouraging the students to engage—in showing them how to draw on the slides, add text in a colour of their choice, talk to each other in the chat box—they are starting to take the controls. I realise that they have taken the wheel from me and are now in the driving seat.

It starts with a rogue smiley face that appears on a slide that didn't ask for student engagement.

"Oh, OK" I say, "It's good to see you're getting the hang of the draw tools. Anyone else want to add something?" I figure I might as well go with it and see what happens but I have a rising tide of anxiety starting in the pit of my stomach. This is not on the script—what if this descends into complete chaos? More smileys appear—and then a scribbled flower. I have no idea if this is one maverick having fun or several. I don't know what it means—the smileys don't really relate to what I had been talking about or the content of the slide. I can't read this situation at all—is this meant in good spirit? Or am I being mocked? It's extremely unnerving. I decide to take it as a joke and laugh, "OK, let's move on—what was I talking about? Ah yes..."

I click onto the next slide and try to pick it back up. And then a message pops up in the chat box.

Laura Jones: Anyone else finding this a weird experience?

I'm mid-sentence when I notice it so I decide to finish the end of the sentence before commenting and see what happens in those few seconds. Is 'anyone else' going to respond? My heart is in my mouth, waiting for the imagined tirade of criticism that's about to hit. It's the 'anyone else' that disturbs me—does this address include me or not? To what extent am I visible to these students? Are they about to start talking about me as if I'm not in the room? Have all my attempts to give myself some kind of presence been futile?

Multiple attendees are typing...

Laura Jones: Good though.

Chris Boyle: I'm enjoying it – it's fun!

***

Resisting inevitable change is futile—and the COVID-19 pandemic appears to have accelerated a shift to online working way past the point of return. However, nostalgia has taught me that what is "worth arguing about, even fighting for" (Halpin, 2016) is not face-to-face contact with my fellow scholars or a physical university campus. Rather, I think nostalgia is allowing me to imagine a better virtual environment—a virtual environment that allows real connections with students, meaningful working relationships between colleagues; in short, an environment that acknowledges that we are human. I'm reminded again of hooks, when she says, "Acknowledging that we are bodies in the classroom has been important to me, especially in my efforts to disrupt the notion of professor as omnipotent, all-knowing mind" (hooks, 1994). Acknowledging that we are still bodies in a room—as are our students—when interacting online is becoming an important part of my approach to teaching in the VLE.

***

The cat is scratching persistently at the door, before letting out a long and low wail. I'm in the middle of trying to explain the difference between the theories of Vygotsky and Piaget to a group of students anxious about the forthcoming assignment. The noise is distracting and I'm losing concentration, "Sorry everyone, I just need to let the cat in." A moment later, she's settling down on the chair next to me, I'm slipping my headphones back on and am greeted by the sound of laughter and chatter. While I've been gone the students have started sharing stories of their own experiences of studying at home.

"I've got my baby on one knee and my laptop on the other."

"Me and the kids are all sat round the kitchen table—they're doing their homework, while I'm in this tutorial. We're helping each other study."

"Sorry about the dog barking. He's just seen a pigeon in the garden—he's scared of them, ha ha!"

I join in and tell them about my cat, "She wanted her hot water bottle. Yes, I know. She has her own hot water bottle."

"I love that!"

"Ha ha, little princess!"

We spend a few minutes laughing about the surreal experience of online working—in homes with families and pets vying for our attention, in dining rooms and kitchens, or sat on the bed.

After the tutorial, I take a picture of the cat—now fast asleep with one paw stretched round her hot-water bottle, hugging it to her chest—and post it on our Tutor Group forum. The next morning there are photos of other pets, other tables or floors strewn with course books in other messily human homes. I realise that the virtual world has enabled a new kind of connection to be made—a glimpse into each of our physical realities of distance learning. This is different from the connections I had with students in the past, meeting on the neutral ground of a 'Study Centre'. It's closer.

***

Nostalgia for my past working life has shown me that the values at the heart of my identity as an academic are unshakeable—a commitment to the radical potential of Higher Education and a desire to achieve what hooks calls a "mutual recognition" with my students (1994). While I have been grieving the loss of my professional identity, I've realised that it was never lost at all but has been there all along. I'll be carrying that into the future.

References

Bonnett, A. (2010). *Left in the Past: Radicalism and the Politics of Nostalgia.* London, Continuum.

Clarke, J. (2010). So many strategies, so little time... making universities modern. *Learning and Teaching*, 3:3, 91-116.

Halpin, D. (2016). Dancing with eyes wide open: On the role of nostalgia in education. *London Review of Education*, 14 (3), pp. 31-40.

Hanson, J. (2009). Displaced but not replaced: the impact of e-learning on academic identities in higher education. *Teaching in Higher Education*, 14:5, 553-564.

hooks, b. (1994). *Teaching to Transgress: Education as the Practice of Freedom.* Abingdon, Routledge

McNaughton, S. M. and Billott, J. (2016). Negotiating academic teacher identity shifts during higher education contextual change. *Teaching in Higher Education*, 21 (6), 644–658.

Mitchell, C. and Weber, S. (1999). *Reinventing Ourselves as Teachers: Beyond Nostalgia.* London, Falmer Press

Sedikides, C. and Wildschut, T. (2017). Finding Meaning in Nostalgia, *Review of General Psychology*, Vol. 22 (1), 48–61.

Smith, J. (2010). Academic Identities for the Twenty-First Century. *Teaching in Higher Education*, 15 (6), 721-727.

Suddenly There's Me

Sean Michael Morris

1969 – Suddenly, there's me.

1978 – Paper deliverer for the Boulder Daily Camera

1979 – Created school newspaper for Columbine Elementary

1983 – Library shelver at Boulder Public Library

1984 – Shipping and Receiving at Into the Wind kites

1988 – Sales clerk for WaldenKids

1990 – Residential assistant, Johnson House, integrated living for autistic and developmentally disabled youth and adults

1992 – House cleaner

1992 – Undergraduate assistant, Metropolitan State College of Denver Writing Center

1993 – Resume writer for Career Services, Inc.

1994 – Bachelor of Arts in English, Creative Writing

1995 – Customer service representative at Amrion, Inc.

1996 – Direct mail copywriter for Amrion, Inc.

1998 – Public Relations director, PrideFest Denver

1999 – Creative Director, Achieve.com

1999 – Web Communications Manager, ServiceMagic.com

1999 – Instructional Designer, Alva Learning Systems

2000 – Quality Assurance Manager, Alva Learning Systems

2002 – Graduate teacher, Creative Writing Program, University of Colorado at Boulder

2003 – Lead Graduate Teacher

2004 – Adjunct instructor, Community Colleges of Colorado Online

2004 – Documentary videographer, untitled Michael Jackson project

2005 – Master of Arts in English, Creative Writing

2005 – Certified Massage Therapist

2006 – Program Chair, Community Colleges of Colorado Online

2007 – Assistant tour manager, Matt Morris

2009 – Self-employed life coach

2012 – Director of Educational Outreach, Hybrid Pedagogy

2012 – Managing Editor, Hybrid Pedagogy

2014 – Co-Founder, Digital Pedagogy Lab

2014 – Digital Community Coordinator, SEIU

2015 – Senior Editor, Education Research at Instructure

2016 – Instructional Designer, Office of Digital Learning, Middlebury College

2016 – Director, Digital Pedagogy Lab

2017 – Co-Author, Bramblepaw (forthcoming)

2017 – Lead Instructional Designer, Division of Teaching and Learning Technologies, University of Mary Washington

2018 – Director of Digital Learning, University of Mary Washington

2018 – Author, An Urgency of Teachers

2019 – Senior Instructor, Learning Design & Technology at the University of Colorado at Denver

Interwoven Trajectories

Susannah Wilson

Wenger (1998) describes identity as "multiple interwoven trajectories," linking membership to different communities simultaneously. This essay is partially a plea for help: my trajectories are unravelling. Halfway through the first year of a Professional Doctorate, if I can use the term 'academic' at all, it must be preceded by 'novice'. But I'd be more comfortable altogether if I didn't use the term at all. I have failed, so far, to weave the identity of academic into my sense of self.

I had not realised that the new role of researcher would be so difficult to incorporate. I knew—instinctively as well as theoretically—that our identities are being negotiated all the time; I had recognised and embraced my multiple role identities of (amongst others) mother, teacher, wife, friend, runner. The prospect of adding one more role identity into the mix did not ring any alarm bells. I was unaware, at the time of applying for the programme, that the specific identity roles of teaching and research are cited as potentially in conflict with each other (Xerri, 2017); I was blissfully unaware of the tensions I was about to unleash within my sense of self.

I am not someone for whom identity is usually an issue—especially with reference to my teaching role. My identity as a teaching practitioner is clear, strong and confident. I have a confidence in the decisions I make as a practitioner—a confidence bordering on arrogance, sometimes—born of my experience and the knowledge I have in my field. I deliver training as a practitioner to other teaching practitioners; I lead a curriculum area and feel confident in my ability to do so. But within my identity as a practitioner, my social bases of identity (Barnard, 2019) clearly align: characteristics of my personal identity (I am logical; I am systematic; I am capable) align well with my role identity of practitioner. As a researcher, the same cannot be said. In the role of researcher, I am filled with self-doubt—I flit between ideas and I do not feel capable of the task ahead. I am scared of this role as much as I am excited by it—and I do not feel competent to achieve.

There is a certain irony in these struggles, in that my proposed research area includes an exploration of the extent to which student identities affect the learning and feedback processes. So I read widely about how successful learning is linked to identity (e.g. Brzeski, 2017). I note that learners' understanding of their "possible selves" (Dornyei and Ushodi, 2009) are fundamental to how they act, and how the 'possible self' must include the concept of success within their study. I read, I note, I make links between the literature and my own learners—and I fail to see my reflection in these portrayals of learners.

My confidence in my practitioner identity is born also of the support I receive from practitioners around me. Family gatherings are overrun with teachers, of different subjects and at different levels; many of my closest friends are teachers. I am a teacher living in a world where teachers and the practice of teaching is valued.

Perhaps this more clearly explains the tension that I now experience. It is the practice of teaching that is valued: the hard graft of working with learners; the responsibilities of leading an exam class; the relentless, physically onerous task of performing in the classroom, hour after hour, day after day. Our discussions about our roles are filled with battle metaphors—we are 'frontline' teachers; we face an uphill 'battle' getting our learners to engage. We are fighters, we are grafters, and our work is hard. There is a "sanctioned importance" (Behar, 2014, p. 37) to my work as a practitioner, and I enjoy working in the knowledge that my efforts are sanctioned by my community.

This new identity of researcher does not sit well within these circles. Hargreaves (1996, cited in Rose, 2002) suggests that the agenda for educational research is set by researchers, not practitioners, and this leads to a gap between the requirements of practitioners and the work of researchers. The requirements of academic research—that it is "abstract and theoretical, or in some other way generalised" (McIntyre, 2005)—render it irrelevant to the complex specificity required by practitioners. Knowing this, perhaps, forms the basis of my struggles. Barnard (2019) suggests that identity tensions result from "seeking a unique sense of self while simultaneously wanting to belong and be accepted by others." I want my work to be accepted and understood by the teaching practitioner community that I hold so dear, and my experiences within it suggest that this will not happen. So I will not talk about it—and I resolve these issues by highlighting my practitioner identity—revising my identity to decrease the prominence of researcher.

But, again, my proposed research area should help me. I underline and highlight references to the difficulties students face in expressing their identities in new learning communities (Wenger-Trayner et al., 2015), and how these struggles may jeopardize their learning successes. I walk into the kitchen, make a cup of tea, reflecting on all of this, and fail to recognise myself as a learner researcher in this picture. I stretch my arms, shaking out the student-shaped tensions in my shoulders—and if I do recognise myself, I fail to take the advice that I know I would otherwise give to any other student. I have a blind spot, and am in danger of taking myself out because of it.

We all have such blind spots—areas of weakness which we cannot or will not acknowledge. If I were to interrogate mine, I would note that they relate to a desire to avoid posturing. But my definition of 'posturing' is skewed, I think. When lining up at the start line of a running event, I'll avoid stretching for fear of being the ostentatious athlete. I teach literature, but will avoid conspicuous reading of poetry in a coffee shop—even if it is just preparation for my next class. I don't judge my fellow runners for limbering up; I'm envious of the person on the adjacent table reading Keats with their coffee. And I'm the one who risks an injury, or an insufficient understanding of the canon. But I'm too self-conscious of how it will appear if I were to adopt the same behaviours: I cannot engage with these aspects of my identity in public. My understanding of 'posturing' means that I jeopardize my own success, for fear of appearing to overreach.

Similarly, I reject a public display of 'doctoral researcher' behaviours. Travelling back from the first residential weekend of my studies, I was desperate to look through the reading list, review my notes, read some of the papers towards which I had been directed. I had all the paperwork safely stored in a purple translucent folder, along with a packet of post-it notes, two biros in different colours and a set of highlighters. I wanted to start reading, annotating, making links, planning. But I knew that the label 'doctoral researcher' was emblazoned on the front of the handbook; that the headers and footers were trumpeting 'Doctorate in Education' and 'Professional Doctorate'. In the very busy, very public space of the train carriage, I was physically confined in the window seat: my belongings squeezed onto my share of the table in front of me and another passenger trapping my access to the aisle. I was equally confined in my actions. I was torn between wanting to start my doctorate study—wanting to engage with the ideas and the processes and the content—and not being able to engage with it publically.

Again, though, if I could have but got on with my work, I would have found some reassurance within the literature. Charmaz (2017, p. 36) suggests that qualitative research is "infused with" Anglo-North American viewpoints and assumptions, which favour the individual over the collective. My focus is on an individual here—myself—and my fear of "losing face" is common in the context of the research I hope to do. If I could have but got on with my work, I could have been engaging with these ideas. Such self-consciousness could be moulded into the methodological self-consciousness and reflexivity which qualitative research requires. But, sitting on that train, I couldn't get over the barriers which I had erected for myself. Now, halfway through that first year, they still cause me to stumble.

And yet. My inner researcher is secure in her knowledge that identity is not fixed. She waits, patient and steadfast, for these tensions to dissolve; for me to resolve these issues and allow her back in. She is right to do so. I have just once managed to articulate these concerns clearly, during a meeting with a supervisor designed to provide further academic and pastoral support. I blurted out my concerns—the words tumbling out in fragments, in incomplete sentences complete with emotionally charged gurning and flappy hands. I was unable to gauge his reaction properly—the Skype software unable to fully overcome the barriers to communication caused by our distance—and I was suddenly filled with dread that he'd take my concerns seriously. I had thought that I was speaking a truth—but I realised that, should he recommend that I give up my researcher identity, I would be bereft. I realised that she had become part of me; I realised that I would fight to weave her closer into me. I hope we'll get there.

References

Barnard, A. (2019). Developing Researcherhood: Identity tensions and identity work of women academics reflecting on their researcher identity. *Forum: Qualitative Social Research*, 20 (3).

Behar, R. (2014). *The Vulnerable Observer*. Beacon Press.

Brzeski, A. (2017). Literary practices, identity and engagement: integrating multifaceted identities of college students to support learning. *Research in Post-Compulsory Education*, 22 (3). Pp. 391-408. doi: 10.1080/13596748.2017.1358519.

Charmaz, K. (2017). The Power of Constructivist Grounded Theory for Critical Inquiry. *Qualitative Inquiry*, 23 (1), pp. 34-45. doi: 10.1177/1077800416657105.

Dornyei, Z. and Ushioda, E. (2009). *Motivation, Language Identity and the L2 Self.* Channel View Publications.

McIntyre, D. (2005). Bridging the gap between research and practice. *Cambridge Journal of Education*, 35 (3), pp. 357-382.

Rose, R. (2002). Teaching as a 'research-based profession': encouraging practitioner research in special education, *British Journal of Special Education*, 29 (1).

Wenger-Trayner, E. et al., (2015). *Learning in Landscapes of Practice.* Abingdon: Routledge

Down the Rabbit Hole of Race-Gender-Culture-Being-Faculty: Confessions, Distortions and Extortions

Jeanette Maritz and Paul Prinsloo

Whether to testify or confess, that is the question. The difference between 'to testify' or 'to confess' is guilt. So, when does a testimony about finding oneself in the nexus of race-gender-culture-being-faculty become a confession of guilt, or remain, somewhat academic and aloof, a testimony? We wish we knew. We want to testify about how our race, gender, and culture impact our being faculty, but our testimony is, inherently, a confession of guilt. But, let us start with a confession, and then you, the reader can decide whether it was a testimony or a confession.

Some confessions come easier than others, while other confessions have to be extorted, and in the process, instead of 'truth', a distorted version is offered as appeasement, to stop the torture and/or stay the execution or, in the context of higher education, to get the appointment or tenure, promotion, appease the committee or get the grant. There is ample evidence of how specific metrics and information—such as race, culture, class, performance and gender—play a role in higher educa- tion—whether referring to the cult of performativity (Kenny, 2018), the role of gender and/or gender in an appointment, tenure, promotion (Croom, 2017), or research productivity (Mayer & Rathmann, 2018) feel- ings of being imposter (Akerman, 2020), or just overall, never good enough (Smith & Ulus, 2019). And how confessions are extorted, and how often we would offer confessions in the annual rituals of perfor- mance management, or applications for promotion or tenure.

We offer our testimony/confession of our entanglement in race-gender-culture-being-faculty, knowing well that our testimony/confession may be rejected based on questioning how two privileged, tenured professors can complain when compared to the plight of untenured and ever-more precarious faculty? In offering this testimony/confession we may also be accused of being 'snowflakes, of "white tears" (Moon, 2016), white fragility (DiAngelo, 2018), or that our testimony/confession is an example of "self-indulgent tellings" (Youdell, 2010, p. 92). (Also see Westcott, 2004). We acknowledge the burden of our race-gender-culture-being-faculty on our experiences as tenured faculty may be nothing compared to more precarious and more/differently burdened intersectionalities. We also cannot ignore how our experiences of being white, queer and gay are, despite us sharing a gender, very different from the experiences of, for example, queer and black individuals and groups (Craven, 2011). Our subjectivities and our (dis)comforts cannot be de-contextualised and disentangled "from all class, cultural, racial and economic dimensions" and come-into-being "as an axis of experience and identity" (Ringrose, 2007, p. 480).

We testify/confess in/through/with our entanglement in our race-gender-culture-being-faculty in the context of post-apartheid South Africa where each of these identity tags—being white, queer and gay, Afrikaans and tenured faculty (and their combinations) has its own set of "meaning, penalties and responsibilities" (Chinua Achebe in an interview with Appiah, 1995, p. 103). In this confession/testimony we reflect on the meaning, penalties and responsibilities flowing from the incommensurability of our identities (Boellstorff, 2005) on a continent where one cannot be African and queer and gay (Epprecht, 2013), from a culture where one could not be a member of the 'volk' ("nation") and queer and gay (Falkof, 2018), and where our whiteness made the penalty for these combinations, worse, and, at the same time, less impactful.

In this confession/testimony, we own up. We testify. We confess.

We are two white queer (Jeanette) and gay (Paul) scholars that arrived in academia by accident or default, rather late (in age) and while having the necessary qualifications to be granted tenure, completely unprepared. For both of us, it was a new beginning, in more than one sense. Our new beginnings overlapped with South Africa's dramatic move into democracy, a Constitution and Bill of Rights that created space for our gender, but also the Truth and Reconciliation Commission's (TRC) process, that held our race and culture, and the generations preceding us to account (Falkof, 2018). As the TRC's processes unfolded, we were confronted with what was done during apartheid in the name of our race, culture and language. Of course we were not innocent bystanders. There were no bystanders. Only victims and perpetrators (Minow, 1998). Vengeance and confession were in the air. Vengeance was replaced by reconciliation. Confession was replaced by a Rainbow nation imaginary and rhetoric (Walker, 2005).

The Rainbow rhetoric left whiteness unscathed and as our gender was protected by the Constitution and Bill of Rights we no longer had to confess our gender to employers, our faith communities and society at large. There was no guilt, no need for (more) confessions, only testimony.

Our relationship started with a testimony, a defiant claim. At an academic writing workshop, Paul introduced himself to Jeanette with a simple "Hi, I am Paul and I am gay". As we both negotiated to make sense of how much of identities (and personal histories) we could share, we navigated our way into collaborating in various research initiatives, bringing our identities into a public, scholarly domain and focus. While much of our personal histories and identity were not known to our students or colleagues, we 'came out', making sense of the nexus of our genderised scholarly identity and we wrote our genderised scholarly identity into being (Maritz & Prinsloo, 2015). We testified.

As we became more established in our careers and identity as researchers, South African higher education was (and continue to be) faced with the slow pace of transformation which did, at that time and in many respects, still, not only referred to the fact that the majority of professors at South African universities were white, but also that the curricula were white, and the imaginary of what African universities should represent, was still saturated with white ontologies and epistemologies. Students started to speak out and for many months, if not years, South African higher education was turned upside down as (mostly black) students and staff vented not only their frustration with the continuing colonial project, but also dreamt of a different world of epistemic and economic justice and freedom (Badat, 2016).

As if history was repeating itself we are now, once again, faced with owning up to what was (and continue to be) done in the name of our language, our race and our culture. We confessed. We testified. We navigate our way and negotiate meaning between not speaking, being alliances to a struggle that is not ours, but a struggle that holds us (and should hold us) accountable and living with many of the unresolved tensions in our own understanding and praxis of racism. It often feels as if we are in a state of perpetual confession, as if there is always a new audience that demands a confession, extorting an acknowledgment of our complicity in the injustices of the present and/or past. We are in a state of perpetual coming out, and this time, coming out as white. And then again, we recognise our own discomfort in admitting our white fragility when we see/say/write it. In naming our discomfort, we do not plead innocence, sympathy or absolution or confess being consumed by "colonisers' guilt" (Tuck & Fine, 2007, p.147). Our acknowledgement of our (dis)comfort is also not "false generosity" (Tuck & Fine, 2007, p.154) but part of a "coming clean, coming out ... unforgetting" (Tuck & Fine, 2007, p.155). Recognising that our confessions may "constitute a form of pleasurable relief because what has produced the discomfort of learning about complicity is removed and one is purged of wrongdoing" (Applebaum, 2010, p.19), we are learning to accept white moral responsibility.

While our gender, culture, and whiteness are entangled, it is our whiteness and our becoming and being white that shaped and continue to shape our public performance of being and becoming faculty. Our stories are saturated with affectivities and attachments that we cannot remove from our telling (Youdell & Armstrong 2011, p. 145). We are and remain implicated. This is not a confession; it is a testimony.

Through our scholarly writing we have come to accept that talking as white (and queer/gay) faculty, but also talking white and queer is inherently political and insecure. We came to understand that our performance of our raced-ness and queer/gay-ness does not have moral authority because of the proximity of the performance to the personal and that this performance does not aim to produce "saintly white person[s]" or an act of "self-glorification in which whiteness is equated with moral rectitude" (Butler, 1995, p. 443). We came to acknowledge that by speaking white and queer/gay we may merely have reorganised our white and queer/gay bodies as "sanctioned and sanctified" (Westcott 2004, par. 22). By acknowledging our gender (in contrast to other identity characteristics and constructs) there is a danger that we perpetuate the "epistemology of the closet" (Sedgwick, in de Villiers 2012, 2) and cause certain types of "privileged 'knowledges' to circulate" (de Villiers 2012, 2). Our disclosure is, therefore, both "compulsory and forbidden" (de Villiers 2012, 3). Thus, being white, queer and gay faculty results in an amazing kaleidoscope of guilt, anxiety, privilege, and (dis)comfort that is self-perpetuating.

We are and never have been just one identity—whether white, queer and gay and (late to arrive) faculty. We testify/confess that our narratives are "partial and governed by the discourses of [our] time and place. These recountings cannot, however, ease or resolve the contradictions born in language, the discourses that bind and unleash meanings, and the real made present and absent by [our] efforts" (Britzman, 1995, p. 232). We live our race, class, gender and being-faculty not as separate but jointly (Nichols & Stahl, 2019, p.1256).

***

As we have come to the end of this testimony/confession (but continuing our fall through the rabbit hole), we are held to account by Westcott (2004) who asks "whose interests are vested in the articulation of a self-reflexive whiteness?" (par.1). To testify about or confess our whiteness, we "acknowledge the cumulative force of historical discourse imprinted on the self as subject. It is to discern that the self has derived benefit, be it material or symbolic, from the possession of the skin legally or scopically sanctioned as white" (par.2). There is, however, a danger in confessional writing "that the conflation of utterance and atonement allows for the cathartic pleasure to be enjoyed in the process of writing" (Westcott, 2004, par.31).

***

There has never been a time that we can remember not being white, queer and gay. In some way we would like to celebrate the claim that we have always been white, queer and gay from the start. While both of us had to 'come out' as queer and gay at some point in our life, our whiteness was always a given. As we grew older, we also learned whiteness—how to be white, what privileges were embedded in living in/with a white skin, and inevitably, that we were superior to other races. Contrary to the colour of our skin, our gender remained hidden, in the closet, banned. We learned the language of being queer, being gay in secret—practicing the vowels, learning the language, and paying the penalties when we were found out/came out. But even paying the price for being queer and gay were ameliorated by our whiteness, our privilege. And then we became faculty. We engaged, theorised, and articulated our gender in and through our scholarly and teaching practices. But it was our whiteness, and the stickiness of our whiteness that eluded (and continue to elude) our scholarly grasp— "... race, like sex, is sticky; it sticks to us, or we become 'us' as an effect of how it sticks, even when we think we are beyond it. Beginning to live with that stickiness, to think it, feel it, do it, is about creating a space to deal with the effects of racism" (Ahmed, 2004, par. 49).

We introduced this meditation on race-gender-culture-being-faculty with the question whether to testify or confess. We proposed the difference between confession and testimony is guilt. As we shared our narrative of race-gender-culture-being-faculty, we alternated between confession and testimony, getting lost as we tumbled through the rabbit hole.

> "Identifications are never fully and finally made; they are incessantly reconstituted, and, as such, are subject to the volatile logic of iterability. They are that which is constantly marshaled, consolidated, retrenched, contested, and on occasion, compelled to give way" (Butler 1993, p. 105).

References

Ahmed, S. (2004). Declarations of whiteness: The non-performativity of anti-racism. *borderlands*, 3(2), 1-15.

Akerman, K. (2020). Invisible imposter: identity in institutions. *Perspectives: Policy and Practice in Higher Education*: 1-5.

Appiah, K.A. (1995). African identities. In Social postmodernism. *Beyond identity politics*, edited by Nicholson, L., and Seidman, S (pp. 103-115). Cambridge: Cambridge University Press.

Applebaum, B. (2010). *Being white, being good: White complicity, white moral responsibility and social justice pedagogy*. Plymouth, UK: Lexington Books.

Badat, S. (2016). Deciphering the meanings, and explaining the South African higher education student protests of 2015–16. *Pax Academica*, 1(1), 71-106.

Boellstorff, T. (2005). Between religion and desire: being Muslim and Gay in Indonesia. *American Anthropologist* 107(4), 575-585.

Britzman, D. P. (1995). Is there a queer pedagogy? Or, stop reading straight. *Educational Theory*, 45(2), 151- 165.

Butler, J. (1993). *Bodies that matter: On the discursive limits of 'sex'*. New York: Routledge.

Butler, J. (1995). Collected and fractured: Response to identities. In *Identities*, edited by K.A. Appiah and H.L. Gates (pp. 439-447). Chicago, IL: University of Chicago Press.

Craven, E. (2011). Racial identity and racism in the gay and lesbian community in post-apartheid South Africa. A research report submitted to the Faculty of Humanities, University of the Witwatersrand, Johannesburg in partial fulfillment of the requirements for the degree of Master of Arts in Political Studies. Retrieved from http://wired-space.wits.ac.za/bitstream/handle/10539/11358/ MA_Research_Report_Emily_Craven_Final_corrections%5b1%5d.pdf?sequence=2

Croom, N.N. (2017). Promotion beyond tenure: Unpacking racism and sexism in the experiences of Black woman professors. *The Review of Higher Education*, 40(4), 557-583.

de Villiers, N. (2012). *Opacity and the closet: Queer tactics in Foucault, Barthes, and Warhol.* Minneapolis: University of Minnesota. http://www.jstor.org/stable/10.5749/j.ctttttzs.

DiAngelo, R. (2018). *White fragility: Why it's so hard for white people to talk about racism.* Beacon Press.

Epprecht, M. (2013). *Sexuality and social justice in Africa: Rethinking homophobia and forging resistance.* London, UK: ZedBooks.

Falkof, N. (2018). Sex and the Devil: Homosexuality, Satanism, and moral panic in late apartheid South Africa. *Men and Masculinities*, 1097184X18774097.

Kenny, J. (2018). Re-empowering academics in a corporate culture: An exploration of workload and performativity in a university. *Higher Education*, 75(2), 365-380.

Mayer, S.J., & Rathmann, J.M. (2018). How does research productivity relate to gender? Analysing gender differences for multiple publication dimensions. *Scientometrics*, 117(3):1663-1693.

Maritz, J., & Prinsloo, P. (2015). 'Queering'and querying academic identities in postgraduate education. *Higher Education Research & Development*, 34(4), 695-708.

Minow, M. (1998). Between vengeance and forgiveness: South Africa's truth and reconciliation commission. *Negotiation Journal*, 14(4), 319-355.

Nichols, S., & Stahl, G. (2019). Intersectionality in higher education research: a systematic literature review. *Higher Education Research & Development*, 38(6), 1255-1268.

Ringrose, J. (2007). Successful girls? Complicating post-feminist, neoliberal discourses of educational achievement and gender equality. *Gender and education*, 19(4), 471-489.

Sedgwick, E. K. (1990). *Epistemology of the Closet*. Berkely: University of California.

Smith, C., & Ulus, E. (2019). Who cares for academics? We need to talk about emotional well- being including what we avoid and intellectualize through macro-discourses. *Organization*, p.1350508419867201.

Tuck, E., & Fine, M. (2007). Inner angles. A range of ethical responses to/ with indigenous and decolonising theories. In Ethical futures in qualitative research. *Decolonising the politics of knowledge*, edited by Norman K. Denzin and Michal D. Giardina, (pp. 145-168). Walnut Creek, CA: Left Coast Press, Inc.

Walker*, M. (2005). Rainbow nation or new racism? Theorizing race and identity formation in South African higher education. *Race Ethnicity and Education*, 8(2), 129-146.

Youdell, D. (2010). Queer outings: uncomfortable stories about the subjects of post-structural school ethnography. *International Journal of Qualitative Studies in Education*, 23(1), 87-100.

Youdell, D., & Armstrong, F. (2011). A politics beyond subjects: The affective choreographies and smooth spaces of schooling. *Emotion, Space and Society* 4(3), 144-150. doi:10.1016/j.emospa.2011.01.002.

PART II

Pathways to Academe

Academe is a landscape well-guarded and gated, kept from non-traditional scholars and practitioners by expectations set around the prestige of publishing, the advanced degree—and, more subtly, the postures of scholarship which are in nature like a secret handshake, signals for a closed society that meets in plain sight. In these chapters, authors detail their beginnings, the paths they have chosen to follow, or which they have been given no choice but to trail blaze.

Reflecting on my Journey as a Reader and a Reading Researcher

Teresa Cremin

As an avid childhood reader perhaps it was inevitable that I enjoyed teaching children to read in primary schools and later came to research recreational reading and the practices that support it. Reading took me places as a child—I adventured in fictional worlds, fought dragons, schemed to overthrow the powerful, fell in and out of love and in effect lived vicariously through literature. Years later, still a reader, I find myself intrigued by the connections between my personal and academic identities and interests. How do we come to find the focus of our research journeys and to what extent do our life practices and academic interests feed off one another?

These are some of the questions I want to explore in this chapter as I reflect upon my life history as a reader, as a teacher of reading and as a researcher of children's and teachers' identities as readers. Whilst this is of necessity a personal journey, I trust there will be connections for you. Others' life stories can enable us to make sense of our own experiences, prompting reflection and reminiscence. I hope my narrative will connect to you, enabling you too to revisit your early passions, be they reading, sport, or music for instance, and prompting you to consider how these early interests may have shaped your later life's work in complex and intriguing ways.

Over the years I have studied and researched far more than reading: teachers' identities as writers also fascinate me, and the opportunities offered to young children to write creatively. In addition, creative pedagogy, storytelling, drama and play are aspects of my impassioned research enquiries. However, I recognise that when I am reading,

researching, talking or writing about reading for pleasure—that volitional act of engagement with texts which offers me such satisfaction—I
feel most 'at home' as an educator, a researcher and a human. I may
even be in my 'element' in the words of Robinson (2015) and 'in flow' as
Csikszentmihalyi (2000) describes those spaces where we are deeply and
affectively engaged, aligned with ourselves and able to be creative.

Growing up as a reader

During my formative years I came to love reading. My earliest readerly
memories are of re-reading the relatively sparse collection of books we
had at home, visiting the library in Banstead to feed my appetite and
swapping magazines such as Jackie and Mandy with friends at school.
My mother did not really approve of such reading material, which no
doubt enhanced my interest and commitment to the genre. Under cover
I swapped many of these 'illicit' texts with friends; I delighted in them.
My dad allowed us to spend our pocket money on what we chose, so
I often bought a magazine on Saturday mornings at Chipstead corner
shop, then on our return I'd rush to my bedroom, shut the door and
devour it in private—furtively stuffing it under the bed afterwards out of
mum's sight. In particular I enjoyed the black and white photo-stories
which often ended, after several weeks of tension and discord, in that
longed for teenage kiss.

Years later I happened upon reprinted copies of several such magazines
(offered free with the Observer) and I felt a visceral sense of joy and
re-connection. For four weeks they arrived as part of the Sunday sup-
plement, I rushed to read them like a child and found many strongly
'affective traces' of my past (Waller, 2019). I read and re-read the photo
stories, searched for the kiss in the final frames, and delighted in the
pin ups of Slade (my heart-throb Noddy Holder), and a doe eyed David
Essex (or perhaps that was me!) with long hair curling over their shoulders. The visuals transported me back in time. The colour adverts for
Rimmel make-up targeted at teens, such as a duo of pink eyeshadows
(for just 30 old pence!) that I'd once saved for and then found was out
of stock at Boots took me right back to that moment of disappointment.
The flowing floral midi dresses with frills reminded me of the tartan
wool skirt my mum made for me, (which I had never liked) and discos
in Kingswood community hall, with us girls dancing round a lone hand-
bag. Encountering these magazines as an adult, my reading and my past
came back with an adrenaline rush of pleasure, teenage angst and a tangible sense of particular places. Needless to say I have kept these jewels

of yesteryear, they represent part of my identity as a reader, are much thumbed and well protected.

My childhood pleasure in reading was also sustained by our family holidays. Each year in western Scotland my dad would go fishing with my brother, while my mother and sister would go bird watching or set off on long walks to find wild flowers. Personally, I read. Alone in the bracken (with a meat pie or sausage roll and the promise not to move until they returned), I'd go on adventures far more exciting to me than my siblings' literal realities. Characters from Eleanor Brent Dyer, Alkan Garner, Susan Cooper, Enid Blyton, the Readers' Digest real-life stories and many more became my constant companions. Ulapool, the nearest town, was a full hour away on a single track road and there was no library, so whilst I took new books with me each vacation, I was soon obliged to re-read the books in the little croft in which we stayed. Maybe I drew comfort from the steadfastness of the texts left there, the predictability and consistency of the cast of characters to whom I returned year after year. I enjoyed the peace and privacy of revisiting my reading journey. On our days out too, if it rained, I was often left in the car or at a bothy at my own request, happy to read, eat, relax and imagine. Place was of vital importance in these early encounters, my reading was always situated—both at home (always in my bedroom) and on holiday (always alone and often outdoors).

Context counts in our early text encounters and shapes our experience of reading, as memoirs of childhood reading often show (e.g. Mangan, 2018). Which places were of salience to you as you look back on your early reading? Can you recall even now the smell, sound and sensations of your life at the time? The people around you? The emotions attached ? These are part of our reading histories, of who we were and potentially who we became as readers.

Being a reader at school

Intriguingly, my memory of being a reader at school is not particularly strong. Were we read to? I know not. Did we have reading time? I know not. I do recall that my friends and I swapped our magazines and books and chatted about them sometimes. In secondary school I particularly enjoyed books about love during the Irish troubles, for example, Joan Lingard's Kevin and Sadie's stories— *Across the Barricades*—a series of romantic and political fictions, set during the Irish troubles which were being played out at the time. These resonated with West Side Story and of course Romeo and Juliet . I read many tales of love and hope amidst contexts of war and strife, they filled my days with tension and hoped-for romantic resolutions, as well as political questions which my parents couldn't fully answer. As Mackey highlights, 'we read our own worlds into the words of our books, and these worlds will not be subtracted from the understanding we develop from the texts' (2016, p. 263).

While close attention to the construction of literary texts and the need to memorise 'right answers' for exams sometimes reduced my pleasure, the rich language of *Othello, Nostromo, Paradise Lost, Under Milkwood* and many others remain evocative and enticing to me, even to this day. Music to be read and re-read. I fell in love with poetry at this age too, in part fed by the social and cultural practices in which our family engaged. The musicality and rhythms of church psalms and hymns, Guide songs and chants and 70's lyrics filled my days. My mother directed a Scout and Guide Gang Show every other year and as young people we got to know these songs and tunes by heart, they added to our campfire reper-toires and were cheerfully re-voiced on family holidays (by all but my long-suffering dad!). On church youth club trips—weeklong residentials to the Lake District or Snowdonia—in the presence of friends who didn't attend the same school as me, I chose not to take books—it didn't feel right. Instead I hid my passion for fiction and poetry, not wanting to be seen as overly learned. Retrospectively, I think I was probably trying on a 'take it or leave it' reader identity, to see what difference it might make.

With A levels dominating everything, and English, biology and history texts to study ('wider reading' wasn't celebrated or valued in those days), my pleasure in fiction was diminished at the end of secondary schooling. The environment that had previously supported and challenged my growth as a reader was shrinking to a single focus: get the grades to get into university. No one from my family had ever attended university and I felt a desire and a pressure to break the mould, to be university material. It took time and single-minded determination; freetime fiction reading had to be placed to one side.

Did the same happen to you as you grew up as a reader? Did you expe-rience a sense of distance from the pleasure of being a reader as your life changed and the system obliged you to prioritise academic work? Or did you remain engaged as a reader despite these pressures? Perhaps you didn't experience reading as tempting and delightful in your early years? We are all unique readers on our own journeys with different stories to tell, but through reflecting on our life histories as readers we can learn a great deal, both about reading and ourselves.

Being a reader at university

At Bristol, I read psychology and papered my bedroom walls with the verses of Dylan Thomas, Roger McGough, Helen Steiner Rice, Sylvia Plath, Seamus Heaney, Adrian Mitchell and many other poets whose voices I wanted to capture and possess, but it seemed there was even less time there for fiction, for other worlds, others' lives, loves and magic. Even on holidays I don't recall choosing to read for relaxation. The habit had gone, dusted down perhaps as a passing childhood passion. Looking back, whilst I think I did see myself as a reader then, I framed myself as a serious undergraduate reader of psychology, social anthropology, child development and memory, not as a free reader venturing into imagined worlds. In our flat no-one bought or discussed fiction—we were variously studying politics, psychology, biochemistry and geology and focused on getting good grades (alongside the usual social life and long nights discussing the world). I cannot recall a single conversation about reading novels. Maybe we implicitly viewed such reading as childish, Richard and Judy book clubs had not been conceived and perhaps less profile was given to recreational reading.

Did your peer group also shape your reading practices, as they did mine, not only as a young child but later too? No doubt I shaped my flatmates' reading lives as well, there was no network for us to tap into as fiction readers, nor did we create one. Although now, years later, the five of us do occasionally chat about novels, swap titles and give books for each other's birthdays.

Learning about reading as a teacher

After university I did a PGCE in Cambridge to become a teacher. There I was reintroduced to pleasures of fiction, read children's texts very widely, and learnt about their complexity. Children's texts are not some watered-down version of adult literature, but like all literary texts, have the potential to create aesthetic experiences that enhance our understanding of the human condition. As Bruner (1990) has shown, we use narrative to make sense of experience and to represent and reflect on our broader social world. In my training, I encountered reader response theories which view reading as an active meaning-making process between reader(s) and text(s). As I studied reading for the first time, I began to realise that texts are not fixed, but develop their potentiality through the reader's engagement with them (Rosenblatt,1978/,1994; Iser, 1978) .

In school as an ingenue teacher, I remember trying to help children engage with reading and find themselves in the mirrors of fiction (Bishop, 1990). I read aloud to my classes, shared my newly unquenchable thirst for fiction (and poetry) and tried to help create legacies of past satisfaction for the young. However, some simply didn't want to know, they were already deeply disinterested due to past experiences—even as 7-8 year olds. They eschewed any sense of a reader identity, and labelled those who read as 'boring' and 'geeks'. They had not yet found what reading was good for. Although I worked to get to know these readers, and used my repertoire of children's texts to make recommendations, I feel sure I didn't make positive reader identity positions available to all. Then, the concept of reader identities was unknown to me, I was unaware I was framing the readers in my class. I did however try to offer stories that opened doors and windows to others' worlds, in order for children to develop empathy and awareness of the plight of others, perhaps as I had done through the Irish troubles Kevin and Sadie stories years before. I also shared my own passion for reading with children.

I recall finding *Bridge to Terabithia*, a children's novel by Katherine Patterson, very moving, and was crying when Darren, a boy from my class, encountered me on the pavement outside school at lunchtime. The death in the text resonated with the loss of my closest girlfriend some months before; I was overwrought and propping myself up on a post, unable to move. "It's alright miss' Darren reassured me, "books get you like that sometimes don't they?- like they're real you know—but they're not" . I can still see his face at that moment in my mind's eye, decades later.

If reading is anything, it is surely thinking about meaning, and when we connect the texts we read to the stories of our lives (and vice versa) we bring our memories, experiences, prior knowledge and understanding to bear on whatever we are reading. As Rosenblatt observed:

> The special meaning... the submerged associations that these words and images have for the individual reader will largely determine what the work communicates to him. The reader brings to the work personality traits, memories of past events, present needs and preoccupations, a particular mood of the moment and a particular physical condition... in a never to be duplicated combination (Rosenblatt,1978/1995, p. 30-31).

It is the transaction between readers and texts and these notions of the reader's life, past and present and the 'physical condition' and 'particular mood of the moment' that in large part shape and influence our affective engagement in reading. I feel sure you can recall occasions when you experienced an almost visceral bodily response to a text, and /or a personal and emotional connection that enabled you to re-read your life through the narrative? The black and white marks on the page resonate with the meanings we bring and those we co-create with the author as we read, and that applies to this chapter you are reading, as well as works of fiction.

Researching reading for pleasure

I found the research around reading so intriguing that when I moved to the university sector, I began to explore the role of Reading Teachers, teachers who read and readers who teach (Commeyras et al., 2003). I wanted to understand if positioning oneself more personally as a reader, and teaching from a reader's point of view, might make a difference to children's desire, motivation, and behaviour as readers. My reading journey was beginning to shape the questions I wanted to answer as a new researcher and teacher educator.

So, working with UK Literacy Association colleagues we piloted a Teachers as Readers survey of teachers' reading practices and their knowledge and use of children's texts. 1200 teachers from 11 Local Authorities completed it and we were shocked by the results. The data revealed that whilst these teachers were readers in their adult lives, when it came to school they relied on a limited canon of books from their childhood and celebrity children's authors. Dahl dependency was worryingly rife (Cremin et al., 2008a, b). Incredibly, 22% could not name a single poet and 24% could not name a single picture fiction creator. These findings, which received considerable media and policy interest, created cause for concern, how could teachers possibly foster reader development without such subject knowledge.

So in my next project Teachers as Readers Phase II we foregrounded teachers' experience of texts and their pleasure in them, and prompted teachers not only to read more widely, but also to reflect upon their practices and preferences as readers. We also examined the potential dynamic between teachers and children as readers. Amongst myriad insights, the project revealed that volitional reading is strongly influenced by relationships: between teachers; teachers and children; children and families; and children, teachers, families and communities, and that a reading for pleasure agenda can be developed effectively through the creation of classroom reading communities of reciprocity and interaction (Cremin et al., 2014). Such communities, the research indicated, are most effectively led by Reading Teachers who recognise the significance of reader identity in reader development and frame their practice in responsive ways.

Was I researching my own practice as a teacher from years before, only this time through a more informed socio-cultural lens? Perhaps so, although I don't think I fully appreciated that at the time. Through case studies, we found that those practitioners who developed most fully as Reading Teachers appeared to make the most impact upon the children's attitudes and attainment.

Since then, I have worked on a number of reading research projects. I sought to understand the role librarians play in extracurricular reading groups, (Cremin and Swann, 2016, 2017) and the ways digital library systems position teachers as monitors and curators of children's reading, not as co-readers or mentors (Kucirkova and Cremin, 2017). More recently, working alongside other OU colleagues, we examined the disengagement of young boy readers. Soberingly, this revealed that teachers' perceptions of children's gender, class and ethnicity shape their practice, significantly constraining the boys' engagement as readers (Hempel Jorgensen, Cremin, Harris and Chamberlain, 2018).

In each of these studies, our research questions, though tailored to the project in question, linked in some way to the children and adults reader identities.More recently I've developed a practitioner community website to share some of this research, which has hundreds of examples of teachers' evidence informed practice, developed as a consequence of their engagement with OU/ UKLA Teacher Reading Groups. These inspiring examples, in line with the research, demonstrate that when practitioners read more widely, get to know the children as readers, develop their reading for pleasure pedagogy, and a Reading Teacher stance, they are enabled to build strong communities of engaged readers. These communities have positive consequences for young readers. (See: https://researchrichpedagogies.org/research/reading-for-pleasure.)

Each study and the website have helped me understand more of the complex relationships, identity enactments and interplay between adult and child and child-child readers. In effect, my early pleasure in reading and renewed passion has been examined through this work. The lines between being a reader and researching reading have become blurred. Perhaps this has happened in your life story too? Have your personal practices and intense enthusiasm for something influenced your own scholarly enquiries?

The impact work has raised new questions for me as a researcher too. Teachers in the Reading Groups have shown energy and commitment, but they have found it hard to track the progression and development of children's affective engagement, attitudes and behaviours as readers. So I am working with teachers to understand how to document the subtle nature of readers' identity shifts. We cannot measure their pleasure, but researchers, working in collaboration with the profession, can surely find ways forward.

Conclusion

Looking back, I can see there are intriguing connections between my own childhood passion for reading and my later research enquiries. Fuelled in part by life experience and personal interest, I have come to study an aspect of my own life—my reading identity—and to explore the possibility that our identities as literate adults have salience for those we work with in classrooms. In building reader relationships and sharing their reading identities, Reading Teachers appear to hold up a mirror to their own practices as readers and in the process learn more about what real readers do. They then consider the pedagogical consequence of this new understanding and act to enable young readers to exert their rights as readers. This, my research indicates, impacts on their pleasure.

Writing this chapter has also prompted me to consider if my reading research has fed my personal reading practices. It is certainly the case that I remain an avid reader, I always have an adult and a children's book on the go, spend far too much money on books, and have been a member of a book group for over 20 years. In that context, whilst I can never turn my researcher's mind completely off, I try to participate as an adult reader and friend, not an academic. The group though is undoubtedly a micro community of readers, and attending provokes my thinking, raising new questions about the nature of reading.

Whilst I swapped Jackie and Mandy comics with my friends many years ago and hid them from mum, the emotional pleasure I experienced reading them, the connections I made to my life and the lives of the characters within them—real and fictional—helped shape me as a reader. At the time of reading and sharing them with friends I was unaware of the place these texts would play on my life journey, but I can see now that the social, affective and relational nature of this small weekly reading practice helped sustain us, both as readers and as friends.

Such retrospective insights about the highly social, situated and contextual nature of reading have been evidenced in much of my empirical research in classrooms, although it has taken the writing of this chapter to fully recognise this. It is now clearer to me that the social environment, our literacy histories, others' perceptions of us as readers and our interactions around reading, influence our attitudes to and understanding of what it might mean to be a reader in particular contexts. As this chapter documents, my sense of identity as a reader waxed and waned, burgeoned and bloomed at different times over the decades depending on my relationships and work contexts. As educators and researchers, we need to pay more attention to this complexity and enable policy makers to acknowledge this too. Readers' identities matter.

I wonder if my writing has caused you too to recollect your own reading history and identity and consider not dissimilar issues? Perhaps in encountering my journey as a child reader to a reading researcher, you have begun to look back on your life story, to consider the passions and pleasures which shaped your life journey—whether that be an enthusiasm for music, sport, reading, or a concern with injustice or equality for instance. Can we really leave our childhood selves, our early passions and practices behind? I am not sure, though perhaps some people deliberately do so, eschewing the narratives of the past in order to shape alternative futures which allow new interests to blossom. Our life stories are not unlike the narratives found in fiction—rich, diverse and intriguing and there are always new stories waiting to be told.

References

Bishop, R.S. (1990). Mirrors, Windows and Sliding Glass Doors. *Perspectives: Choosing and Using Books for the Classroom*, 6 (3), pp. x-xi.

Clark, C. (2013). Children's and Young People's Reading Today. Findings from the 2012 National Literacy Trust's annual survey. London: National Trust.

Commeyras, M., Bisplinghoff, B.S. and Olson, J. (2003). *Teachers as Readers: Perspectives on the importance of reading in teachers' classrooms and lives.* Newark: International Reading Association.

Cremin, T., Bearne, E., Mottram, M. and Goodwin, P. (2008b). Exploring teachers' knowledge of children's literature. *Cambridge Journal of Education*, 38(4): 449–64.

Cremin, T., Mottram, M., Collins, F., Powell, S. and Safford, K. (2009a). Teachers as readers: building communities of readers. *Literacy* 43 (1), pp. 11-19.

Cremin, T. Mottram, M. Powell, S, Collins R and Safford K. (2014). *Building Communities of Engaged Readers: Reading for pleasure*. London and NY: Routledge

Cremin, T. and Swann, J. (2016). Literature in Common: Reading for Pleasure in School Reading Groups' in Rothbauer , P., Skjerdingstad, K.I., McKechnie, L.. Oterholm, K. (Eds). *Plotting the Reading Experience: Theory/Practice/ Politics*. pp. 279-300. Ontario: Wilfrid Laurier University Press.

Cremin, T. and Swann, J. (2017). School librarians as facilitators of extracurricular reading groups in J. Pihl, K. Skinstad van der Kooij and T.C. Carlsten (Eds). *Teacher and Librarian Partnerships in Literacy Education in the 21st Century*, pp. 118-137. Olso: Sense Publishers: New Voices and New Knowledge in Educational Research.

Csikszentmihalyi, M. (2002). *Flow: The Classic Work on How to Achieve Happiness*. London: Rider.

Hempel-Jorgensen, A., Cremin, T., Harris D. and Chamberlain, L. (2018). Pedagogy for reading for pleasure in low socio-economic primary schools: beyond 'pedagogy of poverty'? *Literacy* 52 (2): 86-94.

Kucirkova, N. and Cremin, T. (2017) Personalised reading for pleasure with digital libraries: Towards a pedagogy of practice and design. *Cambridge Journal of Education* 1-19.

Mackey, M. (2016). *One Child Reading: My Auto-bibliography*. Edmonton: the University of Alberta Press.

Robinson, K. (2009). *The Element: How finding your passion changes everything*. London, Allen lane.

Rosenblatt, L. (1995). *Literature as Exploration*. New York: Modern Languages Association of America.

Twist, L., Schagan, I. and Hogson, C. (2007). Progress in International Reading Literacy Study (PIRLS): Reader and Reading National Report for England 2006. London: NFER and DCSF.

Waller, A. (2019). *Rereading Childhood Books: A Poetics: Perspectives on children's literature.* London, Bloomsbury.

Moving to See

Fay Akindes

I carry with me a scene from the documentary film *Naked Spaces: Living is Round*. The camera's eye/I, guided by filmmaker Trinh T. minh-ha, enters a womb-like house in the remote West African village of Konkomba, Togo. The movement from outside to inside creates an intermittent blindness; eyes/I adjust to the sudden shift from an abundance of sunlight to a near absence of light, to light again.

This movement from darkness to light, from not seeing to seeing, is one that I have experienced countless times as I entered academic spaces from the margins. It is an experience I've lived again and again in academe—first as a graduate student, then a full-time novice instructor (still ABD), to earning my Ph.D. and navigating and negotiating my way to tenure then promotion to full professor and most recently to a system administrator. The visual metaphor that Trinh T. minh-ha gifted me is a comforting source of strength, a smooth stone in my pocket. When encountering unfamiliar and potentially terrifying passages, Trinh reminds me to keep moving. Eyes/I will eventually be recentered in light. I *will* see again.

Trinh T. minh-ha is a post-colonial feminist scholar who theorizes with film. She provided an entry point into academe when I was a graduate student. Trinh, bell hooks, and Haunani-Kay Trask are three scholars who inform my understanding of working in broadcast marketing and promotion in television (PBS and CBS affiliates in Honolulu) and radio (NPR affiliate in San Diego), my seduction by theory into graduate school, and joining the University of Wisconsin-Parkside where I taught for 20 years. Since 2017, I have served as an administrator at the UW System in Madison; in a sense, I have circled back to my life before graduate school.

Grad School—1992 to 1997

Graduate school was an opportunity to redeem myself as a student. My undergraduate studies at the University of Hawaii at Manoa were a blurry distraction of concerts, parties, backgammon games, and frisbee, with occasional studying. I managed to complete my degree once I realized no one would save me, that I was dependent on myself. And grad school was my second chance to succeed as a student.

It made a dramatic difference to be a 30-something married adult. I was attending a university far away from home in a place I had never been where no one knew me. It was the perfect place and time to reinvent myself, to start clean. I spent at least a year preparing myself—studying for the GRE, paying off debts, saving money for a computer, boombox, and winter clothes. I was moving from the touristy military city of San Diego where for nearly six years I worked as a marketing/promotion director at the public radio station. My new academic home was Ohio University in Athens, the foothills of Appalachia. I was awarded a public broadcasting fellowship in telecommunication management (M.A.) with a tuition waiver and stipend.

Before leaving San Diego, I scanned the *Athens News'* classified ads and found a basement flat in a house with two undergraduate women. When I first moved into the blue house on Verona Lane, which was next to an elementary school, I sat on the stoop watching the school children play, struck by their carefree and loud laughter. A few weeks later I had a shocking experience : I could no longer hear the children : my brain had adjusted the decibel level of children's laughter without my conscious knowledge. What other adjustments was my brain making?

In graduate school, I stopped wearing contact lenses and got prescribed glasses, wore jeans instead of dresses, comfortable walking shoes instead of toe-pinching heels, utility jackets in place of shoulder-padded blazers. I didn't have a car so walked everywhere and occasionally, when sidewalks were icy or I needed groceries, I called a cab which charged $2. After the Fall term, I moved into a Victorian-style house across the playground, house-sitting for a professor teaching in Malaysia. The house had a piano, a library of alphabetized CDs, and a writing room with a wall of windows overlooking back yards, including a tree with a windchime that could be measured in feet, not inches. Snow blizzards were fierce that year; the world was quiet and white.

What does it mean to be a scholar?

On Friday afternoons I visited Alden Library and browsed the stacks. This is how I discovered a collection of books by bell hooks. She saved me from the dense academese of cultural studies and suggested that, perhaps, I could belong in academe. Like her, I came from a working family in a rural communit—though she grew up in Kentucky, and I was from Hawaii. bell hooks' essays in *Yearning* and *Black Looks* introduced me to the interlocking relationship of gender, race, and class, and systems of white supremacist capitalist patriarchy. Soon bell hooks and filmmaker Trinh T. minh-ha (*Woman Native Other* and *Framer Framed*) were joined on my bookshelf by Hawaiian scholar Haunani-Kay Trask (*From a Native Daughter*), whose writing called me home. Importantly, Haunani-Kay positioned Hawaii as a U.S. colonized state and suggested why my undergraduate experience at the University of Hawaii-Manoa was alienating. While 75% of the students were brown-skinned, 75% of the faculty were white, many from the U.S. "mainland."

Collectively these three women scholars gave me the language to make meaning of my life experiences.

Before my first Thanksgiving in graduate school, I was seduced by theory and decided to pursue a Ph.D. When I shared my decision with my then husband Dan, he said—"But you're a **doer!**" I had spent 11 years working in broadcast marketing and promotion, honing my skills as a marketing strategist, writer, editor, event planner, publicist, and even a one-time producer of a live, call-in show with Radio Moscow. In my last position at KPBS-FM, we mined data from Arbitron and NPR, sketching a round portrait of our listeners. An important realization was that our public radio audience was fundamentally different from that of our sister TV (PBS) station. Our communication approaches, then, needed to be different. Arbitron survey data indicated that our largest audiences tuned in for NPR's *Morning Edition* and *All Things Considered* and that the demographics reflected a predominantly white male college-educated listener who had eclectic tastes in music. So, I forged relationships with local concert promoters, theatre companies, and university activity boards that shared common goals and audiences. KPBS-FM gave away tickets to Eric Clapton, Spalding Gray, Thomas Mapfumo, Laurie Anderson, Bobby McFerrin, and the annual multi-stage Street Fest downtown. (This was a sharp turn from classical music.) We staged the first Afropop Dance Party with Georges Collinet who taught us how to dance the Cameroonian bikutsi, hosted monthly foreign film previews at the Landmark Theatre and, in the process, expanded our database for membership and fundraising drives. The backward design of our marketing/promotion efforts was one that subsequently became common sense when designing a class.

Dan's (mis)perception of academe did little to dissuade me. After all, I knew little about the process of earning a Ph.D. and, moreover, what I would do with a Ph.D.

After moving cross country from San Diego to the college town of Athens, Ohio, I was in love with academe and the idyllic college town next to the Hocking River. It was surprisingly cosmopolitan with students from Africa, the Mid-East, Asia, and South America. In my communication theory class, I found myself in a group where I was the only U.S. American. My group partners were from India, Taiwan, China, and the United Arab Emirates. A few students were sponsored by their governments, some were from elite families, the children of academics and professionals, and a few were former Peace Corps volunteers. Social class differences were prominent.

I was from a working family from a rural community. My parents were the children or grandchildren of immigrants and their home language was Japanese. I grew up speaking Creole English—a chop suey mix of Hawaiian, Japanese, Chinese, Filipino words mixed with English. It was the language of the sugar plantation where laborers converged from different ethnic cultures and English-speaking managers needed a common language, a lingua franca, to communicate across ethnic borders. What emerged was Hawaiian *Pidgin English*. I learned to speak Standard English as an undergraduate student in Honolulu, constructing sentences in my mind before speaking. I rarely volunteered to speak in class and later, as a professor, empathized with my international, immigrant, and refugee students and colleagues.

The temporal experience of academe was one theme of difference between graduate school and my media work. In my last professional job at San Diego's NPR affiliate, I was responsible for writing articles for the monthly magazine that was sent to members of the KPBS-FM and -TV stations. The articles I wrote typically involved interviewing someone who extended the audio documentaries or sound portraits that we were airing. For example, when we aired a sound portrait on Antarctica, I tracked down a professor at San Diego State University who had conducted research in Antarctica and shared a local perspective to the nationally produced story. The challenge in writing these articles was time; I typically had a week between receiving the program schedule and producing articles. I learned to be nimble and creative on command. In my graduate classes, I was thrilled to learn that we had the entire term to research and write papers.

Doctoral studies

My Ph.D. mentor and academic coach was Prof. Jenny Nelson who shattered my stereotypes of a college professor. She had a short asymmetrical haircut, wore purple Doc Martens, and peppered her speech with the occasional f-bomb. She was a single mom of a biracial (Black/White) daughter Avery. I was immediately drawn to Jenny because of her unconventional authenticity and reputation as an incisive editor. She was brilliant. During my first summer as a doctoral student, she invited me to co-teach *Age, Class, Gender, Race, and Sexual Orientation in Media.* Students kept hand-written journals that intersected the personal, popular, and theoretical. Jenny and I read these journals, writing comments in the margins. Initially I was intimidated by this assignment since some of the students were my peers, including Janice Windborne who was the former news director at KPBS-FM. Jenny assured me that I wasn't judging students, but having a conversation with them. It was a pedagogical alternative to traditional exams. Years later I learned that I was one of many students who benefitted from Jenny's mentoring and that she had paid me (and other students) out of her own pocket to co-teach the summer class. She also supported grad students who lacked funds for conference travel. She fed us confidence and made us believe we belonged in academe without burying our home identities.

Media theorist Douglas Kellner shares a multi-perspectival approach to media studies that I found helpful not only as a graduate student, but also as a professor and administrator. Triangulating media into categories of the political economy (producer, professor, administrator), textual analysis (product, curriculum and pedagogy), and audience reception (consumer, student) helped me to organize and make meaning of my work.

Over time the lines around these three categories blurred as I began to see the nuances that previously were invisible to me. Everyone in the class, for example, is a teacher and student. Currently as an administrator, political economy analysis translates into tracing the funding sources of programs, such as faculty development programs created by for-profit businesses masquerading as non-profit organizations. It didn't escape my eyes to see Charles Koch as the largest sponsor at the Association of American Colleges & Universities (AAC&U) 2020 annual meeting and, not surprisingly, that he was a featured speaker in the program. Koch was a supporter of former Wisconsin Governor Scott Walker and the passage of Act 10 that disenfranchised public teachers in our state.

Teaching—1997 to 2017

My career in broadcast marketing and promotion had an enduring impact on my work as a professor from the start. When applying for a teaching position, I targeted my job search sending out around eight applications as opposed to a classmate who kept an index box of alphabetized cards, each representing a job possibility. The University of Wisconsin-Parkside was the only university to invite me for an interview that included teaching a communication class. I shared an audio performance by Guillermo Gomez-Pena, a social justice artist from the U.S.-Mexican border town of Tijuana just south of San Diego, then facilitated a discussion on identity, communication, and culture. Later the department chair commented on my listening skills, particularly that I wasn't uncomfortable with silence and that I waited for students to speak.

There were a few memorable turning points in my early teaching, particularly in the first fall, 1997. It was the first time I was teaching alone and the first time I had constructed a syllabus. My teaching was complicated by my family life; I was solo-parenting our daughter (two years old) and son (six months old) while Simon taught in Cleveland, OH. One of the classes I taught that first semester was Communication Theory. Typically I over-prepared for the class, using the textbook as a rigid guide. One day, however, I walked into class without copious notes and improvised. I spoke less, engaged students more, and let their comments direct the discussion. It was a turning point, teaching me to trust my students and myself.

Soon after, Carnegie Scholar and Augustana College history professor *Lendol Calder* addressed "Throwing Out the Textbook" at UW-Parkside. He challenged the practice of "coverage" and instead emphasized "concepts." He liberated me from textbooks, inviting me to consider alternative texts and student-centered engagement. He also influenced how I approached my syllabi. In my mind, I was creating an experience, not unlike what a radio or TV producer produces with a sound portrait or weekly series.

Assistant Professor

What my experience working in television and radio taught me was the importance of engaging an audience—including visually provocative images in my syllabi, integrating multi-media and discussions into my classes, organizing experiential field trips, and arranging guest speakers (the most unusual being a Skyped conversation with my grad school friend Hando Sinisalu, now an international marketing expert in Estonia, the country where Skype was developed). In public television and radio, the goal was to turn our audience into members. In commercial TV it was to keep our viewers watching as long as possible, to ensure high ratings that translated into advertising revenue. When teaching undergraduates, my goal was to engage students—to capture their interest and attention, to make class time interesting, to motivate students to read and write and learn whatever objectives/outcomes had been established, to make my teaching role less tedious and never one of policing their attendance or behavior. My challenge was to make class sessions interesting, engaging, relevant, and somewhat unpredictable especially during the first five minutes of class.

Sometimes, I imagined I was producing a season of TV episodes. The first class set the tone, establishing the context for what followed. It gave students a sense of what to expect and what I expected of them—to engage and participate in open discussion, to question and consider a different point of view. One semester I opened my Media & Culture class by playing Radiohead's Weird Fishes while students filled out a survey. Why Radiohead? They were the first band to release a new CD—*In Rainbows*—online with a "Pay what you want" pricetag. (At the end of class, a student revealed that he was in the wrong class but stayed because he liked the music. He was wearing a Radiohead t-shirt.) The semester culminated in a season finale which took on an important air—final presentations with invited guests, or a special venue, such as the campus cinema.

Associate to Full Professor

I was told a lie after I earned my Ph.D.: that my tenure clock started ticking when I was initially hired ABD as an Instructor. This reduced my time to tenure from five to three years. Consequently I worked evenings and weekends, sacrificing familial time for job security. I published three essays in a single year and continued presenting papers at academic conferences around the country. Upon receiving tenure, I reclaimed weekends for my family and me. Learning that I had been lied to by someone

I trusted was a threshold moment—I walked through the threshold and never turned back. If I look in the rear-view mirror, that person is invisible.

More than 10 years after tenure, I was motivated to seek full professorship when the salary bump was increased from $2,500 to $5,000 for full professors. We had not received raises in years—in fact we had experienced furloughs, pay cuts, and accusations of not working hard enough from the State Legislature. My goal when producing my dossier was to leave no doubt among my peers that I was worthy of promotion; this was the same impetus when I prepared my dossier for tenure and promotion to assistant professor. In some ways, I exceeded the minimal requirements. Was I performing the Asian American "model minority"? I recall a white colleague stopping at my open door one day; she was teaching an evening class and I was at my computer. She stopped and said she admired my "work ethic," as though it was a choice. Was I over-performing for fear that my work or perceived productivity was lacking?

When the chair of my promotion committee asked for external reviewer suggestions, I shared names of four women-of-color scholars, including a Choctaw/Cherokee-Japanese American, a Native Hawaiian, an African American, and a South Asian scholar. All four agreed to review my scholarship. Rather than being a dreadful experience, the promotion process turned out to be empowering. I chose my voices of authority; they were not from the "center"—those who maintained power in academe—but embodied "marginality as a site of resistance" (hooks, p. 152). In 2015, I was officially promoted to full professor. Two years later after a restorative semester teaching in Dalkeith, Scotland, I ended my 20-year teaching career and joined the UW System Administration.

Once again, I surrendered to intermittent blindness. I was and am moving to see.

***

The author is grateful to the late *Ian Donnachie*, Professor Emeritus of History, Open University, Scotland, for conversations that inform this chapter. Thanks to *Jenny Nelson* (Ohio University) and *Adrienne Viramontes* (University of Wisconsin-Parkside) for reading early drafts of this chapter.

References

hooks, bell. (1990). *Yearning: race, gender, and cultural politics*. Boston: South End Press.

Kellner, D. (2018). Cultural studies, multiculturalism, and media culture. *Gender, Race, and Class in Media: A Critical Reader*. Dines G., Humez, J.M., Yousman, B. and Yousman, LB. (Eds.). Thousand Oaks: Sage.

Trask, H.K. (1993). *From a native daughter: Colonialism and sovereignty in Hawai'i*. Honolulu: University of Hawaii Press.

Trinh, m.h. (1989). *Woman, native, other: Writing postcolonialism and feminism*. Bloomington: Indiana University Press.

Trinh, m.h. (1992). *Framer framed*. New York: Routledge.

Always the Practitioner: Reflections on a Journey into the Academy

John Parry

"When we make a commitment to become critical thinkers, we are already making a choice that places us in opposition to any system of education or culture that would have us be passive recipients of ways of knowing." (hooks 2009, p. 185)

Settling down to write this piece in the small room where I do such work, leaning books on the shelves to my right, CDs stacked to my left, a creaky angle-poise on the desk and a Ramones poster circa 1977 in my gazing space, I listened to the academic inside me and returned to the literature. *Teaching Critical Thinking: Practical Wisdom* by bell hooks (2009) seemed a useful starting point, a grounding for any personal reflections on my own learning journey. On re-reading the book it was clear many of the discussions around theory, practice, knowledge and experience could frame parts of my story but there were other passages that raised some prickly questions. One sentence that I kept revisiting opens this chapter, thirty-eight words eloquently written that poked at my preconceptions. Could I pinpoint when I first made that 'commitment to become' a critical thinker, to move beyond being a knowledge recipient? My initial assumption was that my switch from practice to academia ten years ago represented that turning point, the beginnings of a transition from the experienced, well-trained professional into the more questioning and insightful academic. Yet as I leaned back in my swivel chair doubts began to arise that spoiled this convenient narrative. Were my years as a practitioner really devoid of critical thinking? Did my previous practice experience have any residual impact on me as I have become part of the academic world? Is there an important part of me that will always identify as a practitioner?

I entered the world of practice on leaving school, a choice which I recognise now was shaped to a large extent by my upbringing rather than any clear sense of purpose. My parents were newly elevated professionals, a local government officer and a nurse, who had broken away from their solid working-class roots in mining and mill towns buoyed by the heady optimism of the post-war years. Yet, although the 1970's represented an era of further social mobility when many young people became the first in their family to enter university, I was reluctant to join this next generation of pioneers. Instead I chose a direction with an emphasis on vocation rather than academic study which unimaginatively mirrored my parents' occupations, firstly for a brief period as an accountant and then into nursing. From qualifying as a nurse in a large residential hospital for people with disabilities I then took what was to be a defining step for me, training as a teacher in special education.

Teacher training was in some ways my introduction to degree level study although, as was common practice at the time, this took place in a separate college and provided a very different experience to being part of a university community. There were no faculties or college lawns, no fraternising with other students studying exotic histories or cutting-edge sciences. Consequently, I gained little appreciation of what immersive academic study involved or what the academy represented. Yes, in creaky lecture halls and seminar rooms we covered the concepts and paradigms, the theories of learning, communication and child development, the conceptual underpinnings for any pedagogue. However, those theoretical foundations had little time to settle because we were almost immediately thrown into blocks of teaching practice in schools. Learning to become a teacher was therefore shaped primarily by experience, through reflections on our stumbling encounters with children in those restless classrooms and corridors.

Following training I immediately took up my first teaching post in a school for children with learning difficulties on the edge of the city that had become my home as a student. From this familiar starting point I embarked on a teaching career in special schools before moving into peripatetic work, providing early intervention and learning support to preschool aged disabled children in their homes. I settled in this niche area of education practice for nearly twenty years until in 2010 my journey reached its current destination when I became a lecturer in early childhood at the Open University.

It would be tempting to see my eventual transition from the world of practice into academia as pivotal in shaping my awareness of the interdependence between theory and fact, knowledge and experience (hooks 2009). From this perspective January 2010 would signify my inauguration into the critical thinking club, a seminal moment in my quest for some deeper understanding. Yet looking back on my years of practice I now recognise that there were periods which involved some rigorous self-examination and critical reflection on my values and beliefs. When thinking about my move from nursing to teaching I recollect becoming increasingly unsettled by the injustice and hopelessness of long-term hospitalisation of disabled people. Those I supported as a nurse, from young children to the elderly, were conduits for my caring but their access to education offered a way forward, a re-focusing from the inevitable to the possible. Over time I recognised that I wanted to be part of the shift away from the medical model and this realisation, more than any clear professional ambitions, motivated my move into teaching.

Whilst in practice, in addition to such phases which marked gradual shifts in my awareness, there were also other more distinct moments that jolted the principled, comfortable assumptions that I held about being a practitioner. During my second teaching appointment at a small special school in southern England, I was invited to dinner by one of the children's parents because they wanted to thank me for the work that I was doing with their son. I had met the family briefly at parents' evenings but outside those formalities my only regular contact with them was through the stilted written communications of the home-school book. Every day I would record their son's achievements and misdemeanours at school whilst attempting to keep a delicate balance between professional distance and supportive informality. Then each morning I would read their brief polite replies expressing their gratitude to the school and occasionally noting that their son had been 'a good boy'. So, I accepted the invitation thinking that I could build on this tentative relationship and gain some insights that might enhance my support of their son's learning.

I still recall feeling slightly embarrassed at the sight of the crisp table-cloth and best cutlery that greeted me in their dining room that evening. As we sat down to eat, I noticed that their son was curled in the corner of the cramped living room under a blanket. He never came to the table and when I asked if my presence had fractured his safe personal routine they answered "no, he always needs to take time." The parents then told me that mealtimes with their son would usually involve several hours of patient coaxing and that often he would refuse to eat anything. I had never known this; at school he was sometimes fussy with his food but usually would sit happily for lunch alongside his classmates. The revelation shook me.

From that point on I tried to work more in partnership with parents, to tune into their everyday priorities, to think beyond the home-school divide. I also began to question the structures of special education, the limitations it imposed on young people and the system's tendency to separate children from their local community. Reflecting on the incident now it clearly disrupted my professional passivity and enhanced my 'practical wisdom', that capacity where "as critical thinkers we are to think for ourselves and be able to take action on behalf of ourselves" (hooks 2009, p.185). For me taking such action soon meant making the move out of the special school environment into teaching much younger disabled children before they started formal education and supporting them within their family home. Yet although I became settled within this particular practice world for almost twenty years, my understanding of the value of my role and critical awareness of its limitations continued to be stretched by seemingly routine day to day experiences.

As the Coordinator of the home teaching team I was responsible for making the introductory visits to families whose young child had been referred to the service so that I could explain what support we could provide. I particularly enjoyed this part of my work, offering what I saw as something tangible and positive to parents who often felt confused and compromised, uncertain about what the future might bring for them and their young child who was now deemed to be 'different'. For me this aspect of the job represented a concrete example of my 'helping' and in many ways reaffirmed what I regarded as my professional worth.

I still remember one such visit on a parched summer evening to a small terraced house on an anonymous new town street. There was no doorbell, so I tapped the glass. A young man, who I assumed to be the father of the child I was going to meet for the first time, opened the door. Smiling, I introduced myself and held up my ID. He glanced briefly at my photograph then at me, bowed his head and, with a softly spoken "Welcome," gestured for me to cross the threshold. I was shown into a bustling front room crammed with grandparents, other children and, sinking in a huge armchair, the mother holding her tiny baby. After a round of introductions, I began to explain how the home visits would work. At one point I remember the mother delicately passing the baby to Dad as she insisted on preparing tea and sweetmeats for me. I took this as the moment to say hello to the young person who up until now

I had only seen as a bundle of blankets. The baby boy stared up at me from the safety of his father's arms and wriggled his arm free. Sensing an opportunity to do something I fished a small dangling toy from my bag and suspended it close to the baby's fingers. Almost immediately, with tiny digits flexing he ignored the toy, looked away and reached up to tug at his Dad's beard.

Soon after, having explained all I needed to, it was time to leave. We agreed that I would phone the following morning to confirm which day the home visits would start. As I turned to say goodnight to the father at the front door he held my arm. I could sense his grip, calm but firm. "Would it be ok to wait another month, maybe two so that we can get to know him as a family." he asked. I paused before replying "no problem," then retreated to my car to take in the impact of his polite and reverent door-step plea. Any notions I held about the significance of early intervention and the sanctity of professional expertise had been sharply deflated.

For me vivid stories such as these from my time as a teacher exemplify that practice is an experience of becoming "knowledgeable in a special way' through the 'spontaneous, intuitive performance of the actions of everyday life" (Schon 1983, p.49). This 'special way' involves not only developing expertise and skills but also a level of critical thinking driven by self-reflection. Such criticality may not be as informed by theory or conceptual understanding, but it is shaped by the powerful encounters with daily realities. Comparable experiences were also common within the community of practice (Lave and Wenger 1991) in which I worked. My colleagues were professionals from different therapeutic, sociological and educational mindsets and although tensions were inevitable, joint solutions were found as we endeavoured to support children and families. Reflecting on these times now through my academic lens I can see that being part of such a community meant that I was included in participatory learning relationships rich with critical thinking. However because such learning happened tacitly and to a large degree unconsciously (Rogoff and Gardner 1984) I entered academia in 2010 unsure whether the ideas shaped during my years as a practitioner would have any relevance, value or currency.

The first time that I walked onto the sculptured modernism of the campus was for my interview. It was October, a chill morning mist hung over the building tops while a works team cleared the first Autumn leaves from the pavements. Everything seemed so organised. Anxiously early I went to the canteen for a coffee and to listen into some conversations.

I was curious, what do academics talk about over their cappuccinos? Catching the chat about road works and weather, families and football I began to relax. I carried that reassurance into the interview room and sitting in front of the panel of five draped my arm casually over the back of the empty chair next to me as if seeking support from an invisible ally. To my relief everything unravelled amicably, each person asked questions in turn, nothing proved too difficult, there were nods, smiles and we all laughed in the right places. The Chair of the panel was sitting to my far right. I had glanced in her direction occasionally noticing that she appeared to be concentrating on the paperwork in front of her. As Chair she was privileged with asking me the final interview questions one of which I can still recall in cold detail, "so John what have been the theoretical influences on your work as a practitioner?" It was a tumble-weed moment, the longest silence in the whole forty-five minutes hung in the air before I could form some garbled response that failed to make even the slightest connection to theory.

Reflecting back I can recognise that the question encapsulated the shift that was expected of me as I stepped into the shoes of an early career academic. The critical thinking in this new world drew from a frame of reference, conceptual and theoretical, with which I felt at the time I had very little connection. The question also signalled that my professional standing had reduced relevance in this context and my working identity had shifted from being a highly experienced professional to someone who was 'beginning again', whose authenticity was going to be redefined (Tomkins and Nicholds 2017). From now on I would need to transform the way that I thought about the complexities of early childhood and commit to ways of knowing that extended beyond the encounters within everyday practice.

The decade of participation within an academic culture which followed my move from practice has in many ways been personally transformative (Rogoff 2003). From an intellectual perspective, developing a deeper understanding of the sociology of childhood, socio-cultural theories of learning and concepts of disability has been an enriching experience. I have published journal articles, chapters, co-authored and edited books, led research projects, made successful funding bids and presented at academic conferences in dreamily wonderful locations. To borrow from Bourdieu's sociological analysis of the academy my long apprenticeship has involved a shift in my cultural capital where I have acquired new skills, knowledge and subconsciously a re-shaped way of being (Bourdieu 1988). Yet much of my research work has continued to focus on the practitioner world and developing practice rather than more conceptual or theoretical concerns. For example, my most recent projects have explored how an observational tool called 'In-the-Picture', originally developed for research purposes, can be used by practitioners in their own settings (Rix, Parry, and Malibha-Pinchbeck 2020). Such prioritisation suggests that the knowledge and experience I developed as a teacher, my practical wisdom, continues to have a huge influence on the way that I work. It may also be symptomatic of where I position myself within the academy, as someone whose transformation has some way to go, who still sees himself as a practitioner adapting to the academic world rather than an academic who used to be a practitioner.

Of course, continuing to identify so strongly with my practitioner roots has been a personal choice. Early on in my academic career I decided not to follow the conventional path of studying for a doctorate despite the encouragement from my colleagues and superiors. Indeed I have never been swayed from that original decision even though in some respects my promotion to Senior Lecturer in 2018 could be seen as a signifier that I was developing a 'feel for the game' (Enright, Rynne, and Alfrey 2017, p. 25). I am not sure whether this intransigence was driven by a lack of confidence, pragmatism, laziness or something more fundamental. In many ways the academy appears to shape participation of inductees within its own parameters of established values, procedures, systems and hierarchical structures (Bourdieu 1988 in Enright, Rynne, and Alfrey 2017). In my experience there is less emphasis on exploring the potential of interdependent learning between well-established members and any new entrants whatever their previous background or experiences (Nind and Vinha 2017). Consequently academic criticality and rigour seems to occupy an elevated status over practical wisdom with little of the synergy that bell hooks celebrates. Perhaps that is why I have rarely told my practice stories as a contribution to academic discussions and why, faced with such rigid conditions that determine inclusion (Enright, Rynne, and Alfrey 2017), I have found feeling part of the community to be a more complex and drawn out process than expected.

Looking to the future for some form of personal resolution, maybe for me it is simply a question of time? Perhaps in another fifteen years when my time spent in practice and the academy match up, my identity as a scholar and practitioner will merge imperceptibly. Unfortunately, however interesting this might seem, I think I may not be around to check out the premise. By then I will be nearly 80 years old and well into days spent giving the garden the attention that it has long deserved.

———————————

References

Bourdieu, P. (1988). *Homo academicus*. Stanford: Stanford University Press.

Enright, E., Rynne, S.B., and Alfrey, L. (2017). 'Letters to an early career academic': learning from the advice of the physical education and sport pedagogy professoriate. *Sport, Education and Society*, 22:1, 22-39.

hooks, bell (2009). *Teaching critical thinking: practical wisdom*. New York: Abingdon.

Lave, J. and Wenger, E. (1991). *Situated Learning: Legitimate Peripheral Participation*. Cambridge: Cambridge University Press.

Nind, M. and Vinha, H. (2014). Doing research inclusively: bridges to multiple possibilities in inclusive research. *British Journal of Learning Disabilities*, vol. 42, no. 2, pp. 102–9.

Rix, J., Parry, J. and Malibha-Pinchbeck,M.(2020). Building a better picture: practitioners' views of using a listening approach with young disabled children. *Journal of Early Childhood Research* 18(1): pp.1-15

Rogoff, B. and Gardner, W. (1984). Adult guidance of cognitive development. In Rogoff, B. and Lave, J. (eds) *Everyday Cognition: Its Development in Social Contexts*, Cambridge, MA: Harvard University Press, pp. 95–116.

Rogoff, B. (2003.) *The Cultural Nature of Human Development*. New York: Oxford University Press.

Schon, D. (1983). *The Reflective Practitioner: How Professionals Think in Action*. New York: Basic Books.

Tomkins, L. and Nicholds, A. (2017). Make me Authentic but not here: Reflexive struggles with academic identity and authentic leadership. *Management Learning*, 48 (3) pp 253-270.

Ups and Downs of A Second Career

Jim Wolper

The passenger climbed the steps to the airplane. I waited at the top, in my pilot's uniform, smiling a greeting. She looked up and blurted out "You look like a professor!"

"I am." I don't usually tell passengers this, but she asked. "And you're the pilot?"

"I am."

She started toward the cabin and stopped. "Of what?"

"Math."

No reply. I gave her the safety briefing, walked into the cockpit, and started the engines.

For 25 years I have been both a Mathematics professor and a professional pilot. Most of my professional flying comes in the summer, with some weekends and nights during the school year. I teach flying all year. I have never missed a class because I was flying. Nor is it a hobby: I have the highest grade of pilot certification, and am held to the same standards as the full–time pilots. Most pilots flying the King Air I fly make it a career.

***

I started as an unimaginably abstract Math major. My electives were literature and history courses, not the courses associated with mathematical applications. I barely passed Freshman Physics. The low grade was partly because I didn't find it abstract enough, but mostly because I was an irresponsible first year student. I took no other science courses. The Computer Science courses I took were also theoretical and abstract, covering few of the techniques I used at the summer programming job that their presence on my transcript made possible.

Former Harvard Dean Harry Lewis, himself a computer scientist, said that the apparent purpose of a Harvard education was to never study anything useful (2006). That was true for me: my limited experience with hands–on applications did not come from school. I studied wonderful abstract things with amazing people, but learned far more about how to do things from the campus radio station than I did in class.

Flying was a long–standing interest, in the abstract—even though it's safe to say there is no abstraction in flying! I started learning when my post–doc salary meant I could afford it, and I quickly learned that when it came to aviation everything I knew from school was wrong. I had done and taught dozens of textbook problems in which airplanes flew due North at fixed speeds and altitudes. As a student pilot I learned that this is difficult, if not impossible. North? The compass is subject to all kinds of errors, some of which depend on whether you're in the northern or southern hemisphere. Speed? The number on the airspeed dial, isn't speed through the air at all, or speed over the ground. Altitude? Altitude is, at best, a fuzzy concept we gave up on decades ago. The Earth is not the perfect sphere the textbooks assume it to be, either. And then there was weather—but more about that later.

This was a different kind of reasoning from what my education taught me.

Let me explain. Many people are familiar with weather radar from television or internet reports. Watch it and decide whether the rain is coming. That's the most abstract view: a mathematics textbook might say "the storm is 15 miles away and moving at 20 miles per hour," setting up some practice calculations. In this context those are given, Platonic numbers, with no regard to how one comes to know them.

In truth, measuring distance and speed is a genuine problem that abstract mathematics does not address. It does not even acknowledge that, in fact, a measurement was made, or how (textbooks are full of measurements that are impossible or even silly to try to make). Measurement requires looking at the technical aspects of sending, receiving, and processing the radar signal. Where mathematics renders measurements in concrete values, in fact measurements of distance and speed are presented with some kind of plus–or–minus tolerance. That's a big difference in approach. On the one hand, the number is known—concrete, without abstraction; on the other, the number is an interpretation of radar signals.

Larger airplanes have their own weather radar that helps pilots avoid the hazards of hail or heavy rain. But it takes skill to operate and interpret radar signals effectively.

There are four kinds of reasoning here; and representations of their practitioners can be seen as:

- a mathematician, who doesn't need to measure (measurement is a foregone conclusion);

- an applied mathematician, who uses measurements but not instruments;

- an engineer, who knows the instruments, but can't calibrate them; and

- a technician, who can calibrate instruments.

A mathematics professor is only the first type; a pilot must, at times, be any of the three, which are all very mathematical. In other words, my education missed a large amount of what people view as Mathematics.

Flying's lack of abstraction changed my Mathematics teaching. I start 100– and 200–level classes with a measurement exercise: while the students fill out the little cards with name and class and major, I ask them to measure the textbook. They all use the same ruler. The numbers they come up with are close, but are never identical. "That happens with every number in this course," I tell them. Flying means dealing with weather, and weather provides a lot of problems in applied mathematics. And so knowing how to fly—being more than a mathematician—changes teaching, and affects content.

The kinds of insights and calculations that weather analysis demands are exemplified in a research paper (Lorenz 1963) whose results on "The Butterfly Effect" and Chaos Theory have become part of popular culture. Students can read this paper from a mathematics perspective, some of its discussion as abstract as anything in the typical junior level "introduction to the major" course. Or they can read it for applications, learning computer methods for solving equations. Because I fly, I can help them read it as an engineer, predicting the range of validity of a model. And can show both Mathematics and flying students the technique of using one of the parameters in the study to predict the likelihood of thunderstorms.

Teaching can be affected in other ways, too. My flying career started with teaching students to fly in airplanes. "Math Anxiety" is a real thing, but in flying some students' anxiety is fear for their very lives. Recognizing life or death anxiety has improved my ability to sense when a student is overwhelmed.

***

Research is an important part of an academic career—and flying influences my research, too. The influence of flying on academia appears on my curriculum vitae. I developed a course in the mathematics of navigation, which also featured readings from Antoine de Saint-Exupéry and Futurist poets, and works by artists such as Robert Delaunay. I set aside the book I developed from designing that course—it's not the kind of thing that leads to tenure—waiting until my first tenured summer to complete it.

When I published "Understanding Mathematics for Aircraft Navigation" (2001), the book drew mixed reactions from academics. My department chair as much as spat on it; his successor praised it heartily. Both a major airline and the Australian Civil Aeronautics Authority recommended it to pilots. I don't think this success resonates with academics, however.

I have not abandoned abstraction, and my research includes both abstract mathematics and ineffably abstract mathematics. Flying has influenced these as well. I now use applied techniques, especially statistical techniques, in my abstract geometric research, finding useful information about abstract questions by studying the data they generate in the context of measurement and signals.

That flying has changed the most abstract parts of my research surprises even me. Part of the influence comes from the study of computing, but I have also begun to explore the relationship between Calculus (especially the mathematics of the infinite) and the real-world in a kind of Kantian sense: what is the nature of space and time? My essay "The Queen of Limits" (2019), explicitly uses a common solution to a flying problem to address a foundational, abstract problem.

***

More broadly, it is easy for those who are expert at one thing to imagine themselves experts in many things. I have observed this in non-academics who enter academia, and in academic discussions of non-academic affairs. This is worse for someone with expertise in two fields. The realms of my expertise are so separate as to almost be antagonistic: pilots, mechanics, and dispatchers have little use for the knowledge of academics (although it might serve them well), and academics have little use for the knowledge of pilots, mechanics, and dispatchers (although it might serve them well).

It is tempting to overwhelm students with all this expertise, whether from inside of or outside of academia. We rush to introduce students to fancy ideas before they are in a position to grasp or use them. But there are always core concepts that are necessary to keep students safe—in the air or in the classroom.

For example, when teaching flying to beginners I focus on turning a complete circle without changing altitude. This seems simple, but in fact it uses all of the flight controls. It's the core knowledge that every pilot at every level must master. Academic flight instruction (yes, there is such a thing) puts more emphasis on more advanced topics that professional pilots have to master; but I remind my students that crashing exactly on course still makes them dead.

The emphasis on basics is almost abstract—as if this basic maneuver is an axiom of flying—and thus mathematics influences flying. On the other hand, I am currently writing a Calculus book, and asking about basics—motivated by teaching flying—is central to its philosophy and content. The book begins "Pilots work with air; sailors work with water; knitters work with wool; potters work with clay. Those who do Calculus work with numbers and functions."

What are the basic maneuvers, analogous to an airplane's level turn, in Calculus? The standard textbook answer is that Calculus depends on two basic concepts, maneuvers if you will, "derivatives" and "integrals". Through my real-world work I have come to think that these are too abstract to be useful. The first of the actual basic topics is linear approximation, which my book introduces before students study derivatives. Later, derivatives enable more precise approximations, but precision is an "advanced maneuver" that obscures the concept. Sometimes, the correct level of precision is "fly toward the blue sky."

I understand this because I fly.

As much as I love abstract reasoning and being a Mathematics professor, it is not enough for me. I need balance between action and contemplation. The two are not incompatible. This should be well-known—after all, Wittgenstein started as an aeronautical engineer (Biletzki and Matar 2020).

A few years ago I was at a conference listening to a talk on a deep mathematical subject that very few have the background to understand when I got a text from a former Air Force fighter pilot I worked with asking a really obscure question about an airplane that very few pilots have the background to fly. I found the contrast satisfying, and my ability to discuss both a result of my capacity to fly as much as teach, to do research as much as stay aloft.

References

Biletzki, A. and Matar, A. (2020) Ludwig Wittgenstein. *The Stanford Encyclopedia of Philosophy*, E. Zalta (ed.), https://plato.stan- ford.edu/ archives/spr2020/entries/wittgenstein/.

Lewis, H. R. (2006). Excellence Without A Soul: How a Great University Forgot Education. *Public Affairs*.

Lorenz, E. N. Deterministic (1963). Nonperiodic Flow. *Journal of Atmospheric Sciences*, vol. 20.

Wolper, J. S. (2001). *Understanding Mathematics for Aircraft Navigation.* McGraw–Hill.

Wolper, J. S. (2019). The Queen of Limits. Manuscript.

Discovering Success through Education: The Gentle Whisper of Planting Acorns

Kathleen Harris

Don Herold (1926) stated, 'Work is the greatest thing in the world, so we should always save some of it for tomorrow.' *The Man Who Planted Trees* is the story of Elzeard Bouffier. Bouffier is portrayed as a man of great determination who lives a very simple lifestyle. After losing both his son and wife at an early age, Bouffier travels to Provence, in southern France. His only possessions being his sheep and dog, Bouffier builds a stone house to live in and embarks on a new vision, a significant mission which is to plant one hundred perfect and fine acorns a year. This mission takes a lifetime which allows the reader to manifest and watch as the character makes a transformation of this region over several decades. Like a father, he works hard and nurtures to bring new life into a region which was once barren, cold, dark, and lifeless. Each time I read this piece of literature, I find myself as the character gently planting acorns. I see my roles as a pre-school teacher, a catechist, a professor, and a mother in so many ways throughout the story.

For a human character to reveal truly exceptional qualities, one must have the good fortune to be able to observe its performance over many years (Giono, p. 3). In so many ways, Bouffier brought light to the darkness by planting and caring for the acorns he planted. He carefully observed their growth and watched carefully as all of these seedlings turned into a forest. In my career as a preschool teacher, it was exciting for me to see the positive influence I could have on young children's lives by observing the progress they made day by day.

Just as acorns are first planted when they are very small—but will grow into oaks—young children are natural, vital human beings who haven't had much experience in getting along with peers. Young children are strong willed and self-centered, as well as affectionate and trusting. Throughout my teaching, I've worked as a supportive 'educarer' for young children, respecting and honoring the child's strengths and unique capabilities. Just as Bouffier had to cultivate care when nurturing his seedlings, so does an educarer need boundless patience, good judgment, character, and maturity to exercise the balance of control and latitude that young children require. But the skills of nurture must be learned. You have to know how to select the right acorns for planting, the right weather and soil conditions. For me, that meant acquiring a solid knowledge of child development and curriculum pedagogy from several avenues including a community college, liberal arts Catholic college, and research university.

One of the most valuable lessons and gifts of education is the love of learning. During my preschool career, I took time to listen to children's ideas (although at times, it was hard to listen to fifteen three-year olds all at once!). I also loved to engage in conversations and laugh with them, because I might learn as much from them as they might learn from me. Early childhood author and teacher, Mimi Chenfeld (1993) believes young children invite us on a journey to our individual beginnings when the world was fresh and waiting to be discovered.

My classrooms were a place where laughter and bear hunts occurred daily. You didn't need a ticket or money to ride a special magic carpet or to take a train ride on the Polar Express. Each magic carpet was personalized and could take you anywhere. I was the star polisher making sure all my shining stars felt happy, safe, and could be the shiniest stars in the heavens. The world would be a better place because of them. My goal was to make every aspect of the preschool day an experience to rejoice and find joy. I would do this by using childrens' interests and strengths to develop emotional, social, cognitive, physical, and spiritual domains to their fullest. And I did this by using compassion.

In order for Elzeard Bouffier to bring new life and hope to people who lived in his community, he had to work with compassion for the mission he was committed to. Though that mission was simply planting acorns, it was the care he had for those acorns that made the difference. Compassion works hard to make today's real world tomorrow's better one. Elzeard Bouffier did this by transforming a barren town into one with beauty and hope for the future for those who lived there. Teachers do this by providing a service—one that lifts up, carries us to safety, and provides shelter.

Service leadership has always been a passion of mine. During the past twenty-five years, I have been active with many organizations that have contributed to my teaching profession. While I attended college, I served as a Vice-President for Pi Lambda Theta Educational Honor Society, and Vice-President of Affiliates for the Ohio Association for the Education of Young Children. These roles gave me opportunities to empower members to use their talents and strengths to participate in service projects for the community. I believe leaders must have clear values with a vision. These professional development opportunities gave me opportunities to grow stronger as a professional teacher and also ignited the flame of inspiration for future teachers to become tomorrow's leaders. Edith Wharton states, "There are two ways of spreading light: to be the candle or the mirror that reflects it." I worked to do both as a visionary and servant leader.

My greatest honor was to receive in 1999 the OAEYC Early Childhood Award for the State of Ohio. This award recognizes an Ohioan in the field of early childhood education who has made significant career contributions to the field which have had an impact on the needs, rights, and well-being of children throughout the state. The honor is awarded based on the recommendations and testimonials of the families who have been affected by the nominee.

"It is the joy she projects and the love that she shares with these children that truly distinguishes her as a teacher. She fosters an environment where our son is safe to explore, encouraged to experiment, and challenged to learn."

"I have come to appreciate and learn from her. I've learned how certain activities help to develop "eye-hand coordination," how scrapes of paper are not trash but… confetti, and how much "fun" glitter really is! Mrs. Harris is not only my daughters' preschool teacher, she's my teacher as well. She challenges us, the parents, to be good role models and first teachers for our children. And most of all, to have fun!"

But there are always more acorns to plant. Shortly following receiving this honor, I completed my undergraduate degree in early childhood education and psychology and began a new journey towards a graduate degree in early childhood education and doctoral degree of philosophy in special education.

I'm sure along the way, Bouffier ran into troubled spots during his course of yearly plantings. Bouffier made sure the land he planted was on community land. Conditions of the soil and rough hilly areas may have been a problem for Bouffier when he did his yearly plantings, and also weather conditions may have been unfavorable during spring plantings with either too much rain or not enough. Similarly, in any career there are critical incidents which are unfavorable, but which can lead us in new and important directions.

In my late twenties, after having a healthy pregnancy for nine months, I lost my first child. Who would have ever thought the moment of birth and death would happen so close together within a 24-hour period? This troubled spot during my late twenties made me realize that life isn't always sunshine and roses. During these moments I tried to count my blessings, reflect, pray, and pick myself up to travel the journey, finding the positive moments and laying low focusing on the negativity. Within these moments of change, difficulty, and taking risks, I found new hope and serenity of spirit to travel on. I did my best to focus and live in the moment; and this brought peace and joy to my soul. In addition to the philosophical and spiritual awakening I experienced during this troubled spot, I was aware that it was time for me to make a change in my career and follow my passion in life which was to teach young children. I always wanted to be a teacher. To satisfy my love for teaching, I taught catechism religion classes on the weekends. After taking time to grieve and move ahead with my life, I decided to start taking classes in early childhood education and volunteer with professional organizations.

As an early childhood and special education professor, teaching with compassion encompasses the way I teach classes, conduct myself as a professional, build relationships with colleagues and students and embrace the mission of our university culture with spirit and pride. Compassion brings light into the darkness. Just as Bouffier brought life and light into a once lifeless and barren community, so I also want to be a teacher who brings light to the darkness by sharing my light to my college students and my love of learning. This beautiful story is practical for all of us in a society where everyone wants to achieve more and become better at a new or current career. It proclaims to the reader: you can do it! The story of Elzeard Bouffier offers a reflective and practical formula for following our dream, and allows each of us to dream where there are no limits because all of us have the possibility and power to make it happen.

References

Chenfeld, M. (1993). *Teaching in the key of life*. National Association for the Education of Young Children.

Giono, J. (2005). *The man who planted trees*. Chelsea Green Publishing.

Keller, H. (2011). *To live, to think, to hope: Inspirational quotes by Helen Keller*. Matthew B. Gordon.

Don Herold Quotes. (n.d.). BrainyQuote.com. From BrainyQuote.com: https://www.brainyquote.com/quotes/don_herold_152388

Ten Years in Academia: A Journey of Exploration and Development

Xia Zhu

"The Journey of a thousand miles begins with a single step." ~ Lao-Tzu

It was August 2010 that I started my first full-time lectureship at a Higher Education Institute (HEI) in the UK. Ten years is a good span to look back and reflect on the journey that I have travelled so far.

***

I was still writing up my PhD dissertation at that time, new in academia and young in age and experience, when I gave my first lecture. I can barely remember that class, but I can still feel the nerves vividly today. The sense of uncertainty is still sharp and lively, not knowing what the students would be like, what they would expect from me and how much I could teach them.

Aside from the nerves, what I remember is the grappling with the change of my role from sitting in a room as a student to teaching in front of the class as a lecturer. What I remember is the madness of reading textbooks late into the night with an attempt to feel secure, certain. What I remember is the typing and printing out every word and sentence that was going to be delivered at each of my lectures.

Preparing those scripts, despite being laboursome, seemed to work as a coping mechanism. It provided me with the courage and confidence needed to stand in front of each class and deliver what was carefully planned instead of shying away. Yet the downside of this strategy was the tendency to develop monologues when overly relying on those scripts. On one occasion, a student approached me after a lecture and asked whether she could have a copy of my scripts for her exam revision. That might have been flattering; nevertheless it urged me to reflect on my practice and drove me to write outlines and bullet points instead.

Over the years, as I delivered more and more lectures and repeated some similar ones, I became less dependent on those notes; yet today when I click on those files, revisiting the scripts developed from the early years, they still bring a smile to my face together with those unquenchable memories. Those are the footprints of the baby steps that I made at the beginning of my academic journey. They witness my adaptation to a new role in academia and my exploration into a new territory.

***

My journey in academia involves a self-exploration of being a learner and an educator, as well as a discovery of how theory and practice may work hand-in-hand. When I was a student, it was challenging to understand business-to-business marketing theories. Concepts such as 'coopetition', 'power' and 'relationship' were foreign and remote to my experience. These distant theories came alive and made sense to me when I started working in a company to help them expand their business into the Far East (which was before my entry into academia as a lecturer). I could relate those alien concepts to my work experience in the organisation and appreciate how theories may explain real-life issues in practice. Now as I teach MBA students working from different industries, I hope that they will also have these light bulb moments of 'Ah! That makes sense!' as they see the connection between theory and practice. The joy of discovery shared is doubled.

My exploration in academia is not limited to the offline environment—I eventually ventured into the territory of open distance learning. Looking back, my first eight years' experience in higher education were mainly in traditional campus-based universities. I greatly valued face-to-face interactions and instant feedback from students. Although I was aware of the rapid development of MOOCs and online courses, with limited exposure to online teaching and learning, I doubted their effectiveness in the virtual environment. I was uncertain what students' learning experience may be like online compared to those offline.

When I joined the Open University in 2018, in order to gain a better understanding of open distance learning, I enrolled a 60-credit first-year undergraduate module at the Faculty of Arts and Humanities. Wearing a student's hat, I attended day schools, mingled with other students (I even joined the module's Facebook group!) and submitted all assignments. I purposefully chose a mix of online and offline tutorials in order to make some comparison.

This practical study experience overturned my perceptions about open distance learning. I had not anticipated the enjoyment of studying remotely at my own time. The level of engagement and interaction in the virtual environment was likewise unexpected. For instance, in the first online tutorial the tutor shared a UK map on the screen and asked students to put a 'star' on the map to indicate their locations. It was a joy to find people from many different parts of the UK studying this module together. At the same time, some students drew a line out of the map and wrote down 'Iceland', 'Switzerland' etc. to show where they were based. It was a delightful discovery of belonging to a great learning community with people from all over the world, and a pleasant surprise that student engagement and group diversity could be easily captured through such a simple online activity. It was also a valuable realisation that I preferred online tutorials to offline in-person sessions which corrected my bias towards learning experiences in the virtual environment.

However, this does not mean that open distance learning is without its own challenge, as my learning diary noted that,

> "The module forum is open. I am a bit overwhelmed by how many posts are there...I do not have time to read each post – it takes far too much time."

> "I am very much behind...I don't know how other students manage to be on top of things alongside their work and life."

Along with my personal joy and pain in studying this module, I developed some understanding of students' open distance learning experience: the pleasure of being able to study flexibly in time and place, the ecstasy of an 'ah-ha' moment, a sense of achievement through learning and self-development, as well as the challenge and struggle of balancing work, life and study.

As I progress in my academic role of working with colleagues across the university to design and produce an open distance learning module, I have gained many more insights behind the scenes. It's been a remarkable discovery of a sophisticated systematic mechanism behind open distance teaching and learning. For instance, designers thoughtfully calculate reading speed (i.e. how many words per minute), and this is considered in planning students' study hours each week. Each student activity and every piece of reading have been carefully selected and designed. A tremendous amount of effort has been put into the production and delivery of a module in order to give students a rewarding and enjoyable learning experience in the unconventional environment. Although my encounter with open distance teaching and learning is recent, I am excited about the opportunities and development in the new territory.

***

My venture in academia would have been audacious without good company. Issues such as students requesting extensions for assignment deadlines, asking for help with their group work or complaining about their exam grades were not part of my anticipation about academic work in a Higher Education Institution. Fortunately, my first office was in an open space shared with another six colleagues. The layout of the space offered great opportunities for small talks. A line such as "I just received an enquiry..." could open up a conversation and lead to an informal mentoring session in the office. Colleagues never hesitated to share the mistakes they had made which helped me to understand the nature of those issues and alerted me to the consequences of mishandling those problems. Their valuable advice has helped me to avoid many pitfalls at the start of my academic journey. As an educator, I hope students might also appreciate their peers' contribution and value the great opportunity of encouraging, sharing and building each other up in a learning community.

As I moved to an individual office later on, the casual and helpful conversations with colleagues now take place in the form of having a faculty tea and coffee instead. These informal exchanges are still much appreciated and treasured, and I am hoping to relay what I have received and learned from senior colleagues to new starters as we travel together in Higher Education.

***

As I embark on the 11th year in academia, looking back at the past ten years, it is a journey of exploration, discovery and development in the company of many friends. Looking forward, with much pleasure, I will travel on to 'learn and live' as the Open University motto stated.

'From schoolboy to interdependent learner': An auto-ethnography of deconstructions and reconstructions of the self as a learner

Neil Summers

This chapter explores the constructs of self and how learning has been influenced over my lifespan. Living and learning is dependent on connections, compassion and a willingness to embrace our own vulnerabilities. These themes for this chapter illuminated the impact poor learning environments have on learners and the need for compassionate, supported networks that enable people to maximise their potential.

Junior School 1969

Headmistress talking to me in her office with my parents after I was caught with a group of boys pushing another boy into a girl's toilet.

"...we are moving Neil into the class 1 (3 years below my current class) as a punishment for behaving this way, we hope this will teach him to behave and act his age!"

I spent 6 months in class with children who were 3 years younger than me, sat at a desk at the back of the class, I was lonely and afraid. This shameful and humiliating experience was part of the negative constructions of myself as a learner that haunt me to this day.

I recall that I was rarely comfortable with relationships as a child; my memories as a child were punctuated by not feeling a part of, or understanding the world I was living in. Not feeling wanted, understood or heard is a lonely and confusing world to live in. Especially as an infant, child and adolescent, when children are thought to be developing secure attachments and sense of self (Winnicott 1988). What feels fundamental about these relationships is what I learnt about myself and others via the relationships I was part of and observed. I was told by my parents and teachers that I was a "sensitive child" and that my behaviours were diffi-cult to control; that I found it hard to grasp some of the essential knowl-edge and skills needed to be "doing what the other kids do", reading, writing, talking, playing, having fun! My sense of myself, and the way I have lived and learned has been fundamentally influenced by these early constructions about myself as a boy, man, nurse, lecturer, son, brother, father, husband and friend (Stahl and Garth 2013). How these truths were constructed interests me as a learner and trainee counsel-lor; the ways in which society controls and chooses what it prefers and tolerates as "human" (Bauman 2005). I want to explore and understand questions about the constructs of self and how my learning has been influenced by what some refer to as "othering," (Meekums 2008). I am choosing to focus on certain elements of your learning journey, as these elements represent the way that you have been 'constructed' and recon-structed.

The Constructed Self

My sense of my self started at home with my family. It is claimed that this process is influenced by the mother with her love of her baby (Win-nicott 1988). Everything a mother does for a baby, from feeding, bathing and "holding" contributes to the child's first idea of the "mother" and helps a child learn about the experiences of the body as a place of secu-rity. Winnicott (1969), developed this theory to include the concept of self, stating that the self is an important part of a person's mental and emotional well-being which also plays a fundamental role in human creativity. These early constructions of self are shaped by what Gergen (2010) refers to as deeply held western beliefs that we hold "mental con-cepts" of ourselves. Societies speak and refer to these concepts of self as potentially being faulty or dysfunctional with the individual self simply being the processes related to conscious choice. The self is represented commonly as... "individual knower, the rational, self-directing, morally centered and knowledgeable agent of action." (Grugen 2010, pg. 2). The constructionist view challenges these beliefs by attempting to develop an ontology the discounts the notion of a bounded self as a singular identity in a social world with relational process (Gergen 2010). This construct suggests that it is not the self that individuals bring to form relationships, it is that the psychological self emerges as result of the relational process.

The Construction of Learning Difficulties

This process continued at school where my aspirations and needs were neglected in what felt like an emerging construction by others of "me" having issues with learning. Dudley-Marling (2004) suggest that this is part of the technical gaze that has permeated the theory and practice of education that assumes that learning disabilities can be explained pathologically and exist in individual students. This left me uninspired and lacking in confidence and believing that the issues I faced as a learning with some sort of dysfunction on my part: "I was the problem." These experiences continue to shape my early constructions of self and stayed with me until I began to build secure and meaningful relationships with mentors in and out of education where I was given the opportunity to develop a sense of myself as a skilful insightful person that had the ability to learn. These mentors gave me confidence and nurtured my abilities and gave me a secure unconditional basis to explore and learn. It is interesting to note that it was the relational aspects of learning I needed and when these secure relationships were not available to me, my confidence waned and the earlier construction of myself as a dysfunctional learner prevailed. These varying constructions and deconstructions of self continued throughout my adult life and culminated in me identifying some very specific learning needs that opened new opportunities and experiences. I was again able to form strong relationships with people around me and could use a technology to enhance and support my learning. I have had to continually fight against the response to my learning needs from others and from my internal critic that asks, "What's wrong with you? Why can't you do this? Why can't you do this Neil?" and the search for a cure or a fix to these issues (Dudley-Marling 2004).

This search led to my decision to train as a therapist and to a fundamental change in my personal and professional self. I found a professional and academic home that has enabled me to re-frame my uniqueness and to start to explore what my relationship is with this perceived "problem" (Freedom and Coombs 1996). These life events have led me to explore how social constructions of masculinity, nursing, therapy training and dyslexia have impacted on my identity throughout my learning journey. While this exploration has not answered these questions, it has provided me with the time and space to explore these existential questions. This exploration feels important as it will allow me to explore my journey as a learner and how different constructions of my self have influenced what I have done so far and who I am to become. This study will also add to the research literature in the field that is limited in relation to identity formation (Riddick 2000), impact of education on learners (Stahl and Dale, 2013), and men becoming therapists (Decker 2001, Smaller and Finlay 2016).

Procedure

I wanted to keep the methods for this study and analysis open as I was unsure about what I would find when I explored, mapped, collected and reflected on the significant aspects of my learning experiences and how these experiences contributed to my many constructions of self (Meekums 1993). My ambition was to free my mind and think about creative ways of collecting and reflecting on historical data that would allow me to shape and develop themes related to living and learning. I also kept a reflexive diary and recorded my feelings and ideas related to immersing myself in my life history. The analysis and reflections began as soon as I started articulating my intentions to pursue this method at the end of the first year of the module in year one.

I initiated this process by plotting my life timeline detailing what I felt were useful aspects of my learning experiences. This details my age, where I was born, where I lived, whom I lived with, the institutions I have studied at. A cacophony of feelings and memories have flooded in and out of my life and my reflexive diary captured my feelings and reflections. The development of the timeline was a creative, exhilarating and empowering experience as opposed to the writing. It is interesting to note that even before I started writing I felt anxious as it appears to be associated with the negative constructions of myself as a learner.

What was I reading, seeing, feeling and learning during these periods of my life?

I recorded personal narratives related to these areas by using pictures, music, books and identifying key relationships in these phases of my life. I also wanted to do some experiential work and recorded some videos of me taking the walk to school that I did as a six-year-old and other visits to homes where I lived and key institutions where my learning experiences unfolded in areas where I spent time being human.

I immersed myself in the data, using all my senses to explore significant life events, relationships and contexts that linked to the many identities I have occupied in my life. I wanted to focus on my subjective experience

(Ellis and Bochner, 2006), with the focus on where links should be made. It is suggested that the use of this storytelling unearths meaning without trying to define it (Arendt 1973).

The following themes are a representation of this iterative process and are closely aligned to phases in my life. I have chosen to explore 3 aspects of my learning experience and how these have influenced the construction of myself.

Themes

He's a Sensitive Boy—Learning to Hide!

My first real memory as a child was how exciting and fascinating the world was, with so much to learn, so much to see. I was born at home July 10th 1963 and my mother, father and older brother (by three years) lived in a council house in an industrial working town in the West of England. My father was a plumber, my mum was a housewife, with my dad working in a local car factory and in the evenings installing central heating to save for our first house. My early memories are punctuated by exploration, excitement and fear as I learnt to walk and talk and develop relationships with my family. One of my earliest memories was when I was about four years old and was taken to Playschool which was in a nearby church. I remember feeling very insecure about being away from my mother and not wanting to go to Playschool and feeling very uncomfortable with being there. I became tearful on arrival and just did not get the idea of why my mother was there and why she was leaving me. I can remember not wanting to play with other children and not finding the environment at all stimulating or comforting. I was so distressed by these events daily; I attempted to run home and would give any opportunity to run away from the playgroup to my house that was only five minutes away. My recollections lead me to believe that my mum wasn't too happy about me leaving the playgroup and of course the staff were very concerned and I can remember being told off for attempting to leave and staff trying to encourage me to take part in the activities in the group. My mum and dad would also encourage me to go to Playschool, my dad saying "you are being a silly boy you must go to playschool."

This is one of the many encounters I experienced in my childhood, that I feel shaped my first construction of self, the construction of what I believe on reflection relates to a term that was frequently used by my mother and significant others "sensitivity." I can recall my mother telling me (repeatedly) that I was "too sensitive." My mother constantly tried to get me to control what she called "my sensitivity" as she thought that this may result in me being hurt. I am now beginning to understand what she meant by sensitivity, this sensitivity was referring to my feelings and she and others were giving me strong messages to shut down my feelings and not share these with others. The way I was taught and learnt to deal with feelings was to push them away and "shut them down" and this is very much part of unconsciousness and appears to have developed into some well-rehearsed templates (Curtis 2010). I believed that if I shared my feelings I would be shut down, I feared that people would treat me harshly, as the nursery did, and I would be made to go back to the nursery and told to stop being "silly." These experiences affected my construction of self as a boy and spilled over to me as a man. What I believed to be "my sensitivity" ultimately led me to believe that I must not be "silly" or "sensitive" to be accepted as worthy of love or positive regard by my parents and significant others (Rogers 2007). I had learnt as a child the things I needed to do to please my parents and I endeavoured to repress "sensitivity" and "silliness "and to be a "good boy."

I always had strong feelings that I often felt weird inside, these feelings would come and go and were paradoxical. My feelings would swing from happy to sad, confident to insecure, loved and unloved, insightful and completely empty. These feelings were always hidden, never expressed for fear of making my difference more instance.

Help through Others—I Can Learn!

Moving through early childhood into school up until the age of 18 my learning experiences didn't improve. I have very many recollections of being bored, unconnected and somewhat perplexed by human emotions and learning experiences. I struggled to read and write; all my junior school reports used terminology like Neil must try harder, Neil needs to concentrate, Neil appears to be too worried about what others think of him, he often daydreams and can be quite rude when he is asked to get on with his work. I did not like going to school and even now thinking back to my school experiences it makes me feel anxious. I never felt part of anything, I joined the chess group, I was unable to hold my own and lost my confidence. I joined the football team, I was stuck in goal, I didn't enjoy that very much. The narrative was set by others; that suggested, I was unable or unwilling to learn. My learning needs were being constructed by others in the "figured" space of 1960-80 school system, where significance was placed on academic ability that was measured by rote learning teaching methods and children were tested via exams like the 11+ that streamed children into ability groups and types of schools, for example, secondary modern and grammar schools (Holland et al. 1998). My position as a learner in school occupied the space that identified me as a passive, resistant learner (Jenkins 2008). I was streamed into the bottom sets in all subjects and at one stage at junior school (because of an incident where me and some other boys pushed a boy into the girl's toilet against his will) I was put into a younger year group as punishment. This as a young boy was a shaming experience and further compounded my negative sense of self, I wasn't even capable of learning with other children of the same age. I was constructed as a "deviant" learner and the difficulties I was facing did not reflect what I could achieve, they were a direct result of how I was reacting and being treated by teachers (Dudley-Marling 2004).

It wasn't until I stayed on in the sixth form that I met and was encouraged by teachers who believed that I had the ability to learn. The sixth form was very liberating, no uniforms, access to a common room with a pool table and snack bar, a flexible timetable where you could come and go between lessons. It was at that time I was taught by an English teacher who encouraged me to read, encouraged me to write, and spent an inordinate amount of time with me. It was this relationship that challenged my internal beliefs about myself as a learner and motivated me to pursue exciting ways to learn.

During this time, I was also growing into a man and noticed that people wanted to develop friendships with me, that others liked me and I began to like myself. This was a beautiful time in my life where I became a confident young man and indulged in the pleasures of life developing passions for music, alcohol, ideas and love. This lust for life and learning kick-started my passion for working with others and developing a real interest in social justice, humanitarian and environmental causes.

Much to the displeasure of my parents and extended family I took a position as a student nurse and a local hospital for people with learning disabilities. I volunteered at this hospital as a sixth former and was struck by the institutional nature of people's lives, that up until this time I was never aware of. Whilst studying as a student nurse I developed a lifelong relationship with my nurse tutor who to this day is my mentor, friend and hero. Together with other students and committed staff we challenged, supported and developed ideas in relation to improving the lives of people with learning disabilities, in the communities we lived in.

I enjoyed studying and the key difference between these experiences and my experiences as a child, was the positive and nurturing relationships that were around me and the engaging nature of the theories and ideas that supported our shared vision. This was the empowering phase of my life, a phase that reflects the belief that people are able, if they are supported and nurtured and in the right context, to learn and thrive in communities (Stahl and Dale, 2013).

I was beginning to take personal control over aspects of my life. It took the form of an almost spiritual element: "...at the level of feelings...at the level of being able to make a difference in the world around us" (Rappaport 1985, p.17). I was being supported and exposed to a wide range of experiences that maintain and built mine and others' competencies. Being empowered related to my sense of being in control and to be in control gave me choices and I could act on matters that affect my life (Zimmerman, 1998).

I worked closely with a young man with significant learning disabilities, who was also totally blind. This young man was led and assisted with his daily activities and did not have much control over his life. We were out on a walk one afternoon and I was learning him through a forest. I loved sticks as a boy and would spend hours in imagery play, reenacting Robin Hood tales and other combat scenarios, the stick became a bow and arrow and gun and lance. I wondered whether this young man, if offered , would use a stick. I placed the stick in his hand and after a couple of attempts he began to use it to guide his way. After prompting him again to sweep the stick across his path and walk unaided. I will never forget his smiling face and his delight as he began to negotiate the walk independently and this experience led me to believe that the key to learning is compassion, connection and love.

Re-Construction—Restoration and Healing

The contribution of significant others in helping me to feel secure, loved and able to live and learn alongside my colleagues and friends became a stable aspect of my middle years, between the ages of 30 and 45. On reflection and looking back at the many aspects of my experience of learning during that time has become clear that what I thought I needed in order to function was praise and acknowledgement from others; this is the only way at that time I felt competent as a man, father, son, husband, friend and teacher. I moved from a job as a practitioner working with families with children with learning disabilities to a nurse teacher as I had a passion for working with others to share common goals around supporting peoples' ability to learn. It was at this time that my early child experiences of being too sensitive and not being able to learn once again came to the fore as it was suggested that you can't be a teacher if you can't spell, write and deal with all forms of communication competently. As a child, I had learned many ways to hide what I thought to be my failings and weaknesses and again I had to retreat and think about very many ways I could stop others from what I thought at that time as the inability to read and write that appeared to be needed at that time to teach. Technological support was not available for me at that time and it wasn't until the introduction of the first personal computer alongside word processing that had spell checks I could confidently function in a teaching environment. My feelings of inadequacy were compounded by others urging me to seek help and support for what was constructed as a dysfunction (Grugen 2010).

I underwent a psychological assessment and was diagnosed with 'attention deficit disorder with associated "learning difficulties". This diagnosis was a double-edged sword as it constructed a new version of me as "Neil with ADD". On reflection, it did help explain some of the issues I have with learning but compounded my insecurities by "othering" me. The diagnosis came with recommendations about technology that could help with my 'condition' with significant others around me suggesting that they always knew there was something 'wrong' with me; my diagnosis gave them the label that they could use to satisfy their long-held beliefs about me.

This label and the lived experience of being me are in conflict as I've come to realise that attention deficit disorder is not an actual pathology. It's one of the many socially constructed explanations to describe behaviours that do not meet societal norms (Parens and Johnston 2009). Timimi (2004) suggests that the pathologizing of the symptoms of ADD is influenced by societal values where passivity is constructed as the norm and where those on the active/ passive spectrum are seen by society as different; their behaviour constructed as problematic. The process of defining this behaviour against a set of symptoms absolves society from any blame related to what the causes of these perceived problems are. I believe that diagnosis does not in any way explain the causes of the differences and emotions that I feel, just differences in behaviour. However, the differences are being reinforced by my relationships as a child and the social context in which I was living and learning at the time. My family and social environments were key determinants in my success as a learner and consequently my internalised notion of self. I was in danger of believing the self-fulfilling prophecy that I didn't can learn and this was somehow part of my DNA, fixed and absolute and I have struggled with the confidence, support and the belief that I can be loved and learn unconditionally (Riddick, 2000).

The struggles led me to counselling training and over the last three years I've been exploring my sense of self and challenging long-held beliefs about who I am and how I learn. I now reject my diagnosis and see no meaning to disclosing all telling others of this crass pathological reductionist view of myself. I take the position that I have a unique learning style and, if provided with support in the right context, I am capable of learning and succeeding (Sebastiane et al, 2016). I am now learning to reconstruct myself as I continue to challenge myself, learn new skills and use my life experiences to develop new ways of supporting my clients. The learning environment and the relationships I've developed over the last three years have helped me to come out of hiding, and close all the doors that I had used to protect myself from feelings of hurt and disappointment. The most difficult aspect of this journey is to combat old constructions of myself that still haunt me at times but more recently are fleeting feelings that come and go and which are countered by the strength I have developed with the support of others in shaping and developing the new me. I've chosen to just use my name not prefaced by Mr, counsellor, teacher or father just Neil. A confident, skilled capable learner who wants to learn with you.

Conclusion

I have explored and developed an in-depth understanding of the constructions of me how my learning has been influenced by what some refer to as "othering" (Meekums 2008). I have traced my learning experiences as a boy and man and this exploration has been both joyous and sad and has illuminated the highly damaging consequences of what society controls, prefers and tolerates of the human self.

This exploration has been both joyous and sad and has illuminated the highly damaging consequences of what society controls, prefers and tolerates of the human self. I have learnt that effective learning is contingent on secure attachments and nurturing, enabling relationships that collectively embrace person centered compassionate models of support. This exploration adds to the research in demonstrating how autoethnography can be used to explore constructions of male learners and counsellors. In tracing my experiences. In undertaking this study, I have been able to strengthen the emerging construction of myself as a learner, a person who is curious, bright, compassionate looking forward to continuing to learn with others.

————————

References

Aguilar, J (1981). Insider Research: an ethnography of a debate in Messer-schmidt. *Anthropologists at Home in North America: Methods and Issues in the Study of One's own Society,* Cambridge and New York: Cambridge University Press, pp 15-28.

Barnes, J (1979). *Who should know what? Social science, privacy and ethics,* Penguin.

Bauman, Z. (2005). *Work, consumerism and the new poor* (2nd ed.), Maidenhead: Open University Press.

Bourdieu, P (1983). Forms of Capital. *Handbook of Theory and Research for the Sociology of Education.* New York Press: Greenwood Press.

Cheater, A.P (1987). The Anthropologist as Citizen: the diffracted self? *Anthropology at Home,* ASA Monographs 25. London and New York: Tavistock Publications, pp 164-80

Curtis, R., and Hirsch, I. (2003). *Essential Psychotherapies: Theory and Practice,* Gurman, A.S., and Messer, S. B. (Eds), New York: Guilford Press.

Decker, N (2001). Gender Battles I Have Known and Loved: The Evolution of My Development as a Therapist Treating Men and Couples. *Reflections: Narratives of Professional Helping,* Vol 7, No 1.

Dudley-Marling, C. (2004). The Social Construction of Learning Disabilities. *Journal of Learning Disabilities,* Nov/Dec 37,6,482.

Dryden, W., and Spurling, L. (1989). *On becoming a psychotherapist.* London: Routledge.

Ellis, C, and Bochner, A, (2006). Analysing Analytic Autoethnography: An autopsy. *Journal of Contemporary Ethnography,* Vol 35 (4).

Ellis, C. (1996). Maternal connections. *Composing ethnography: Alternative forms of qualitative writing,* C. Ellis and A. Bochner (Eds.). Walnut Creek, CA pp. 240-243.

Freedman, J. and Combs, G. (1996). *Narrative therapy: The social construction of preferred realities.* New York: Norton.

Gergen, K. J. (2011). The Self as Social Construction. *Psychology Studies* 56 (1):108–116.

Marechal, G. (2010). Autoethnography. Encyclopaedia of case study research, A. J. Mills, G. Durepos and E. Wiebe (Eds.), Vol. 2, Thousand Oaks, CA: Sage Publications, pp. 43-45.

Medford, K. (2006). Caught with a fake ID: Ethical questions about slippage in autoethnography. *Qualitative Inquiry*, 12, 853-864.

Meekums, B. (2008). Embodied narratives in becoming a counselling trainer: an autoethnographic study. *British Journal of Guidance & Counselling* [online]. 36 (3), pp.287-301.

McLeod, S. A. (2009). Attachment Theory. Retrieved from www.simplypsychology.org/attachment.html.

Parens E., Johnston J. (2009). Facts, values, and Attention-Deficit Hyperactivity Disorder (ADHD): an update on the controversies. *Child Adolescent Psychiatry Mental Health*, 3 (1): 1.

Parlett, M. and Hamilton, D. (1987). Evaluation as Illumination. *Evaluating Education: Issues and Methods*, R. Murphy and H. Torrance (eds), Milton Keynes: Open University Press.

Rappaport, J. (1985). The Power of Empowerment Language. *Social Policy*, 16 (2), pp.15-21.

Riddick, B. (2000). An Examination of the Relationship Between Labelling and Stigmatisation with Special Reference to Dyslexia. *Disability & Society* [online]. 15 (4), pp.653-667.

Shaw, S. S. K. and Anderson, J. L. (2016). Studying Medicine with Dyslexia: A Collaborative Autoethnography, *The Qualitative Report*, Vol. 21, Number 11, Article 2, pp.2036-2054.

Rogers, C.R. (2007). The necessary and sufficient conditions of therapeutic personality change. *Psychotherapy: Theory, Research, Practice, Training* [online]. 44 (3), pp.240-248.

Russell, C. (1999). Autoethnography: Journeys of the Self. *Experimental Ethnography*, Duke University Press.

Smaller, N and Finlay, L. (2016). Becoming a pilgrim: the lived experience of men becoming therapists following a former career. *Self & Society*, 44:3, 215-225.

Stahl, G. and Dale, P. (2013). Success on the decks: working-class boys, education and turning the tables on perceptions of failure. *Gender and Education* [online]. 25 (3), pp.357-372.

Stake, R. E (2004). *Responsive Evaluation*, London: Sage.

Thomas, G (2011). *How to do your Case Study*. Sage Publications.

Timimi, S. and Taylor, E. (2004). In Debate: ADHD is best understood as a cultural construct. *British Journal of Psychiatry*, 184 (1): 8–9. doi:10.1192/bjp.184.1.8. PMID 14702221.

Winnicott, D.W. (1988). *Babies and their Mothers*.

"Your husband doesn't seem like an English professor": Choices, context, and work on the outside

Ed Nagelhout

In order to reflect effectively on my professional scholarly career, I wanted to craft an apt metaphor. My first attempt was the hackneyed image of a gravel road that stretches on indefinitely through the countryside. This gravel road might represent the acceptable path to a scholarly identity. My stories could then show that this is not the only path, for there are other paths, along the berm or through the brambles in the ditch at the side of the road. But I grew up on a cul-de-sac in a blue collar neighborhood in Southern California, where the fathers went to work on assembly lines, in service bays, or on construction sites. My father was a Teamster, working at a Firestone tire and retread plant in Paramount. There was only one way in and one way out of our cul-de-sac. There were no berms, no ditches by the side of the road, no scholarly pursuits. Only concrete and asphalt.

As a child, my grandmother once told me that there were no wrong choices; instead, she stated, "There is the right choice or there is the hard choice." I asked her if the right choice, then, was the easy choice. She was adamant that the right choice wasn't necessarily easy, rather it was expected and acceptable: the choice that insiders get to make. The hard choice, she insisted, is the one that we have to make based on our hopes and dreams, but that falls outside our realm of normal understanding. Grandma was rarely concrete.

At this point, my formal training requires I insert a preview paragraph here, one that states my thesis, summarizes the key points, and establishes signposts for the rest of the essay. And, now, after more than thirty years of writing professional academic papers, that would be the right choice. But this paper resides in a different academic context, and demands something different, maybe less concrete to tell my simple set of stories about choices that I have made along the way to a scholarly identity. Some were the right choice. Some were the hard choice. Some seemed like no choice at all. But each of these choices reveals a small piece of my whole experience as a professional in academia. Each of these choices provides a glimpse of my work from an outside. Each, hopefully, shows a moment when I tried to put insider expectations into a context that I could understand.

I need to go back to school

I earned my PhD from Purdue University in 1996, specializing in Rhetoric and Composition, a discipline I didn't even know existed when I started graduate school in 1989. Before that, I was a Sears Service Technician: punching a clock, driving a white van around Southern California, and fixing a range of appliances, from washing machines to refrigerators. I was a different kind of professional.

I was fully vested (at 27), accumulating Sears stock options, saving for retirement, meeting the expectations of my blue-collar upbringing. But I knew I could not keep driving a white van around Southern California for 40 more years until I retired. The day I decided to make a change, I walked into our mobile home in Ontario after work, on another cul-de-sac, dressed in my brown uniform. My wife, Sondra, pregnant with our third child, was already home from her job as a bookkeeper at a local Toyota dealership and preparing dinner. "I have to go back to school." She turned, putting her hands on her belly, and smiled: "OK."

My mother may have been skeptical about our union, but Sondra was not a hard choice. With her is the only true inside I have ever known.

When I visited the guidance counselor at Cal-State Fullerton in December of 1986, I had more than 100 transferable credits, but as a former scholarship athlete from 1978-1982, these credits were all over the map. My first four years in college were about eligibility, not study plan. I had no declared major, and only chose courses that I knew I could pass so that I could focus on what was important. Baseball. Getting in the cages every day and hitting until my blisters bled. Again. Again. Cliche, but true. I wanted to be a different kind of professional. Surprisingly, the guidance counselor, having evaluated my academic record to date, declared my best choice, and quickest path to graduation, was as an English major. My teammates always called me a weirdo for bringing books to practice.

I walked into her classroom on the first day

Upon graduation, I was accepted into the literature graduate program at Purdue University. My wife and I packed up the three boys and all of our belongings into a mid-sized Penske moving truck and our white Toyota van, and relocated from Southern California to West Lafayette, Indiana. My Teamster father was disappointed since, according to him, I was letting my family down by quitting a good job with good benefits to chase insecurity. My choices were completely outside his realm of understanding.

When we arrived in West Lafayette, one of the first people I met was Bob Johnson, a PhD candidate in Rhetoric and Composition. He described the program in some detail. I was fascinated, and wanted to learn more. So the next day I made an appointment with Dr. Janice Lauer, the head of the program, and asked to enroll in her course, Contemporary Composition Theory. Her reply: "Well, if you would have applied to our program, you would not have been accepted, but since you're already here, and since Bud [Dr. Irwin Weiser] is your first-year composition mentor, you can enroll in my course, and we'll see how you do."

I walked into her classroom on the first day, and Dr. Lauer had written on the board:

An Sit
Quid Sit
Quale Sit

I was hooked. This, simply, showed me what I was about, in a context I could understand.

While I was hooked, I soon discovered that the work, the ideas, did not come naturally, and I struggled to catch up, struggled to make up for too many days in the batting cage, too many days in a cul-de-sac with only one way in and one way out.

But I was hooked. Plodding along seemed like no choice at all. And learning became something different, a daily discovery rather than simply a means to an end. I made progress, sometimes passing, sometimes barely passing. When I met with my cohort to study, I felt like the little brother tagging along, always asking questions and never quite under-standing the jokes. But they were patient, and took me by the hand when I needed it, and I will love them forever. The kindness of community should never be a hard choice.

I moved through the program until the time came to begin casting about for a dissertation topic. This seemed like no choice at all, for the guid-ing question to my entire graduate career (besides, "What the hell am I doing?") seemed to be, "How does a person learn to write like a scholar, like a disciplinary insider?"

And I soon discovered researchers who described the ways that insiders became insiders and the ways that insiders perform like insiders. I began reading about activity theory and legitimate peripheral participation, and I tried desperately to put these insider theories and practices for learning into a context that I could understand. I grappled with the con-cept of master/apprentice structures in the liberal arts and the asymmet-rical relationships inherent in intentional instruction. I tried to picture what learning might look like when it occurs during the immersion of an apprentice in the context of day-to-day work. I read about air traffic con-trollers, what they saw when they looked at a screen or out a tower win-dow, and the right choices that they made. Yet, even at this point in my graduate education, understanding insider thinking still arose from the outside: my first attempt at articulating for myself the production, con-sumption, exchange, and distribution described by activity theory was a model using batting practice as a framework. It seemed for me there remained only one way in and one way out.

I play softball with them

While trying to get a handle on my own legitimate peripheral partici-pation, I was also playing tournament softball. One weekend in the late spring, a local team picked up a few ringers (like me) for a major tourna-ment in Kokomo. On the first day of the tournament, I packed lunches, toys, and softball equipment, loaded the boys into our white Toyota van, and took off down the road through the countryside (giving Sondra a well-deserved day of rest, relaxation, and QUIET). In between games, I struck up a conversation with a teammate who happened to be a PhD candidate in Biology (yes, we were the only two graduate students on the team, probably in the whole tournament). When he found out my area of study, he went into an extended rant about his major professor's inability to write and therefore to help him effectively with his disserta-tion. I was fascinated, and wanted to learn more. So, of course, he invited me to play on the Biology summer softball team, the Celluloid Heroes. Apparently, some faculty members in the department were hyper-competitive in the Purdue Summer Softball League and were always looking to try out new players.

I enjoyed meeting the Biology professors on the team in a context, technically, outside of academia, and my ability to hit a softball 400 feet allowed me to easily fit in as an insider. My curiosity and enthusiasm for studying writing, and my endless string of questions after games over the course of that summer about their own writing practices, however, gave those professors the confidence to recommend a variety of labs in their department to contact about my work. And, so, with advice from Bud, who remained my mentor, I took my research show on the road, for the first time, outside the English department. I met with the Chair of Biology and their Director of Graduate Studies. I pitched my research plan to 11 different professors (none of whom had an interest in softball), formally presented my research design to 8 labs, and got the go-ahead from 6 of them.

I eventually chose one lab for a pilot study and two others for the full study. They accepted my work as their work inside their labs. And, in turn, I learned more about drosophila, the Ross River virus, the Sindbis virus, the scientific method, and IMRAD than I ever thought possible. This was a whole learning experience for me, and helped springboard my thinking on program development, on the whole learning experience of undergraduate students, and the ideas that should push us to see beyond the single course, beyond courses in a program or major that are too often disparate and delivered in isolation as insider information.

I completed my dissertation and defense ahead of schedule. Some still tell stories about those weeks before graduation of me wandering through Heavilon Hall or hanging out in the Writing Lab, baseball hat on my head and coffee cup in hand, looking content but just a little bit lost. Maybe there was more than one way out. As a newly-minted PhD from one of the best rhetoric and composition graduate programs in the country, I was prepared as an insider for my future work. They explained the right choices, but I could only nod my head from the outside, struggling to put those insider instructions into a context that I could understand. I no longer lived on a cul-de-sac, surrounded by concrete and asphalt, but the choices seemed just as hard, just as far outside the realm of my understanding.

"You won't get tenure without it"

I have always worked in English departments, where the scholarship of writing studies has traditionally been deemed irrelevant by my literature colleagues. Likewise, their choices were completely outside the realm of my understanding. I grew up a library kid, riding my bike to the Stanton library 2-3 times a week. Since I didn't have to buy the books, I could put a book down or quit reading if it was no longer interesting. School tried its best to break me of this un-scholarly habit: to press on through the boredom, to overcome my ignorance, to appreciate truth and beauty to the very end, to understand what was important. I have never finished a book by Jane Austen, but I have read each book by Rainbow Rowell more than once from cover to cover.

Since the time of my dissertation study, my work and research has remained collaborative and interdisciplinary. Very un-scholarly in English. On my campus visit to UNLV, the Dean of the College of Liberal Arts and the Chair of the English Department both emphasized that tenure and promotion meant a single-authored scholarly monograph. "You won't get tenure without it." I could only nod my head from the outside, struggling to put those insider requirements into a context that I could understand.

I work to promote writing in all of its applications and iterations. My scholarship seems far-reaching and expansive, to me, but my daily work too often feels like just so much shouting about the same things from too many outsides; and so my most satisfying research has grown out of some local context, or blossomed from some chance encounter, driven by a desire to understand how writing operates in some specific academic or professional rhetorical situation, and I tell my stories in the disciplinary spaces that are important to my work, even if those spaces are deemed less legitimate choices in my department. I can only make choices in a context that I understand, no matter the context of my immediate surroundings.

I write every single day, but I have yet to write a single word towards a single-authored book. Very un-scholarly in English. Instead, I take my show on the road, outside the department. To date, I have published work with 34 different scholars from 12 different disciplines. I have presented more than 100 papers at a wide range of disciplinary, interdisciplinary, and multidisciplinary venues. When I applied for promotion to full professor, a literature colleague came up to me after the department vote and said, "You have so much stuff. I voted for you, but I still don't understand what it is you do." My choices are completely outside their realm of understanding.

He broke his wrist trying to dunk a basketball

Inside and outside are too often talismanic when we are growing up because simple binaries can define our world more concretely. As a teenager, it too often feels like the only choice. As I grew older, understanding how I fit in became tempered by reflecting on why I wanted in. This felt like a better choice. In graduate school, getting in often felt like a survival mechanism. Sometimes, that can be painful.

When my youngest son was eight years old, he wanted to be a professional basketball player. He played every day. He watched games on TV. He was tall for his age, so he was going to be a center like Shaquille O'Neal. And he was going to dunk. Just like Shaq. Of course, when you are eight years old, and not over seven feet tall, you have to adapt. He broke his wrist trying to dunk a basketball by jumping off a picnic table. Eventually, we all run into our limitations. Sometimes, that can be painful.

At this stage in my career, looking forward to retirement, I find that I have been the happiest and the most productive in spaces where my limitations are accepted, even encouraged, where inside is engaged and engaging, and the expectations are a part of the experience, rather than a prescription. Sometimes the inside is fleeting, a mere glimpse from the outside. Maybe that can be painful, but if we are kind and do our best to share the inside with the outside, to blur those arbitrary lines, no matter how fleeting, our work, and our world, can be the better for it.

I grew up in a cul-de-sac, surrounded by concrete and asphalt. There were no lessons, no brilliant insights, no scholarly pursuits. Ultimately, the inside is what we make it, the sum total of all of our choices, the place where we feel at home. This is not news because at the end of the day, we all go home to a life. This should be no choice at all.

With Sondra is the only true inside I have ever known.

"Your husband doesn't seem like an English professor"

I was the first person in my extended family to get a Bachelor's degree. That was something to be proud of. Getting a PhD just made me suspect in their eyes. My wife's extended family, mostly living in rural Wisconsin, were uncertain how to react when they heard Sondra was married

118 Voices of Practice

to an English professor. When they met me, they really weren't much interested in hearing about what I did. They only told her, "Your husband doesn't seem like an English professor." My colleagues in the English department tell her the same thing.

PART III

Scholarship and Practice

Once inside academe, how does the the marginal scholar "fit in"? What opportunities are given for utilizing the skills learned in their fields within the more theoretical landscapes of traditional scholarly discourse? There are deeply affective narratives of the balancing act of being both a practitioner and an academic, of making one's way simultaneously inside and outside of the university. In these chapters, authors discover their voices—voices informed by trying to fit in, by learning to code switch, or by recognizing the performativity of life and career inside the ivory tower.

Striving for a place on the inside: one story of finding a scholarship community in a 'research intensive' University

Bryony Black, Gareth Bramley, Kate Campbell Pilling, Louise Glover, Zoe Ollerenshaw, Laurence Pattacini, and Joan Upson

Introduction

This chapter is written by a group of University Teachers from a range of disciplines in the social sciences, based at a 'research intensive' university in the UK. We came together through a university initiative designed to both kick start, and to support pedagogic research and scholarship activity for staff on teaching-focused or non-research contracts.

In this chapter we discuss our reasons for joining the group, the benefits we found from being part of this community, and its impact upon our own scholarship practice, jointly and individually, beyond the group. We also explore, by reference to individual perspectives, the experience of the journey from 'outsider' to 'insider', and our surprise at finding ourselves within a new scholarly community which we, and the University initiative, have created or allowed to emerge.

The Scholarship Circle discussed in this chapter was an initiative of the Faculty of Social Sciences seeking to facilitate the development of scholarship and pedagogic research within teaching-focused staff across the faculty. The Circle was not the first incentive focused upon the scholarly development of teaching-focused staff, but it has proved to be the most effective so far in terms of facilitating the skill set and confidence necessary for this group to develop as individuals, and as an effective community of scholars. Previous initiatives had brought pedagogic expertise from within, and outside the University, together with our University teaching staff and certainly sparked our enthusiasm, but none had the means of following through by providing ongoing support and the development of the necessary skills set for our scholarship to take off.

All of the individuals within the Circle had accumulated knowledge, experience and 'know how' as professionals practising within their respective fields prior to taking on roles as University Teachers. It was this breadth and depth of experience that led us to understand that we could contribute to academic life and scholarship by harnessing existing 'know how', developed through technical and professional experience outside of the academy to solve 'real life' problems, and the accompanying 'soft skills' developed with that experience.

Within the body of this chapter/discussion we will further explore and share the development of the members of the Circle as individual scholars, and the group as a model for the development of scholarship within a department, Faculty or more broadly at institutional level, at a time when the measurement and narrative of Teaching Excellence within the UK Higher Education Sector has never been more prominent.

Gareth's story: becoming an insider

I came to this scholarship circle with excitement and trepidation in equal measure. I felt extremely lucky to form such a support network with like-minded peers, as well as having access to dedicated support from our mentor David. However, this set up also led to doubt swimming around my head about my own ability to undertake scholarship, particularly in the form of published work. My experience of the circle took me on a magical mystery ride through stress, productivity, enthusiasm, doubt, understanding, weariness, nervousness and eventually to fulfillment! I would absolutely say that the ability to focus on a defined circle of scholarship was an extremely positive experience for me, and I particularly valued the openness and honesty of the circle combined with the musketeer like 'all for one and one for all' mentality. Looking back at the end, with published article in hand, I cannot thank our mentor and my fellow participants enough.

Scholarship confusion

Whilst as University Teachers we were acutely aware of the 'need' to undertake 'scholarship' as part of our contracts, prior to joining the group our primary challenge lay in defining the meaning of scholarship in this context. Had the teaching-focused label created its own mythology of a teaching 'expert' which University Teachers are then assumed to have to conform with? Did 'scholarship' mean simply embracing the general importance of best practice in teaching, or should it go much further than this to suggest tangible output and impact or a specific set of scholarly 'spurs' to earn?

As individuals we were unclear, not only about a definition of scholarship, but also about the purpose of scholarship in our subject areas. The confusion exhibited itself in three ways:

- A doubt whether scholarship is viewed as important and useful, particularly when balanced against teaching content, knowledge and skills to students

- A lack of clarity as to whether it is ultimately worthwhile for us as teaching-focused staff to invest the time in scholarship

- The lack of tools available to individuals to develop their scholarship.

Despite the confusion as to both the meaning of scholarship, and the way in which this fits in with the role of a teaching-focused academic, everyone who joined the Circle expressed a desire to undertake scholarship in some form. Unfortunately, desire did not create an obstacle free path for any of us.

Laurence's story: becoming an insider

The scholarship circle initiative gave me the confidence and the impetus to engage with pedagogical research, apply for small research grants and collaborate with students to reflect on my own practice and practices in our department. The support and knowledge provided, enabled me to submit and present papers at learning and teaching conferences, lead discussions at learning and teaching awaydays and write papers.

A major and thorny obstacle to overcome was that of time. We were each committed to our area of expertise (the content, knowledge and expert subject viewpoint of our teaching); however the push towards having more engagement with pedagogical research, or other scholarly output, conflicted with the need to keep up with the priorities, such as constantly evolving developments within a particular profession or subject area. This obstacle was exacerbated as most of us were expected to teach across a diverse range of subject areas at differing levels. Although many of us did recognise that exploring best practice in learning and teaching is essential, we also needed to develop and keep up to date with core knowledge which, in addition to all other facets of our teaching roles, could be all-consuming.

A further significant obstacle to overcome was both the perception, and the reality, of a lack of access to or awareness of scholarship-shaped tools to help us develop our skills. These tools could be the provision of specific guidance and support as to how to actually start along the journey of achieving scholarship, in light of our backgrounds and previous experience, together with solving the conundrum of how our teaching focused work could successfully form a more symbiotic relationship with scholarship. An unfortunate perception we carried, that is perhaps often a reality, is that research-focused staff may have clearer access to such tools.

Furthermore, some of us felt that becoming a 'scholarly academic' made us feel like outsiders from the profession or expertise base in which we began, but never truly insiders with more traditional academics. This feeling was deep-rooted because of a lack of confidence that scholarship is as intrinsically valuable as more traditional research. We all shared experiences of being perceived as not sufficiently skilled as an expert to challenge or to join academic educationalists; thus the feeling grew that we fell into a 'no man's land' attempting mysterious scholarship without a clear appreciation of its value and purpose. Such a viewpoint of an outsider was perpetuated by our own teaching-focused employment contracts and career promotion pathways not including or specifically referring to 'research'.

Despite, or perhaps because of the challenges outlined here, the ten of us that joined the Scholarship Circle were enthusiastic to engage with some form of scholarship of teaching and recognised the benefits of doing so. As one participant noted:

I both appreciate and respect this initiative as an essential tool in getting the ball rolling for us as individuals, and for those who will follow... There is an important pioneering aspect of our Circle, and we, individually and collectively have much to learn. (Participant A)

As time went on, we began to feel that the Scholarship Circle, rather than being the answer to our confusion, instead allowed for foundations to be established within the world of scholarship. One participant summarised this:

Once more, let me say at this point, that I both appreciate and respect this initiative as an essential tool in getting the ball rolling for us as individuals, and for those who will follow...There is an important pioneering aspect of our Circle, and we, individually and collectively have much to learn. (Participant C)

Bryony's story: becoming an insider

Taking part in the Scholarship Circle gave me the confidence to take the lead on scholarship within my own department. Having identified a gap in professional development opportunities for the increasing number of people on teaching only contracts, I led a session at an away day, focusing on developing a shared understanding of 'scholarship' and the range of activities this could involve. Following this session I set up a Scholarship Group within my department to encourage others to set aside time for this important element of their work. It took us a while to find an appropriate direction for the group, but it continues to thrive.

Discovering a scholarship community

We came to the Scholarship Circle for a range of reasons, but through it we had, almost accidentally, discovered a group of people with whom we shared common issues and a desire for scholarship that was not previously fulfilled or supported. We all felt in some ways like outsiders, and this status was not just a question of not belonging to the 'research active' norm of our chosen disciplines, but also feeling an amateur within the realm of the educational specialists.

Many of the concerns and confusions discussed in Section 2 were dealt with through the Circle. The Circle consisted of regular meetings which were structured around key tasks and outputs such as conducting a literature review or seeking ethical approval for a project. In addition to our group meetings we were each paired with another member of the circle with whom we had contact between meetings and who, as well as the Circle coordinator, reviewed our work. The mutual feedback of the buddy system together with the regular Circle tasks provided the motivation, tools and support needed to build confidence, facilitated a meaningful and efficient collaborative dynamic and provided further incentive to produce the work set up by the coordinator. Perhaps unexpectedly, the buddy system did not merely give us support but gave us an additional motivation to continue in order to support our buddy. Typical quotes from our contemporaneous reflections illustrate the importance of the structure put in place by the coordinator:

> a good supportive framework to encourage ways forward to write academic articles related to learning and teaching (Participant I)

> the buddy system is also very motivating as you don't want to let them down. (Participant G)

A vital achievement of the Circle was the creation of a forum in which participants felt recognised not merely for their existing professional achievements but also for their intellectual potential as scholars and as members of a community. One participant reflected on their feelings following the first meeting:

> Excitement! – an active scholarly group which is motivated and positive in its contribution to learning and teaching related scholarship (Participant B)

This shared understanding and enthusiasm was useful to us in a number of ways; from practical constraints of ever-present issues with time management – as a group tasked with teaching and pastoral and administrative support for teaching it was easy to discuss this openly – to hidden issues such as lack of knowledge of the 'tools' of academic writing and the personal failure that we had not managed to chart our own academic progress, given our roles at a prestigious Russell Group university.

The individual vulnerabilities we all showed from day one gave us some confidence as a group, and again, this is evidenced in reflections from our group:

> I am grateful for the comradeship of others in the circle, because we each understand what we mean when referring to the difficulties that we face as a group, whilst the rest of the world would have less/no sympathy (Participant D)

Joan's story: becoming an insider

When the invitation went out to prospective members I ignored it. I
assumed that it was a general circular and not directed at me. After all,
why should it be? Then came the follow up and the enquiry about my
availability, and by the time that we met over coffee in the Students
Union my head was buzzing. In the weeks that followed it was like
emerging out of a deep fog. I was not alone in assuming that there were
mysteries that others knew but that I did not, and could not. One by one
they would be revealed to the group and we could look round the room
as each of us had that 'light bulb' moment of self belief.

No less important was the expert input from our Circle leader about the
process and tools of scholarship, which helped us develop our understanding of scholarship itself and suspend our insecurities and open up
to constructive criticism. We felt, and continue to feel, 'behind the curve'
compared to research active colleagues, and the Scholarship Circle gave
some of the tools that we needed to develop our skills. We felt that a
veil was removed to allow us to see the building blocks that had been
kept 'secret' from us regarding our own research and writing. Some of
the resources were new to us. For example, as one participant reflects:

"Reading the Four Rhetorical Questions (Golden-Biddle and Locke, 2007)
was like a 'light bulb' moment for me in showing the way forward" (Participant F)

Other resources were already known to us but the Circle helped us to
chart a course through more generic scholarship tools and gave us a
forum in which to raise specific questions.

Being 'behind the curve', we had little understanding of the time taken to
develop an article and how that time might reduce with experience. We
were quick to blame ourselves, as we perceived our 'insider' colleagues
were able to create high quality research at pace. The supportive structure of the Circle allowed us open and realistic discussion and perhaps,
rather than seeking to navigate the existing insider/outsider landscape,
it gave us confidence in becoming insiders of our own new gang.

Louise's story: becoming an insider

The Circle helped to underline for me what teaching specialist colleagues such as our group can bring to University life and work using our experience plus how we can develop and evolve our skills including scholarship to meet new challenges within HE. I moved to higher education after a career to partner level as a solicitor in private practice. I teach on core modules related to my practice area and have leadership roles in the School on employability and civic engagement (including pro bono clinical education) – issues whose importance is increasingly recognised but which are perhaps traditionally less valued. My work with the TESS Circle has helped me to run a roundtable event on commercial legal clinics attended by many other universities and to give a strong role within that event to the voice of our respective students. I have also partnered with other colleagues within the University who have strong professional links such as architecture to identify and present on our unique 'value added' element and collaborated with a research-focused colleague on a publication.

What happened next?

We entered the Scholarship Circle on the understanding that it would offer us the chance to produce two academic papers over the course of a year – one solo and one collaborative. Whilst this aim was not fully met, the Scholarship Circle acted as a catalyst for productivity. In a group where none of us had previously had a paper published and few of us had presented at academic conferences, we found that the circle planted seeds, it changed perspectives, and it allowed us to see that which was previously hidden from us – in any given year our research-focused colleagues may have to cast tasks aside, or put work on hold, and we should not be so quick to judge our own lack of concrete product as failure, rather to see it as part of a natural cadence.

It became evident following the Circle that it had offered us a route to innovation. Whilst three of the group did have papers published, equally as important was the range of other outcomes that came as a result of participation in the Circle. Most importantly, we realised that aiming solely to produce published articles was a limited view of what could be achieved through scholarship. Following membership of the Circle, we presented at conferences locally, nationally and internationally, set up scholarship groups within individual departments and led staff training for teaching-focused colleagues, all of which would have been unlikely prior to engagement with the group.

Whatever the intention of the university in setting up the Scholarship Circle, the very existence of a university-led initiative to support scholarship for teaching-focused academics gave us renewed confidence and the impetus to go and 'do' scholarship. The group element enabled us to realise that scholarship is not necessarily a solo endeavour. We continue to work together and with people we would probably never have met or collaborated with, without the Circle.

Kate's story: becoming an insider

My first big step was seeing that I was a suitable person to be part of a scholarship circle. Our meetings were inclusive and supportive and showed me that I was not alone in my struggles and difficulties with what was deemed to be scholarship and how to evidence it. I found the collaboration with members of the circle rewarding and confidence building. It inspired me to develop other areas where I could carry out my own and collaborative research beyond the circle and that I did belong in the learning and teaching community.

Of course, time is still not on our side, but we have seen the value of making time for our scholarship, for working together, for breaking free from the teaching, leadership and administrative load of our jobs. This is helped by the fact that we have each developed our own definition or understanding of 'scholarship', meaning that when we do create time we know what we want to do with it and we understand how it fits within our own view of our expertise and skill set.

The exciting part for all of us is that, almost two years on, we are all confident to say what we understand as 'scholarship', to tell others about our work and to help others to develop their own understanding of scholarship. We are no longer at the mercy of others who judge whether we have undertaken this mystical activity called 'scholarship'; we have the agency to act as we believe is appropriate. Watch this space!

Reference

Golden-Biddle, K. & Locke, K. (2007). Crafting a theorized storyline. *Composing qualitative research,* Thousand Oaks, CA: SAGE Publications, Inc., pp. 26-46, doi: 10.4135/9781412983709

Hattery: The Many Roles of a First-Time Teacher

Sean Robinson

On the first day of class, half-way between the parking lot and the brick clock tower that houses what will be my classroom, I stop. The building is backlit, campus is quiet. It hits me that in mere minutes, there will be students—paying students—who will enter the class and expect someone to teach them something. They'll expect me to teach them something.

I have never taught before. Not in the way professors teach: in front of a classroom, with twenty sets of eyes watching their every move. I am—I decide, standing on the walkway—a great many things. I am an alumnus of the university. I am a writer, a student, an artist. I am—absolutely—not a professor.

Yet, three days before, I was having coffee with the chair of the English Department, and yup. Yes. I accepted a position as a Teaching Lecturer at my alma mater. Three days before the beginning of the semester. And I have never taught before.

I decide that I will just have to pretend to be a teacher.

It's strange as the students filter in. I am in the same classroom where, eleven years before, I began my own academic journey. In Composition, with Patrick Armstrong teaching the class. Like me, he was an adjunct teacher, and like me, he held a MFA in creative writing. I wonder, as they sit, if he was ever as nervous as I am. I decide that he probably was, and that if he can do it, so can I.

I shuffle papers—the syllabus, the assignments—like some sort of academic Tarot and wait for class to begin.

***

So, how does a person who has never taught before make a meaningful contribution to the students? How when that person is—at heart—a fantasist? I have more in common with Tolkien's elves than I do the Analytical Essay that serves as a backbone for the Composition course at my university. How do I do it when I have three days to do it?

Like any story, you start at the beginning, and make up the rest.

In writing there is an adage: write what you know. With this in mind, I gathered my trusty resources, and forged into battle.

In building the course—indeed in teaching the course—I looked to three books. The first, *On Writing* by Stephen King. In it, King tells the writer that they are a mechanic accompanied by a tool box. The second, Anis Bawarshi's *Genre and the Invention of the Writer*, tells the writer that they are a performer, acting out the parts assigned by genre. And in Peter Elbow's *Writing Without Teachers*, it offers that the writer might be many more things—including a cook. But never, ever, a teacher. Instead, Elbow espouses two writing processes: growing and cooking.

With these three perspectives—tenets, perhaps—the course was designed. In it, I hoped to drive home three goals: the first of which was the emphasis of real-world application for the skills used in class. The second was that the students understand and appreciate that in academia (and in life, probably) sometimes process is as important as product. Lastly, to introduce them to practitioners of writing—folks who write as part of their professional lives.

On that first day in the clock tower classroom, the first thing we do is introductions and this is where, in reflection, another hat becomes clear. I am going to need to be a facilitator. The students—all first year students—do not want to speak. But when prodded, they share their names, their majors.

Once a week we do a check-in. The first time we do it, I tell them it will be the most important thing we do in class all semester and their heads snap up from their smartphones and toward me all at once, like mind-controlled villagers in a horror movie. They rate their weeks one-to-ten and share something about themselves.

I listen to all of them, and as the weeks progress, I make it a point to celebrate with the ones having great weeks, and offer encouragement to the ones who aren't. College is tough.

But on day one, we begin the process of learning. Section 7 Composition was designed (in three days) to speak to the writing perspectives offered by King, Elbow, and Bawarshi.

In *On Writing*, King offers the metaphor of a tool box as the repository for the skills necessary of a writer. He says "The toolbox was what we called a big 'un. It had three levels, the top two removable, all three containing little drawers as cunning as Chinese boxes" (King 1999). King goes on to explain what goes into the tool box: "Common tools go on the top. The commonest of all, the bread of writing, is vocabulary," "You'll also want grammar on the top shelf of your tool box." Further on, King discusses style: the creation of paragraphs and the use of adverbs.

Beginning on day one, we start going through these drawers.

But first, we start with effectiveness—to see how the tools in the metaphorical tool box are used to their best effect.

I ask students to complete an essay describing a piece of effective writing. It's there where the first surprise comes to me as an educator. The essays are thoughtful, interesting. Three students choose "The Road Not Taken" by Robert Frost, but find it effective for different reasons. One talks about his past history as a drug dealer. Another discusses how going to a college out of state was unexpected. He's a football player and he writes that he's scared of college, being far from home.

They're scared of failing.

Even half-way through the class, I'm scared of failing, too. I tell them that, because we're all in this together.

And it's then that I realize that in some ways, my job is more complicated than I'd imagined when I sat in the coffee shop and became a college instructor. If I have to wear the hat of a carpenter, of a cook, of a gardener, I must also wear a hat I don't have a name for. Confessor. Confidant. Anonymous lurker in the comments section of their lives.

But then again, it's the hat of a teacher.

***

We move forward from there.

There are readings: Ann Lamott's "Writing Shitty First Drafts" where they students don't want to say the title out loud. We talk about word effectiveness—analyzing the poetry of Robert Frost ("The Road Not Taken", an activity shamelessly taken from Patrick Armstrong when I took Composition in the same classroom a decade and more before) and the spoken word of Tupac Shakur. We discuss why writing matters and slowly, so slowly I almost don't realize it, they start opening up.

One student shares a free write after weeks of awkward dead air when I ask if anyone wants to. Another talks about wanting to beat a state record in running. More importantly, they start talking to each other about what makes writing good, or bad, or effective, or why we write.

Writing needs to find a happy medium between too simple, and too complicated. The topic has to be engaging, even if the reader isn't interested. Waiting to the last minute to write an essay produces something less effective than one that has gone through drafts.

They buy into the idea of writing as a process, and something worthwhile.

As we roll into research essays, there's a young lady who gathers information of American made pick-up trucks. She provides data and independent analysis. When I tell her she's done the most interesting research essay in the class, she tells me that she's not a writer. Another—probably the most skilled writer in class—completes a reading of Thoreau's *Walden* using two sources. But in those two sources, he wrings seven pages of philosophical analysis, offering it up with clean words and, if I listen, an echo of how he—the student—looks at the world. And the world's a pretty good place. Even at 8am for Composition.

When I mention it to him, he says that he doesn't think he did the essay right.

This parallels what Peter Elbow offers up in *Writing Without Teachers*. In the "Growing" section Elbow discusses how writers generally believe that writing must be tightly controlled and that as a writing student grows, they begin to interact with the written world differently (Elbow 1998).

Further, Elbow goes on to state that this previous idea is backward—that the "meaning-into-language" process is counter to the act of writing. He writes, "Writing is, in fact, a transaction with words whereby you free yourself from what you presently think, feel, and perceive. You make available to yourself something better than what you'd be stuck with if you'd actually succeeded in making your meaning clear." (Elbow 1998)

The student who wrote on Walden never quite believed that he was a good writer, instead focusing on how to become better—as a writer, as a student athlete, as a person. During our correspondence following the course, in the years since he graduated, he cites the Walden essay as his proudest.

While the growing shown in these essays and in the course may not quite be what Elbow is describing, I believe they represent a necessary growth for a burgeoning writer, academic, student, or person.

In this, perhaps, the writing professor must also wear the hat of a gardener. They must believe in our students and their limitless potential. If nothing else, a gardener believes that the garden can grow, should grow, must grow. So too, our students.

***

Two-thirds of the way through the course, one of the quietest students stops coming. He's the one who writes well, and doesn't have to work for it. He's also the least likely to laugh when I make a joke, and be on his phone when he doesn't think I'm paying attention. When I email him, he says that things have been stressful for him emotionally, mentally and physically. He ends it saying he appreciates my concern. No mention that we crossed paths on the Quad: me leaving the class he'd skipped, he avoiding eye contact. Or that his grade is suffering his lack of attendance and participation with his peers.

In *Writing Without Teachers*, Elbow highlights the need for participants sharing their work to avoid arguing or attempting to make meaning out of one another's work or attempting to reach a consensus. Rather, he suggests that each person bring their own experience to the table, to share with the author. He also suggests (which I think inherent to anyone who is sharing their work with other people) that they demonstrate bravery. Which he defines as "Willingness to risk." He also goes on to say that there is a need for "participants to feel a responsibility toward the other members of the class" (Elbow 1998).

Elbow says that a writer must learn from fellow writers, rather than an almighty professor. Since I am neither almighty, nor a professor, we workshop. For each of the five essays Composition writes over the course of the semester, they share with a small group. They comment on each other's work.

This is where, on reflection, I might have done things differently.

In Patrick Armstrong's Composition course, we workshopped exclusively. We read each essay out loud in class under a pseudonym, and only took ownership of our work in public once the critiquing was over. As a writer (who also went to a MFA program) this has always been my preferred method of working. But for the students in Section 7, we go about it a little differently.

On the first workshop day, they pull out their piles of papers, the critique sheets I've asked them to fill out to add some structure to the conversation. They get to work. Ten minutes later, each of the groups is back on their phones. There hasn't even been enough time for me to make my way to each group, let alone for each group to talk about each of the essays.

It is probably a good thing we only do this a few times. Better, is that when we discuss the workshopping process, folks talk about being unsure of what to say, or how to say it. They want to be supportive of one another, not mean. We discuss strategies on how to approach an essay someone's written. We talk about responding as writers, and inch-by-inch, the critique and peer-feedback becomes better.

In the anonymous evaluations at the end of the course, many say that this was the best part of their learning experience, and helped them hone their skills.

The skills they learn are things that can be worked on. Put into the toolbox.

Concurrent to King's toolbox and Elbow's garden, Anis Bawarshi discusses that genre defines and creates the writer, and that the classroom should model that crucible of creation.

He says, "genres are [also] instruments and realms—habits and habitats. Genre are the conceptual realms within which individuals recognize and experience situations at the same time as they are the rhetorical instruments by and through which individuals participate within and enact situations" (Bawarshi 2003).

On the day we begin discussing genre, there are ten (of twenty) students in the class. It's the worst attendance we've had, ever. But we forge on. They're broken up by academic discipline into five, unevenly populated, groups. It's not ideal, but there has been a surge of would-be Nursing majors since the University offered it as a program. There is a group for Psychology, one for education, a third for health science, and a multi-disciplinary group containing an artist, a computer scientist, an environmentalist, a meteorologist.

In these groups, I hope that the students will begin considering the larger framework and context that their future writing will grow in. Bawarshi suggests that "To begin to write is to locate oneself within these genres, to become habituated by their typified rhetorical conventions to recognize and enacted situated desires, relations, practices, and subjectivities in certain ways" (Bawarshi 2003).

While complicated, this passage can be summarized to say that a writer must follow the rules of the genre they're writing in. Their first activity as genred groups echoes this:

I ask them to debate the superiority of their academic discipline, in an echo of what happens—perhaps in a more friendly manner—in academia. By the end of class, they have laughed and challenged one another. They have begun to think about their disciplines as discrete entities beneath a greater academic umbrella. As the course comes to a close, they will complete independent research and put together a "Writing in the Disciplines" essay.

This is the assignment they struggle with the most. In it (running parallel to the genre exercises suggested by Bawarshi) they are asked to look at their academic discipline and identify what sort of writing goes on in it. Afterward, they're asked to look at peer-reviewed journals and periodicals, and share what current trends are in the field. Lastly, they're asked to speak with someone who's employed in the field, to see their perspective on writing day-to-day.

In my mind, it is the perfect synergy of the three perspectives in the class—the real-life practical application of King's Tool Box, the peer-centered Kitchen of Elbow, and the theoretical Genre Land of Bawarshi.

Panic ensues.

***

Two students send rough drafts my way that discuss the importance of writing, which is not the assignment. Some try to explain how a research article is constructed—also not the assignment. The worst is from an English major who says, pointedly, that writing about writing makes no sense, and is a waste of time.

So much for perfect synergy.

In the classes that follow—including a short extension—I get us back on track. I wear each of my many hats: the expert, the cheerleader, mechanic, and taskmaster to get there, but we do. The day before Thanksgiving break begins, they submit these essays with a sigh of relief.

I think, in many ways this embodies some of what *Genre and the Invention of the Writer* says about the genesis of writing. "Invention takes place at the intersection between the acquisition and articulation of desire" (Bawarshi 2003).

By the time the essay is submitted, the students desire to be complete with the project and thus, the project is articulated.

On the last day of the course, we engage in the time-honored tradition of English classes everywhere when the semester is wrapping up: we watch a movie. And when the short films give way to Saturday Night Live skits, I ask them to tell me why the skits, or the film (a reboot of the Power Rangers franchise, laden with profanity, blood, gore, and action) are specifically effective.

The artist, who has written essays on Australia and the use of unicorns in art, says that it wasn't effective. She quotes the Aristotelian Triangle, saying that the film required Pathos and it didn't connect to her as a reader. Another—the oldest in the class, a wrestler with a bum leg—says that the skits were effective because they have a good hook; pulls the viewer in.

Conversation spirals and turns. Some think they're particularly effective, others don't. There is good-natured banter, while talking about what makes writing effective, perspective. They use the tools we've put in their tool boxes throughout the semester, and they do it while I watch on, adding in when it seems appropriate.

This is probably my favorite hat I wear in class: the hat of an observer, a watcher. Perhaps King would say that the role is that of the tool-box maker, or Elbow would say it is the hat of a gardener. It doesn't matter, because when the end of class comes, they're laughing and learning.

When the dust settles, the videos are over, and the students leave the classroom onward to the next semester, I read their last assignments. I asked them to complete a reflection where they comment on what they've learned, where they've grown, and what they still need to work on. It's in this that I have succeeded. Maybe. Hopefully.

One student writes, "This class gave me a safe space to comfortably express my emotions and express what I was thinking without being judged." Five years later, they're a political activist, working on presidential campaigns. Another, now an athletic trainer at a local school says, "I believe in the question for knowledge and masterization. That even when you struggle in something, there is no reason not to get better at it because you never know when a mastered skill will come in handy later on in life." The third, a student who doesn't continue at the University, and has fallen off the map writes, "This class has given me more inspiration, more hope for my future."

It's this that the first class ends on. Whatever hat we wear as a teacher, an instructor, a professor, whatever title, and all the hats we wear, we must provide safety, support, and an environment of growth for our students. So they can find hope and inspiration for their futures.

That's the most important hat we wear.

References

Bawarshi, A. (2003). *Genre and the Invention of the Writer*. Logan, UT: Utah State University Press.

Elbow, P. (1998) *Writing Without Teachers*. New York: Oxford University Press.

King, S. (1999). *On Writing: A Memoir of the Craft*. New York: Scribner.

Finding a Voice

Lucy Rai

My own story is one that I have told many times to colleagues. It is the story that explains how I became involved in scholarship of teaching and it still underpins my work. Just to backtrack a little, I began my career as a social worker working with children at risk. It was a career I was motivated to enter as I wanted to help people change their lives when they were facing disadvantage, discrimination and family instability. The reality of my experience of social work practice, however, was that as an employee of the system I was part of the problem. The people I was working with were not able to claw their way out and my role too often seemed to be at best damage limitation and at worst making the situation worse for people. This was highlighted most strongly for me through an experience which ultimately resulted in me leaving social work practice.

While working in an inner city child protection team, I was allocated responsibility for a young mother who had had all five of her children, aged seven years downwards, removed into the care of the local authority following very serious physical abuse of her eldest, a seven year old boy. This mother was also raised in local authority care after her mother came to the UK from Jamaica and was subsequently detained in a psychiatric hospital under the Mental Health Act 1983. The five children of this mother were placed in three different foster homes, all but one being with white families. Despite precautions put in place following assaults on two previous social workers, I was seriously assaulted by her and experienced post-traumatic stress as a result. This was a very emotionally difficult experience for me personally but it also indicated the level of mental distress this woman was experiencing. She was later diagnosed as having a 'personality disorder', a label which seemed at the time only to indicate to professionals that she was mentally unstable but 'untreatable'.

But this was not the point. The point for me was that I was working with the third generation of a family who were in acute need and, to my mind, the system was failing for a third time as another generation of children entered the care system. I felt I was part of a system which was unable to stop the patterns of personal and institutional harm. These systemic failures of immigration, the impact of racism on care provision, the limitations of hospital and community care provision for those with mental health and parenting needs all provide a context to a story. A story taking place in the context of institutional discrimination which made me aware of the importance of understanding the identities of learners.

So to return to the story—it begins like this. I was working as a tutor and volunteered to take on some additional work to offer a support session to a group of students who had been identified as needing help with their writing. I arrived in the classroom with a pile of grammar books under my arm and a lesson plan based on writing correct sentences, making a plan, structuring an essay with an introduction, main points and conclusion—familiar stuff to most educators. I had not been given any information about the students who would attend my session other than that they were social work students. When my group arrived I looked into the faces of eight women, all of whom were of African Caribbean heritage.

My recent social work background may have contributed to my instinct to stop and listen before I opened any of those grammar books. Two hours later the books remained closed and a door had opened to the scholarship that I have continued working on for the past twenty years. During these two hours I listened to stories from these women and they fundamentally changed my understanding of education and academic writing.

The lesson I learnt that day was in many ways very simple. Learning to participate effectively in higher education is not (only) about acquiring skills and knowledge. It is about developing an identity and ways of communicating which are significantly more accessible to some students than others (Bowel 2000; 2001, Lillis 2001). This is probably not a statement many would argue with, but the institutional practices around teaching, tuition and, in particular, assessment were failing to effectively respond to this challenge, and this is largely still the case (for example

Evans et al 2019; Pitman et al 2019; Pang et al 2019). This was my moment of realisation. My motivation for moving from social work to education was to teach, I had no real interest in research. But this experience changed that. The only way in which I could have an impact on the practice of anyone other than myself was through giving a voice to these students, and the only way to make those voices heard in academia was through research and publishing.

Let me explain. Here are the voices of some of the students who participated in the first scholarship I undertook, which arose directly from that first writing class. These are some of the ways in which they talked about their language, the language they grew up with and used with family and friends:

Broken English

Not exactly academic English

Not proper or the Queen's English.

When writing at University I have to resort to English

Patois is a comfortable dialect which you use with people you're comfortable with

I don't have to explain myself in Patwa

After I recognise your voice (as a relative) I start to speak Patwa, it would be so easy to communicate...you just speak it and then you just laugh about it, you know, make a joke, and you just start laughing! (Rai 2001)

So when I listened to the stories of these women, and the students of African Caribbean heritage who were in my subsequent research, I heard the voices of people who felt their first language was not a language in its own right but a lesser version of English. More importantly it was not a language which enabled them to express their true identity.

As a result of listening to these voices I wanted to find out more about the languages these students spoke, to challenge my own limited understanding of something central to some of my students, I learnt just how unhelpful to think of patois / creoles as dialects or 'broken' forms of English or any other European language. These languages reflect the rich linguistic as well as the social history of their origins. The history of patois goes beyond the scope of this chapter, but I will offer a couple of examples which illustrate my personal learning. Each patois / creole language reflects its individual linguistic roots, which include West African, European languages and languages which predated European colonisation such as the Taíno language (Dalphinis,1985; Edwards, 1991; Sebba 1993). As a result the grammatical structure is significantly different from English so shifting between the two is not just a matter or vocabulary or pronunciation. Writing and speaking in English for native patois / creole speakers involves learning new grammatical structures using both familiar and new vocabulary. The grammar of these languages is not an incorrect version of the colonising European language. It is a grammar of its own.

My early research with this specific student group also raised my awareness of the fact that these students sometimes found it difficult to express themselves freely in an academic context because they needed to speak and write in a language with which they did not identify. This does not only apply to students of African Caribbean heritage. I was particularly significant for students in social work education where so much of the learning and writing was reflective and so required students to draw on their 'use of self' (Rai 2008). Higher education placed an effective additional hurdle in the way of students whose home language was not a standard form of English. Social work as a discipline placed an additional hurdle by requiring not only that student wrote using academic English, but that they also drew on their authentic identity through their reflective writing.

The use of the language we grew up with and use with friends and family is significant for everyone but the impact on identity expression is greater when this language is considered as an imperfect version, as broken or improper and not to be used in the context of work or education (Rai 2001; Rai 2008). The students I interviewed described this sense of exclusion which was reinforced repeatedly across their experiences of education. Painful stories were shared of accusations of cheating in exams when 'correct' English was used, of being placed in special needs classes due to needing language support, of being excluded from academic classes and encouraged to focus on sport. These are all real testimonies shared by students and it was the power of their stories which led me to focus on the themes of identity and emotion in my subsequent research on student writing. Reflecting on these stories also led me to a body of literature which shifted the focus from an individual deficit approach to understanding academic writing to one which took a critical stance on the institutional context in which writing takes place (for example Lillis 2001).

But there was another lesson. The 'problem' here was not individual students with gaps in their academic writing, or even use of English skills.

The problem was institutional, not only in higher education but across the whole education sector (Lillis 2001; Lillis and Tuck 2016; Tuck 2016). There are many barriers which regulate who is heard, whose writing promotes academic success and whose voices are marginalised. Marginalised students include those who enter higher education through a non-traditional route (Bowel 2000; 2001, Lillis 2001). Amongst these are students whose home language, the language which most authentically communicates their identity (Rai 2001) is not the language of education and work.

It took some time for my own scholarly confidence to reach a point when I could reflect on the imposter syndrome that so many of my student research participants described which arose from not having followed the traditional route into higher education (Rai 2008; Chapman 2017). I had been very privileged in my schooling, attending a good university after a productive gap year working as a social work volunteer. As a white British daughter of a doctor who attended a good school and moved on to a good university I had no reason to feel an imposter to the academic world, but this is how I felt. It was the discovery of an old school report that reminded me of the reasons for the emotional resonance I felt with these students. The report said "Lucy is a very able child until she puts pen to paper." That was it. That was the total assessment of my academic ability as a twelve year old. The reason for the comment was that I had always found accuracy in writing very difficult, particularly in relation to spelling. I was very aware that however good my ideas and comprehension were, the presentation of my work would result in criticism. Exercise books covered in red pen marking each error. In my educational experience and ability to write accurately equated to academic ability, so without the former I could not have the latter.

Despite the perceived limitations on my academic abilities, I was able to perform well enough to graduate, to achieve a social work qualification and to be appointed as a lecturer in social work in further and subsequently higher education. However a voice on my shoulder reminded me quietly that I was not a scholar. Although I didn't have a clear rationale at the time, I shared with these women an implicit understanding that written communication was a powerful force to allow or impede participation in the academic world. It was only the experience of listening to the stories of the African Caribbean women talking about their sense of exclusion from education that motivated me to undertake scholarship research in order to make a difference to the opportunities of other non-traditional students.

Writing, which in my childhood seemed like a barrier to academic credibility, became a central focus for my scholarship. My research into the experiences of African Caribbean student writers led to my doctoral studies, focusing on student writing in social work. I learnt that writing has a remarkable potential to regulate the participation of learners, teachers and scholars. To regulate whose ideas and experiences are heard. The codes which govern and legitimise the form of writing which is considered to be effectively academic run across student writing, scholarly publications and professional writing. Marginalised students include those who enter higher education through a non-traditional route (Bowel 2000; 2001, Lillis 2001). Academics can also be marginalised. For example academics for whom English is a second or third language but need to publish in it as English is the required language for international scholarship (Lillis and Curry 2018; Curry and Lillis 2017, Rai 2018). Such marginalisation can arise from the ability to access these technical codes but also from the authenticity which arises from identities which sit easily within the institutionally accepted codes. By codes here I am referring to expectations of academic writing, frequently implicit, which are applied to the writing of students and aspiring authors. These codes span from surface features of language (spelling, syntax and grammar) through to vocabulary and expectations of argumentation and structure which may arise from the discourse of the curriculum or from institutional practices (Rai 2008; 2004). For those who are familiar with these codes they are invisible and self-evident until writing breaches the code, when they jar, they stand out as errors which raise a red flag, questioning the writers competence. Not only competence as a writer, but their competence as a scholar. The validity of their ideas.

As a scholar I have listened to students talk about their feelings of demoralisation and frustration when the feedback on their work focused disproportionately on correcting spelling, grammar and citation methods, to the exclusion of engagement with the ideas. My childhood experiences in school enabled me to empathise strongly with them, but my role as an educator struggling to feel like an insider led me to be cautious about questioning the value of a heavy focus on the surface language errors. As I write this chapter now I am sure that to the outside world I am a comfortable insider to academia. I have a research doctorate. I am a Principal Fellow of the Higher Education Authority. I have published academic articles and books and I have been a university lecturer for over 20 years. On paper I am an insider.

References

Bowl, M. (2000). Listening to the Voices of Non Traditional Students. *Widening Participation in Lifelong Learning*, 2(1) Available at: http://www.staffs.ac.uk/journal/Volume2(1)/contents.htm [Accessed 13.06.03].

Bowl, M. (2002). Experiencing the barriers: non-traditional students entering higher education. *Research Papers in Education*, 16(2), p. 141-160.

Ceryn Evans, C. Rees, G. Taylor, C. & Wright, C. (2019). 'Widening Access' to higher education: the reproduction of university hierarchies through policy enactment. *Journal of Education Policy*, 34:1, 101-116, DOI: 10.1080/02680939.2017.1390165.

Chapman, A. (2017). Using the assessment process to overcome Imposter Syndrome in mature students. *Journal of Further and Higher Education*, 41:2, 112-119, DOI: 10.1080/0309877X.2015.1062851.

Curry, M.J. and Lillis, T. (2017). Problematizing English as the Privileged Language of Global Academic Publishing. *Global Academic Publishing: Policies, Perspectives and Pedagogies,* Curry, Mary Jane and Lillis, Theresa eds. Clevedon: Multilingual Matters, pp. 1–20.

Dalphinis, M. (1985). *Caribbean and African languages: social history language literature and education.* Karia.

Edwards, W. and Winford, D. (1991). V*erb Phrase patterns in Black English & Creole*. Wayne University Press.

Lillis, T. (2001). *Student Writing Access, regulation and desire.* London: Routledge.

Lillis, T. and Curry, M.J. (2018). Trajectories of knowledge and desire: Multilingual women scholars researching and writing in academia. *Journal of English for Academic Purposes*, 32 pp. 53–66.

Lillis, T. and Tuck, J. (2016). Academic Literacies: a critical lens on writing and reading in the academy. *The Routledge Handbook of English for Academic Purposes*, Hyland, Ken and Shaw, Philip eds. Routledge, pp. 30–43.

Pang, B. et al. (2018). Forging Strengths-Based Education with Non-Traditional Students in Higher Education. *Curriculum Studies in Health and Physical Education*. Routledge, 9(2), pp. 174–188. doi: 10.1080/25742981.2018.1444930.

Pitman, T. R., Bennett, D. L. and Richardson, S. (2019). An Australian study of graduate outcomes for disadvantaged students. *Journal of Further and Higher Education*, 43:1, 45-57, DOI: 10.1080/0309877X.2017.1349895.

Rai, L. (2001). An investigation into the language needs of a group of african caribbean open university students. Internal Report for The Open University Student Retention Team.

Rai, L. (2004). Exploring literacy in social work education: a social practices approach to student writing. *Social Work Education*, 23(2) pp. 149–162.

Rai, L. (2008). Student writing in social work. Doctoral Thesis. The Open University

Rai, L. (2018). How to Get Published in a Peer Reviewed Journal: Reflections on Panel Discussion at the International Council for Open and Distance Education: World Conference on Online Learning 16–19th October 2017, Toronto, Canada. *Open Learning: The Journal of Open, Distance and e-Learning*, 33(1) pp. 70–74.

Sebba, M. (1993). *London Jamaican: language systems in interaction*. London: Longman.

Tuck, J. (2016). 'That ain't going to get you a professorship': discourses of writing and the positioning of academics' work with student writers in UK higher education. *Studies in Higher Education*, 41(9) pp. 1612–1626.

Community-as-Method in Prison and College

Joe Stommel

I am writing this as a retiree from Colorado State government with thirty years experience in systems management administration. I also have taught college classes in Psychology over twenty of those years. My expertise was substance abuse programming and mental health. I have worked extensively in intergovernmental planning and program development between institutions with great traditions. I have learned to navigate and critique organizational management. I have learned a lot but I recently turned 70, so I must admit that I've gotten a little crabby over the years. But reflecting in this way teaches me something about who I am and who I've been. More than anything, I see a kernel of myself that has persisted, and carried with me from my work in the classroom to my work in prisons and now to my work as an online teacher.

In the spring of 2017, I was asked to make a complete course redesign for the second part of Introductory Psychology (PSY 102). I was excited to embark on this creative endeavor. I'd be the lead expert to make this an all new and better course. Decades before I was in charge of developing new "therapeutic communities" for the prison system for the State Department of Corrections. In both cases, I knew there would be issues putting an innovative development into the boundaries of a crudely institutional system. So I was prepared and skilled to anticipate and overcome the hurdles of new development in the college system, just like I had pursued in the prison system. Little did I know that in each of these cases the hurdles would become fortified barricades, like thick prison walls.

I have been teaching PSY 102 for nine years online and had previously taught for six years in a face-to-face community college classroom back in the 80s. I had a vision of what the learning process might be in a class like this. I had shed traditional notions of *read the book and take the test.* Instead, I designed a multimedia and multi-dimensional learning experience, much of it self-guided by the student in an interactive community of learners.

My instinct was to reduce the emphasis on individual reading and individual testing, just absorbing someone else's so-called *knowledge.* In the case of my redesign of PSY 102, I knew the course was lacking in self-examination and exploration, interaction with others in a community of learners, and exposure and action in the real world community.

I had a new vision for this class, a balance of some book learning, more self-exploration and group interaction, and a new emphasis on service learning. I wanted to encourage the class to look at current events and complete an experiential learning project. With that vision in mind, I prepared what the college calls "modules" to match up my vision with the various activities in the syllabus.

I first sought to reduce the emphasis on tests and quizzes, but the administration countered with the need for module tests and a final exam as predetermined and immutable requirements. The system (both the technology and processes) was dictating our format. The community college system had undergone a change in administration and with it came new and rigid guidelines for the structure of classes. And, of course, the structure put very specific constraints on the pedagogical possibilities. So required exams were a near ultimatum. But I reduced the points allocated and made exams a smaller part of a more thorough array of course methods. These are the kinds of bureaucratic challenges I had seen as a state administrator, so I was well-prepared for this kind of compromise.

I implemented a system of progressively challenging class discussions where students would first interact supportively with classmates, then participate in community formation, then react to the diverse perspectives of others, and ultimately change one's thinking and each others' perspectives through community interaction. But, even here, my design was subject to bureaucratic requirements: I was told I *must* introduce each discussion with a lengthy prompt. That I *must* provide three or four documents of "topic exploration" before the discussion segment could begin. While I was trying to move toward less solitary reading, less content dissemination, the administration required that I provide more and more of these. They had applauded my innovative vision, but in action were requiring more adherence to standards.

The administration was worried about inconsistencies among instructors and course implementation, so every new course needed to be tighter and more structured into boxes of required content. This was at direct odds with a move across the community college system to make courses more human, more alive to the needs of their diverse student populations. There was indeed a tension between a desire to innovate and to assure that innovation didn't ignore the needs of real students.

For the new PSY 102, even something as simple (and pedagogically sound) as replacing research papers with service learning projects was put under scrutiny. I could do it, I was told, but I'd still have to *also* run students through the gauntlet of a research paper.

"But the goal of this course is not to teach research paper writing."

"Okay," the administration responded, "you can reduce the research requirement by half and each report submission for the experiential learning project has to be graded by a complicated rubric scaling their score from 0 – 75 points."

It was clear that the more I implemented my vision of a new format, the more I was crashing against an incredibly backwards set of design parameters.

"This is the way we have to do things."

No discussion.

I distinctly remember a similar narrative from when I implemented therapeutic community (TC) treatment programs in the State prison system. In the 90s, therapeutic communities were becoming the most highly researched and effective approach for drug-addicted inmates. They grew out of the self-help movement to provide a comprehensive and intensive prison program removed from other inmates and using an innovative practice called "community-as-method." As I wrote in "Correctional Pedagogy: Prison Reform and Life-or-Death Learning" (2014): "[Therapeutic communities] encourage simple and necessary values for good citizenship—honesty, accountability, work ethic, and community responsibility."

The therapeutic community is designed as an intensive 24/7 program of living a new and responsible life with ongoing support, encouragement and correction by fellow residents. Morning meetings were daily inspiration sessions led by residents as were the group therapy sessions. Behavioral improvement used a system of what we called "pull-ups" by fellow residents as reminders of improved behaviors, followed by learning experiences agreed upon with senior residents. The philosophy is based on a community-learning model of addiction recovery and responsible living that is staff-led but implemented by the community members themselves. The community itself is seen as the vehicle for change in the prisoners' lives.

Correctional officers overseeing the residence units were forward-looking in their unanimous vocal support in how well the TC units were self-managed by participant members of the program. The belief that inmates should not be *running the cell block* was revealed to be nothing but a misconception and a misguided fear. Just like students leading discussions in college classes should not be seen as less than instructors, the best group therapists in TC encounters were the inmate participants, not the therapists.

Whereas a therapeutic community is a separate living unit designed to keep the program residents away from a negative prison environment, the conventional prison system is set up to discourage self-efficacy, self-management, and participant-driven community. When implementing a new and intensive program there was always the perceived conflict with the main mission of the prison system: to keep the inmates quiet, controlled, and secure. So at each proposed program implementation the mission of 'security' and conforming to long standing day to day operations would take precedence. The prison subverts success if they adapt a wing or unit to accommodate the program but then require many other daily activities mixed with the general population. In this case, meals and recreation times would be mixed with other inmates who would harass the TC members as coddled or "square" or "submissive to the man."

There were elements of a TC approach that didn't fit in a traditional prison environment.

Fortunately, inspiring leaders were able to convince the system to bend. A number of separate units were set aside. TC activities were *mostly* kept apart from the general population. A new work site was designed for program participants. Correctional officers were recruited to take a thoughtful security stance that supported the communal behavior management of the TC. These real innovations took hold, and these new programs were found in a five-year federal research study to result in the highest reductions in participant relapse and recidivism (Sacks, et.al., 2010).

In both my experience with the community college online system and with the State Prison system, each step of the development process showed the philosophical support for, but also enormous bureaucratic resistance to, changing any of the fixtures of the institution. The idea that "our prisons must be schools" has a corollary, that "our schools cannot be prisons." (Stommel 2014). But this is what I faced when attempting to innovate. The prison walls that hold people inside and block interaction with the outside world are similar to the college system walls of instructional requirements that often cannot be breached for the sake of authentic experiential learning.

As I worked to design a new PSY102, I experienced almost daily stress, feeling constantly that I had to justify my methods and every innovation I was advocating for. Again, the seemingly simple pedagogical moves I was making were scrutinized in absurd ways. And the responses were erratic.

- When I wanted 20 simple pass-fail tasks, the college wanted elaborate evaluation rubrics with five scalable items for each.
- I asked for original written content to be shorter and geared toward student participation and personal exploration. This was accepted.
- When I wanted to de-emphasize module tests and the final exam, this was met with strong resistance. But a system was devised by my Department Chair to have open-book exams.
- The interpretation of federal requirements about public work and access were not nuanced. And where my design required additional support for accessibility, no help was offered by Instructional Design, only limits.
- The college system had previously used a system encouraging "student-led discussions" that I found now had to have special authorization.

Each of my pedagogical approaches tested or stretched a very rigid set of boundaries. But I found that with some sensible pressure, the walls could be breached.

Organizational change requires a recognition of the distinction between verbal support and active support. Verbal support disguises itself as positive when it is usually neutral and often turns out to be negative. Active support involves sustained effort toward a cause or plan. Without active support, little can get done within a system. Fortunately, my department chair was helpful in my course design and offered meaningful, active support. He intervened frequently to soften some of the rigid requirements, and he provided a vote of confidence.

Most of my course revision was accepted, and my vision found its way into a very worthy final product in the Fall semester 2017. (And that course now continues to be taught by myself and many other instructors in the program.) The students embraced the additional discussion emphasis and experiential learning project with genuinely advanced work and wonderful accomplishments in service learning. The Department Chair nominated me to receive the annual Instructional Excellence Award in Behavioral Sciences.

***

I have learned about leadership over the years that you provide enthusiastic vision and communicate it clearly. But beyond that someone in a leadership role must recognize the assets and strengths they do not possess and cannot impose. Instead, they must find those strengths in peak contributors, the *culture carriers* of an organization. In spite of all the obstacles I faced, I found those in my chair, the instructors who handled the first iteration of the course and, and in the peers in the community of learners we call the class.

What the work of this course has become depends on the community who now inhabits it. That is truly what community-as-method is all about.

References

Sacks, S., McKendrick, K., Sacks, J.Y., & Cleland, C. (2010). Modified therapeutic community for co-occurring disorders: Single investigator meta-analysis. *Substance Abuse*, 31(3), 146-161.

Stommel, J. (2020). Correctional pedagogy: Prison reform and life-or-death learning. *Hybrid Pedagogy*, June 21. https://hybridpedagogy.org/correctional-pedagogy-prison-reform-life-death-learning/

A Narrative of Discontent: On Interrogating What It Means to be Scholar

Chloe de los Reyes

"Our survival depended on an ongoing public awareness of the separation between margin and centre and an ongoing private acknowledgement that we were necessary, vital part of that whole." ~ bell hooks

Many of these chapters describe academics' moves from practice outside of the academy to inside of it as scholars/researchers. However, I want to foreground an often-disregarded outsider-to-insider experience of moving from being considered a professional to being seen as an academic, a scholar, and a knowledge producer. For me, that has involved moving from being an undergraduate, graduate student, and then adjunct faculty member on a four-year campus to a tenure-track faculty member on a two-year campus. Very simply, as I moved along this trajectory, I saw myself continuing to grow as an academic and knowledge producer, while it became increasingly clear to me that in the eyes of most tenure-track faculty and perhaps the larger composition field, once I left my graduate student status, I was becoming only an increasingly professional teacher of writing. Even when I began my appointment as a tenure-track community college faculty member, thinking then that being on the tenure-track would cause me to be seen as an academic, I still felt resistance, as four-year campuses and the larger composition field still seemed to struggle with the idea of two-year faculty as real academics.

And so my project uses my own trajectory in academia, how I came to be here, how I am experiencing it, and how I might "engage in my own imagination" to make a place for me, to explore what it means to be an academic, a scholar, a researcher (brown). I am asking these questions as someone who has inhabited, and arguably still inhabits, the position of an outsider—then, as an non-PhD adjunct at a four-year university, and now, as a newly-hired tenure-track faculty at a community college. I am asking these questions because I believe that our community's prevailing caste system that relies on degrees, memberships, and affiliations seriously limits the contributions—and most importantly, the growth and development—of both faculty and students.

Both Donald Murray and Jan Blommaert speak helpfully to the ways we understand the interplay of our personal and professional lives. Murray (1991) maintains that all writing is in some way autobiographical, growing "from a few deep taproots that are set down into our past in childhood," and Blommaert (2020) asserts that the professional and personal are always intertwined, sometimes in complementary ways and others in "uneasy or poorly balanced ways." And so I begin with the ways my professional life is rooted in my personal history, in my observations, and in my experiences in making sense of the world around me, moving then to the professional questions that have troubled me into writing this chapter.

***

My story begins as a rather inquisitive child growing up in a devoutly Catholic family in Iloilo City, Philippines. Our lives centered on being Catholics: We went to mass every Sunday, every feast day, and every holiday of obligation. We prayed the rosary every evening after dinner during the month of October. Both my maternal and paternal grandmothers were quite active in the church—one would even volunteer my sisters and me for whatever activity she felt we ought to be part of. All three of us sisters, for instance, played the role of the angel who announced Jesus' resurrection on Easter Sunday. My dad was part of a couple church committees. My mother, to this day, still often jokes about wishing for one of her daughters being called to serve as a nun.

For me, Murray's taproots arise from always having been curious as a child. In fact, my inquisitiveness always got me into trouble. I asked a lot of questions—and what always seemed to be the wrong questions: "Why do we have to pray the rosary?" "Why is it an obligation?" "What does obligation mean?" "Wouldn't God prefer that we pray the rosary because we wanted to rather than because we are obligated to?"

However, even though my family didn't really discourage my curiosity, they didn't really encourage it either—or at least they did so selectively. They encouraged reading, playing, trying new things, and actively playing a role in our community. They wanted me to do well in school and to be smart, even to question things—just not certain things, especially things tied to religion, cultural values, gender roles, and the like. Nevertheless, the underlying curiosity and eagerness to learn is at my core. I read as much as I could; I hung around and eavesdropped on the grown-up table as much as possible.

***

When I was around 12, my parents decided to move to the United States. This move only strengthened even more my inclination to figure things out, as the stakes are now even higher. When my family and I arrived in the US, we needed to figure out how to fit in and how to navigate this new country. I suppose a majority of my life was spent trying to figure things out—who I was and where I belonged. And that may be how I stumbled upon the field of Composition Studies.

Upon receiving my B.A. in English Literature, I decided to keep going to school and chose an M.A. in Composition program because it was local and because I thought it could help me improve my English. Little did I know that this field is far more rich than just learning about grammar and that writing and language is tied to our ways of seeing the world.

Composition Studies offered me ways of making sense of my experiences. Much like Christine W. Nganga in "Emerging as a Scholar Practitioner: A Reflective Essay Review," graduate school was "a time when [my] passion intersect[ed] with opportunities for inquiry that lead to finding solutions for educational dilemmas" (p. 243). I learned about language acquisition, the ways people viewed multilingual students, and language politics. I learned that many would put under me the umbrella category called English as Second Language (ESL) and confirmed my earlier observations that there is a stigma attached to those who belonged in this category. Most importantly, my graduate program helped me realize that there was nothing wrong with me, and that I didn't need to change. Instead, the world needed to change the way they see me and others like me.

And that's how I fell in love with this field. Even though my entry to the field of Composition Studies was somewhat accidental, I stayed because it gave me an avenue to pursue my questions and turn them into research projects, and these research projects, in turn, helped me understand who I am and how I can best contribute to the world. I worked in my university's writing center, where I was able to wrestle with what it means to be "ESL" from multiple points of inquiry: my tutoring practices, scholarship on ESL students or variations of it (Second Language Writing, Multilingualism, Translingualism, etc.), and my own understanding as a person who was labeled as ESL for most of her life. By then, I started to see how "[b]ecoming a scholar practitioner is a process that requires continuous discovery of one's passions as linked to inquiry" (Nganga, p. 245). I wanted to understand language, writing, and labels, and how these have been powerful forces in my life.

***

My mentors—one in particular—was able to model for me what it means to be a scholar—how not settle for easy answers, how to continue to ask questions, how to ask the right questions, and how to reflect on one's views and to be open to changing one's mind. She did so by inviting me to work alongside her on projects or to help me develop my own. At that time, I was interested in learning more about how we can best tutor multilingual students. And so "[m]y learning curve has been a composite of spending extended periods of time at the university working on different projects with professors in addition to my coursework. These activities shaped my identity and the avenues through which I enact my scholarship and practice" (Nganga p. 245).

As a graduate student, I was presented with opportunities that allowed me to grow and to develop as an academic. In 2007, our writing center director arranged for two tutors to spend one term as visiting tutors, one in a writing center in Germany and another in Sweden. In Germany, I was able to get a different view of what it means to learn English as foreign language. I was also able to see language learning or acquisition from the perspective of an observer, which helped nuance my own understandings. The Germany experience then gave way to multiple conference presentations and a chapter in Bruce and Rafoth's *ESL Writers: A Guide for Writing Center Tutors*. I mention this not to list my achievements, but instead to show that I was constantly learning, that "I was involved in some kind of study, collecting and selecting writings from which I wanted to draw advanced insights, useful for the research projects I was engaged in" (Blommaert).

In fact, one of my favorite things to do was to listen in on my professors' and other scholars' conversations. Whenever an opportunity arose to participate in an academic conference, I was the first one to sign-up. I felt like a child again eavesdropping on the adult table. Moreover, this first-hand participation in the field allowed me to nuance my understanding and to move beyond what I learned from books and in the classroom. I saw for myself how ideas are teased out, challenged, and eventually evolve and spark new ideas.

In such contexts of collective sharing, conditioned by maximum generosity, changing one's mind is self-evident. The very point of having a discussion or brainstorm – an "exchange of ideas" – is that ideas can be exchanged and changed, and that one leaves the session with better things in one's head than before the session.

***

However, as I moved from graduate student to adjunct faculty member, my view of myself changed abruptly. Instead of being recognized for my move from student to faculty status, I struggled to be fully recognized as a "colleague," as someone who is valued, has expertise, and who is welcome to all the tables, in the four-year institutional context." After receiving my MA in English Composition, I stayed at my alma mater and continued to teach at several programs in that institution: in the English Department's First-Year Writing Program, the International Extension Programs, and the Educational Opportunity Program. Over time, I was able to build my course entitlement to a full-time load; however, despite the arguably good contract (I had benefits and retirement) and an arguably adjunct friendly-English department, "even these good practices are beset by the challenges of the contingent system," as Amy Lynch-Biniek points out.

In fact, although I was now "faculty," I felt less like an academic than I did as a graduate student. My experience and observation have been such that most adjuncts "are defined by a work schedule (part-time) and by a single trait of teaching (lecturer) because [adjuncts] are not expected to be or do more than that" (Hanson and de los Reyes). Herb Childress (2019) said it best: "the peculiar cruelty of higher education is its third option — the vast purgatory of contingent life, in which we are neither welcomed nor rejected, but merely held adjacent to the mansion, to do the work that our betters would prefer not to do." I'd been able to work around this and carved out a role for myself in the department through sheer doggedness—I just kept signing up for committees and projects that didn't preclude adjuncts, and despite the scarcity of funding, I was able to attend conferences through the charity of friends (lots of frequent flyer miles donations and hotel room rollaway beds). I did so even, when at times, it felt like my contributions weren't really valued, or much less heard. I needed to create "a dysfunctional story in which [I] have at least some role, in which [I] can name a way that [I]belong" (Childress).

***

However, in late August of 2018, while everyone was finishing up their curricula for the upcoming academic year, I was, instead, writing a resignation letter, filling out a leave of absence form, and crying my eyes out, because I had decided to step away from my adjunct position, even though it now included some administrative responsibilities. Very simply, even though I can cite the layers of explanation of how I arrived at this decision, I just felt deadened by the everyday politics and the uncertainty and marginality that came with adjuncting. I felt disillusioned upon the realization that the system is stacked against persons like me who are not tenured and who don't have the right degrees.

***

During this time, however, I was encouraged by my mentor to hold steadfast and to not give up entirely on academia. She suggested I explore the possibility of working at local community colleges. After some consideration, I decided to make an inquiry and submitted an application to one closest to me; however, I was told that classes have already been filled for the upcoming spring semester and that I would need to wait to see if something else opened up in the following academic year. So I kept plodding along. I applied for several administrative support positions at various local universities and colleges and applied to a couple of parallel positions to the one I had left. I also thought of doing something completely different, so I also submitted numerous applications for everything and anything I was remotely qualified for outside of academia, including an application for a part-time position at our local nursery. I thought about going back to retail again. I even considered going back to school to become a librarian. Nothing really panned out. Maybe that was a good thing. Deep inside, I knew that I wasn't going to be as happy anywhere else.

Fortunately, about a month or so into my job search, out of the blue, I was contacted by that close-by community college because two classes had opened up at the last minute. So just like that—I was back in academia once again. Only this time, in a completely different context.

***

My new context complicated my already convoluted professional life. I needed to start over, and I was not sure how to bring with me the professional and scholarly identity that I'd worked so hard to build over the years, as the community college context is much different than that of universities. Moreover, there wasn't an established program that would allow me to continue my previous specialized work. However, by the end of that term, by good fortune, several full-time positions opened up in the English Department, and I was offered a tenure-track position.

Oddly, when I began my appointment as a tenure-track faculty, I thought that being on the tenure-track would allow me to do the work of, and be regarded as, an academic, but once again, I was wrong. Many of my community college colleagues had been conditioned to see their roles as teachers who looked at times at others' research but were not expected to conduct or publish their own and who were expected to follow curricular designs handed down from the top. Moreover, my observations echoes Howard Tinberg's (2010) in that I, too, "rarely witnes[s] campus discussions on scholarly or theoretical matters" as a majority of the conversations often revolve around the more practical ones: creating student learning outcomes, developing support structures, and such. This is not to say that the practical are unimportant, as they are an integral part in serving the needs of our students; however, it does foreground Tinberg's questions: "Can research and publication enhance our teaching? I believe so. Can theory inform practice and practice shape theory? Absolutely" (p. 8).

***

In "We Value Teaching Too Much to Keep Devaluing It", Seth Kahn (2020) writes:

> In English studies, both faculty and those who practice in the field expend an abundance of energy attending to instruction and research. Despite all of this, we risk seeing our efforts undercut by a handful of recurring riffs, like those in jazz music, that reinforce a disparity in status between some kinds of teaching in relation to others, between teaching in relation to research, and between teaching faculty in relation to research faculty.

Reading Khan's observations is disheartening especially as someone who has spent years working as contingent faculty. However, the conversations about such disparities, particularly with regards to contingent faculty, always revolve around pay and labor, but I argue that these conditions are mere symptoms of a larger issue, as similar symptoms are occurring at two-year institutions as well in the form of professional disparity. As Jeff Andelora (2005) writes:

> Despite the fact that all of these two-year institutions were expected to provide a college-level curriculum, the very appellation of junior college designated them as something not to be taken too seriously, as almost as if they would forever be the university's kid sibling. (p. 309)

Even though the label has since changed from junior to community college, the perceptions have stayed and so has the construction of the identity and thus the work of community college professors: teachers firstly and scholars rarely, and the "lack of participation in research, theorizing and knowledge-building" has only solidified existing academic class structures and hierarchy (Andelora).

Neither contingent nor two-year faculty are expected to contribute to the field, and this practice not only contradicts our belief that all teaching involves learning and creating knowledge but also severely limits our value to the field. Such disparities will continue to occur if we don't support or encourage our colleagues to do the work that it takes to be a scholar, and by extension, to be a teacher. Once again, I amplify Andelora's words:

> Ultimately, if faculty stay divorced from their disciplines too long, it becomes increasingly difficult for them to meet the needs of their students. In our own field of composition, if faculty members have not kept pace with the changes we have seen over the last thirty years, what they have to offer their students is limited. (p. 315)

Faculty owe this much to those we are called to serve: our students.

To do this, it is imperative that we rethink the necessary intersections of teaching, learning, scholarship as embodied, fluid, and non-hierarchical. Along with Howard Tinberg, Seth Kahn, Jeff Andelora, and many others, I want to challenge traditional separations between teaching and research faculty and to rethink the narrative and the current structures we have created for ourselves. Simply put: If we believe that learning must always be a component of teaching, it follows that questioning and researching those questions must be a part of all teachers' teaching. In turn, this means that we must reexamine the caste system or status markers that differentiate the work of two- and four-year college faculty, of adjunct and tenure-track faculty. It means that all faculty should be engaged in learning and creating rather than expecting that only select professors—the upper tier—and that the rest simply replicate

their work or even follow decontextualized curricular designs handed
down to them.

***

James Bordley in his speech at the Investiture of the Charter Members
of The John Hopkins Society of Scholars in February 22, 1969 describes
a scholar as someone who

> possesses learning in depth in one or more fields, and whose activities
> include, on the one hand, reading, observation, experimentation and reflec-
> tion; and, on the other hand, the communication of the acquired learning to
> others by teaching, writing or other means. This type of scholar is usually a
> student during most of his life, and a teacher during part of it.

Although James Bordley can easily be dismissed as applying fifty years
ago to an elite group of Hopkins faculty, I want to use it today to challenge faculty in all positions to take seriously the rich learning, teaching,
knowledge-creating circuit they encourage their students to hop into
and to apply that same imperative to themselves. I am compelled to
teach because the act of learning especially about writing excites me, and
I hope to impart my knowledge and my excitement to my students. It is
part of who I am. Taking this challenge means that each of us searches
our own taproots for that eagerness to learn, that curiosity that we may
feel has dampened.

I understand that re-reading Bordley's words is complicated as it
requires revision on multiple fronts: of academic, disciplinary, and institutional cultures, identity construction, professional development,
workload, among others; however, the community college/four-year
university as well as the contingent/tenure divide and the privileging of
select voices in the field's larger conversation can result in missed learning opportunities and an incomplete composition scholarship. It challenges those with institutional power to reconsider the educational caste
system we have inherited so that faculty teaching whomever, wherever,
and under whatever conditions can keep their own and their students'
curiosity and knowledge-creating lives vibrant.

References

Andelora, J. (2005). The Teacher/Scholar: Reconstructing Our Professional Identity in Two-Year Colleges. *Teaching English in the Two-Year
College*, vol. 32, no.3, pp. 307-322.

Blommaert, J. (2020). Looking back: What was important in my academic life? Ctrl+Alt+Dem: https://alternative-democracy-research.org/2020/04/20/what-was-important/.

Bordley J., 3rd (1969). What is a scholar? *The Johns Hopkins medical journal*, 125(1), 1–7.

brown, a. m. (2017). *Emergent Strategy:Shaping, Changing Worlds*. Chico, AK Press.

Childress, H. (2019). This is How You Kill a Profession: How Did We Decide That Professors Don't Deserve Job Security or a Decent Salary? *The   Chronicle   Review:* www.chronicle.com/interactives/2019-03-27-childress?fbclid=IwAR3bedRR-j4qOr9EpE-BYrU6F8Slolkpi65vABITd_mOP43wlF1VEZGZzQ_0. Accessed 1 May 2019.

Hanson, G. and de los Reyes, C. (2019). Identity Crisis: Daring to Identify as More than 'Just' Adjunct Composition Instructors. *Forum: Issues about Part-Time and Contingent Faculty*, vol 22, no. 2, pp. A4-15.

Kahn, S. (2020). We Value Teaching Too Much to Keep Devaluing It. *College English*, vol. 82, no. 6, pp. 591-610.

Murray, D. M. (1991). All Writing Is Autobiography. *College Composition and Communication*, vol. 42, no. 1, pp. 66-74.

Nganga, C. W. (2011). Emerging as a Scholar Practitioner: A Reflective Essay Review. *Mentoring and Tutoring: Partnership in Learning*, vol. 19, no. 2, pp 239-251.

Tinberg, H. and Nadeau, J. (2010). *The Community College Writer: Exceeding Expectations*. Carbondale and Edwardsville, Southern Illinois University Press.

Embracing Entanglements: Exploring possibilities of non-traditional scholarship

Tanya Elias

Oakeshott (1989) described the university as a place made up of three classes of people, "the scholar, the scholar who is also a teacher, and those who come to be taught, the undergraduates" (p. 25). Despite years of ongoing dedication to my studies, however, I cannot comfortably locate myself anywhere in his description. I am neither scholar, nor teacher, nor undergraduate; I most often sit on the fringes of academia. For most of the past 25 years I have studied at a distance, physically and ideologically disconnected from the university as a place.

My open education journey began when I took two courses by correspondence, as it was called at the time. Since then, my non-traditional, non-placebound scholarship has both shaped and been shaped by my life studying outside a classroom while also working full-time and raising five children. What began as study via open education has slowly become the study of open education. I am currently enrolled in a Doctor of Education (EdD) program at the University of Calgary, where I am often reminded that my historical and personal connections to the field of open education are deeper than for most. At the same time, my current scholarship represents a hobby rather than a professional career goal or aspiration. I have been asked many times, "Why would you undertake doctoral studies if you do not want to work in higher education?" I usually struggle to answer. What I do know (or think I know) is that I have found a comfortable-discomfort wedged into a strange space between the "real world" and academia, a space of possibility and agency. The boundaries of this space are blurry, ill-defined and messy. It is my own scholarly universe(ity), complicated and entangled.

University as Open

The meaning of "open education" has shifted over time and continues to lack a consistent definition (Stracke, Downes, Conole, Burgos, & Nascimbeni, 2019). Over the past 25 years, I have experienced this shifting meaning first-hand. Despite the often-cited connection between the beginnings of open education and the advent of the Internet, my early studies were supported by older technologies including telephone, mail and print. This iteration of open education sought to transcend limitations of distance, place and time. Its was an open education of flexible, self-paced learning; an open education that allowed the completion of courses outside a program; and an open education that was interested in reducing the barriers to entry. It was an open education that enabled me to continue my undergraduate studies while living 3,000 km north of the closest university (see Anderson 2008).

As I began my graduate studies, I experienced an open that involved online learning in cohorts. During that time, I researched open as a mechanism for increased accessibility (see Elias 2010, 2011) and participated in research on the use of open educational resources (OER) in a project that I would later come to recognize as a form of open colonialism (see Richards, Marshall, Elias, Quirk, Ives, and Siemens 2010). Later, I explored openness in terms of data (see Cooper, Berg, Sclater, Dorey-Elias and Kitto 2017) and informal online learning spaces (see Poellhuber, Andereson, Racette & Upton 2013). My doctoral work has explored open software, the work of early open pedagogues (see Paquette 1979 and 2005 and Katz 1972) and the implications of scale within open education both big and small (see Elias, Ritchie, Bowles & Gevault 2020). Because of these varied experiences, I use the term "open education" freely, not as a signifier of a singular experience but as a complex system of these many open educations.

Kanuka (2008) pointed out "incongruence and inconsistency in action between and among instructors, administrators, and students, and the ensuing disagreements that revolve around the means rather than the ends of education." (p. 111). Lee (2015) noted that this pre-existing theory-practice gap had been intensified by neoliberal forces to intensify disjunctions "between potentially oppressive power relationships among stakeholders in higher education, unlike the rhetorical claims that simply promote online education as a revolutionary solution" (p. iii). These disjunctions, incongruencies and inconsistencies are the lived experience of my adult life.

My many open educations have defined my educational and career paths and my ability to support my children. They have often governed my sleep schedule; they inform my current doctoral work. They have opened some doors and closed others. I chose to study first general studies, then instructional design and open education largely because that was what was available at reputable, public institutions. Fully online programs were then, and largely remain, the exception. Inevitably, for-profits, foundations and venture capitalists have filled the void, embracing and then driving the open education agenda, often in troubling directions (Elias 2019). As a result, I am keenly aware of the realities, debates and controversies that surround the field of open education.

Throughout my studies, I have been deeply connected to my studies and worked closely with professors; I have developed friendships with other students, and I have connected with researchers and practitioners from around the world. My open educations and the learning opportunities they have provided always seemed like enough. I spent little time thinking about the physical university campuses attached to my studies. It never occurred to me that something significant was missing.

University as a Place

It wasn't until I worked briefly as an educational administrator on a university campus that I learned about the ideological connection between academic scholarship and the university as a place, as described by Oakeshott (1989). For three years, I worked with people who loved physical, *place*-based universities. They saw universities firstly as *places*, physical structures that had been intentionally built away, set apart, from the non-academic world. They further suggested that the ongoing existence of university campuses was, in fact, a testament to their strength, stability and resilience. For them, the university as an institution and as a physical place were inseparable.

I was intrigued by these suggestions of connections between the university as an institution and a physical place; I looked deeper. The literature supported these contentions. Egerton Ryerson, principal of Victoria College in 1842, proclaimed that "the university should be a place of learning; but it must also be a place away from 'the din of controversy'" (as cited in McKillop 2001, p. 16). Almost 150 years later, Oakeshott similarly emphasized the importance of a university as place.

> What distinguishes a university is a special manner of engaging in the pursuit of learning. It is a corporate body of scholars, each devoted to a particular branch of learning: what is characteristic is the pursuit of learning as a co-operative enterprise. The members of this corporation are not spread about the world, meeting occasionally or not at all; they live in permanent proximity to one another. And consequently we should neglect part of the character of a university if we omitted to think of it as a place. A university, moreover, is a home of learning, a place where a tradition of learning is preserved and extended. (Oakeshott 1989, p. 24)

In 2020, echoes of these ideas persist. Weller (2020, April 22) noted that higher education remains organized around several core principles including "bringing people (staff, students) to one main location" and co-locating "all aspects of education…including content (lectures), resources (library), support, socialisation, accommodation." Zimmerman (2020) expressed ongoing skepticism "about whether we can transmit our 'real' selves with our laptops. We're people, not pixels. And teaching—and learning—are personal acts, which simply can't be simulated on a screen." Laporte and Cassuto (2020) went further and concluded that "continuing with virtual learning threatens the entire concept of the college experience." Within the context of the place-based university, the more things have changed, the more they have stayed the same.

University as Suddenly Displaced

Given the traditional focus on the place-based university, it should not be surprising that when the physical place became inaccessible due to Covid-19, universities sought to immediately replicate their set-apartness, or rather have faculty and students replicate it, within the "comfort" of our own homes. "Zoom" and "zoom(call)ing" have suddenly become part of our lexicon. Weller (2020, May 14) lamented the focus on the heavy use of synchronous, online lectures. With this shift, has come a flood of advice on how to behave and what to display. Kiser (2020), for example, wrote a troubling article in which she advocated for keeping up the appearances and endeavoring "to not be the generation that allowed its integrity to crumble as we caved to laziness, disorganization and unprofessionalism." Others have offered advice on how to rigidly structure at home days into rigidly separated work and home blocks of time (Pallavi, 2020). Bowles (2020) suggested that "we're being coached on the propriety of what's in shot because our lives are cluttering the view of the employer's virtual estate." In the emergency online pivot, physicality as represented by our backgrounds have proved to be tremendously important.

University as Classes of People

Beyond the importance of the place for the university, Oakeshott (1989) described three classes of people within it, scholars, scholar teachers and undergraduate students. Each of these classes plays a part within the university. Scholars were those who "may be expected to devote an unbroken leisure to learning" (p. 24); the scholar who was also a teacher "imparts something without having to expressly teach" (p. 27); the undergraduate was the "neither child nor adult... freed for a moment from... the burdensome distinction between work and play (p. 29). As noted in the introduction, I find none of these classes of people as defined by Oakeshott to be a comfortable fit. I have certainly crossed into adulthood and, despite my ongoing involvement in the study of the field of education, I have never taught a formal class. I therefore have nothing to contribute with respect to the "technical" aspects of education. Finally, my scholarship is certainly not one of "unbroken leisure," but rather one that is fragmented and not so neatly tucked around other roles and responsibilities.

Or as People Falling Apart at the Seams?

Bowles (2020) noted:

> We know that the equation of visible domestic demands and "falling apart at the seams" isn't a novel or emergency framing. Parents have known this all along. People who manage work with disability or chronic illness or caring responsibilities or what we coyly call "mental health issues" all know this. We are only ever a heartbeat away from our professional competence being judged as "falling apart at the seams."

In a paragraph, she captured my experience as a student, scholar, professional and parent, one that predates the pandemic by decades. And while her words speak to my lived experience and what I know to be true, such ideas are rarely evident within the scholarly literature. Instead, where matters of emotional labour and care are discussed, they are addressed only insofar as the classroom and work of the teacher, responsibilities outside the scholarly world, rendered invisible.

Bowles continued:

> When we come back from this, let's remember that we learned that having lives beyond our work is neither distracting, ludicrous or embarrassing. Our lives are just what they are. And if we can continue to see the impact of this, we can really start to think about rebooting a much fairer and more inclusive university system, including for our students.

To me, what she is describing is a system of education that is firmly rooted within our own realities, one that not only acknowledges but *embraces* the messiness and complexities of our lives beyond the university as a place.

University as Entangled Education

I do not devote "unbroken leisure to learning," but rather learn in fragments of time. I study and write in between the cracks of my work and life. I work full-time for a technology company. I am a single, and would argue full-time, parent. These are my professions. The former pays the bills, the latter is my life; though they are not without their struggles, I love them both. I fit my scholarly activities into broken bits of time that is not as much "spared" as woven through, entangled with, everything else.

Writing this chapter has been an exercise in embracing these entanglements. I began composing in my head while I worked on converting the garage into an additional bedroom. As I worked, I thought about what it meant to make space for my two not-quite-adult children who had returned suddenly and unexpectedly with their own ideas, needs and judgements. Their school and work and lives had been disrupted, so they came home. For an indeterminate period of time. Suddenly, the house I had bought five months earlier was too small. We needed more space. As a result, the garage conversion project that I had intended to undertake in a few years, began. Early on a Saturday morning while all five kids slept under the same roof for the first time in years, I began the work while they slept. As they awoke, they came down to help, all with their own ideas as to how the project should proceed; my children tend to make my small world better, not easier.

As I worked, I thought about open education. What did it mean to care within the context of open education? Might care in the open involve welcoming the not-quite-invited, making space for unexpected people and ideas that don't quite fit? Maybe it also involves finding ways to balance the needs of these new arrivals with those already comfortably established at home? Doesn't care involve a willingness to start the difficult work alone, while others sleep or are otherwise preoccupied? And then ceding the control to the others because that's how they learn, all the while knowing that if they mess it up or lose interest, they will expect you to fix it or continue on without them? Who wants to undertake that amount of care for strangers? I wondered and smiled.

A few days later, I continued my disjointed writing process in my room. My middle son burst in to inform me that he had completed his Grade 10 English test online. He had written an essay about post-secondary education. I laughed about the similarities in our tasks. I paused from my writing to read him sections from Oakeshott, Bowles and Morrish. He said, "Exactly!" We talked about the ideas for a while and laughed before I turned my attention back to my writing, his ideas still bouncing in my head. I considered the politics of citation (Ahmed, 2017) as I noted that his contributions carry no formal attribution. Not long after, my oldest daughter came in to ask what I was doing. Was it work? Was it school? Well, no... It was just an extra bit of writing because... She looked at me skeptically, rolled her eyes and left. Why *do* I do the the things I do? I wondered and smiled. I kept writing.

Another burst of writing took place on a Sunday morning a week later. I wrote as I listened to song requests from and played by some open educator-friends on ds106radio. My flow paused when *Are you all right?* came across the airwaves.

Am I all right? I wondered. *Yes, I think I am.*

Another pause came later when, in response to my song request *Radio Gaga* (inspired by my son while working on the garage-turned-bedroom), someone else tweeted a video of a conference talk about the benefits of small-scale approaches to radio. My writing became a process of connecting the disparate dots flowing through work, kids, music, voices and the odd flurry of tweets. It is within this entanglement that I find meaning.

Learning as entangled. I should note, that although I have only recently begun using the term "entangled" to describe these connections, this embedded, overlapping and interconnected approach to open education is nothing new. After beginning my studies at a place-based university all those years ago I quit, thinking academic study was not for me. It was only after I accidentally tumbled into open education that I learned that I loved academic study when it is connected to the world, my world.

I fulfilled my undergraduate English requirement not in a lecture hall but reading the books from my children's literature class to my kids at bedtime, the exact place those texts were intended to be read. Up until then, reading had only for me been about the plot. Skim and scan. Gather the details as quickly as possible. Repeat. Reading those stories out loud to my kids, slowed my reading. It forced me to pay attention to the word choice, the cadence. The silences. With my kids, I learned what it really meant to read. It is a lesson I have not forgotten. I recently pulled one of those books off the shelf and started reading it out loud to my youngest daughter.

> Here is Edward Bear, coming downstairs now, bump, bump, bump, on the back of the head behind Christopher Robin. It is, as far as he knows, the only way of coming downstairs, but sometimes he feels that there really is another way, if only he could stop bumping for a moment and think about it. And then he feels perhaps there isn't. (Milne, p. 3)

In a world moving too fast in all the wrong directions, the cadence of reading *Winnie-the-Pooh* as he bumped down the stairs, accepting his fate while also feeling there ought to be a better way, seemed an appropriate response. In that moment, my youngest daughter, not yet born when I first read that book out loud to her siblings fifteen years earlier, became our classmate, learning with us. She brought the book to bed with her that night to keep reading it on her own.

Some time later, I took a women's history course. It included an opportunity to do primary research. I gathered stories from my mother-in-law and her mother about growing up on the land, while they played games and sang songs with my kids. Scholarship became storytelling, or perhaps more to the point, storytelling became scholarship. It was something that we did together, four generations sharing in two languages. In another course, I analyzed my great-grandmother's journal written while homesteading in the Yukon. Several years later, I studied children's media and explored two TV shows, *Lizzie McGuire* and *Arthur*, favorited by my kids at the time. It took ten years for me to complete my undergraduate degree. During that time, my family did not stand by and support my studies, but actively participated, learning with me and teaching me.

My family encourages me. Last year, I thought about quitting my doctoral studies. My son was also struggling in school so he made me a deal: If I didn't quit, he wouldn't either. My studies continue. Later, I joked about writing a long paper that no one would ever read, and he promised that he would read it, even if no one else did. I do not know why my current studies matter to him, but they clearly do. My studies and family and work, intersected and interconnected, have always been defined by tightly woven connections of experience, exploration and relationship. These learning experiences were possible only because they occurred within the entangled "din of controversy" rather than in a university, by a scholar set apart.

Intellectual traditions as entangled scholarship. By embracing my entanglements, my studies have been at least as much about bringing non-academic thought into my studies as sharing in the other direction. I believe in an approach to scholarship that is *set within* a complicated and unstable world, a world full of distractions. An approach to education that is set within the world might be one in which our classmates are our children, our co-workers, our families and our friends; it might be one that pushes us to locate and analyze our own texts and to honour voices in our lives that might otherwise unheard or be forgotten, one in which we create artifacts to be shared with those closest to us. It might encourage critical exploration of the "distractions" and maybe find that the message is in fact in the "mess." Todd (2015) described a desire to "hear a whisper of the lively and deep intellectual traditions borne out in Indigenous Studies departments, community halls, fish camps, classrooms, band offices and Friendship Centres" currently under-represented in the scholarly literature (p. 7). I believe that my entangled scholarship has afforded me exactly that, an opportunity to notice the wisdom that surrounds me, in a variety of non-academic forms. Is it possible that I learned more *because* of the absence of lecturing heads? What if education was more open to these non-traditional forms of wisdom? What about the lively and deep intellectual discussions taking place among Black Lives Matters organizers or Mi'kmaw fishermen exerting their rights? What opportunities to learn are missed in the university as a place set apart from controversy?

Academic freedom as entangled. I have grown increasingly comfortable in my non-traditional scholarly space, one unbounded by either place or specific job expectations. I have also been struck by the stories of prominent women leaving academia. In sharing her story, Ahmed (2016) said: "This is my story. It is personal. *The personal is institutional.*" Similarly, describing her own decision to leave, Morrish (2017) stated, "This capriciousness of managerial commitment to academic freedom means that to be a critical scholar is to live with uncertainty... So I decided to reclaim my academic freedom—outside the academy." As I read the stories of these tremendous women, I wonder why anyone would question my choice to remain comfortably within the world rather than set apart in academia?

As I finished my final edits on this chapter, I was in the process of guest facilitating a discussion forum for an instructional design course at my old school, Athabasca University. The professor who was teaching the course taught me the same course when I was a student. She has included several papers I wrote during and after the course in the syllabus and invited me to participate. Unlike Oakeshott's (1989) classes of university-people, I recognized myself in these students: adult learners balancing busy lives with their online education, drawing on their varied experiences, learning from one another and from others beyond their cohort. It was a privilege to learn with and from them, if only for a week. In the course, I recognized something else, my old student avatar complete with my oldest son sitting with me, then eight. Now at 19, due to limited options he is enrolled in his own online classes. Has he added his own avatar to his course shells? I wonder and smile as more of the disparate dots are connected.

Embracing My Entanglements

My "scholarly hobby" has become the place where all of my carefully constructed contexts collapse, not under the surveilling gaze of a university, but simply because it is time. Time to embrace and celebrate the tremendous value that my many entanglements bring to my studies. Time to appreciate that I have the freedom to follow my interests, unencumbered by worries about tenure and future speaking engagements. Time to shed the guilt about all the other things I am not doing while pursuing critical research and reflection. Beyond my own self-interest, I believe it is time to recognize students, teachers, scholars as well as those in the middle and outside spaces as different, but equal. It is time to embrace the fullness of experiences in ways that extend our agency in our lives and in our studies, in ways that enable us not to preserve but to question and challenge the tradition of learning. Time to actively engage in controversy and celebrate our entanglements.

References

Ahmed, S. (2016, August 27). Resignation is a feminist issue [Web log post]. Retrieved from: https://feministkilljoys.com/2016/08/27/resignation-is-a-feminist-issue/

Ahmed, S. *Living a Feminist Life*. Duke University Press Books, 2017.

Anderson, T. (Ed.). (2008). *The theory and practice of online learning*. Athabasca University Press.

Bowles, K. (2020, May 9). Background [Web log post]. Retrieved from: https://musicfordeckchairs.com/

Cooper, A., Berg, A., Sclater, N., Dorey-Elias, T., and Kitto, K. (2017, March). LAK17 hackathon: getting the right information to the right people so they can take the right action. *Proceedings of the Seventh International Learning Analytics & Knowledge Conference* (pp. 514-515).

Elias, T. (2010). Universal instructional design principles for Moodle. T*he International Review of Research in Open and Distributed Learning,* 11(2), 110-124.

Elias, T. (2011). Universal instructional design principles for mobile learning. *The International Review of Research in Open and Distributed Learning,* 12(2), 143-156.

Elias, T. (2019). Troubling "Technologies": Exploring the Global Learning XPRIZE Using the Frameworks of Skinner and Foucault. *Current Issues in Emerging eLearning,* 6(1), 1.

Elias, T., Ritchie, L., Gevalt, G., and Bowles, K. (2020). A Pedagogy of 'Small': Principles and Values in Small, Open, Online Communities. *Open (ing) Education,* (pp. 364-389). Brill Sense.

Kanuka, H. (2008). Understanding e-learning technologies-in-practice. The theory and practice of online learning, 91.

Kiser, K. (2020, April 16). Instructors, Please wash your hair [Web blog post]. Retrieved from: https://www.insidehighered.com/advice/2020/04/16/teaching-online-should-not-mean-presenting-yourself-less-professionally-or

Laporte, C. & Cassuto, L. (2020, April 16). How to responsibly reopen colleges in the fall [Web log post]. Retrieved from: https://www.insidehighered.com/views/2020/04/16/practical-advice-how-colleges-can-responsibly-reopen-fall-opinion

Lee, K. (2015). Discourses and realities of online higher education: a history of [discourses of] online education in Canada's Open University (Doctoral dissertation, University of Toronto).

McKillop, A. B. (2001). Disciplined Intelligence: Critical Inquiry and Canadian Thought in the Victorian Era (Vol. 193). McGill-Queen's Press-MQUP.

Morrish, L. (2017, March 2). Why the audit culture made me quit [Web log post]. Retrieved from: https://www.timeshighereducation.com/features/why-audit-culture-made-me-quit

Oakeshott, M. (1989). The idea of a university. *The voice of liberal learning: Michael Oakeshott on education*, 95-104.

Pallavi, D. (n.d.). 9-5 and beyond: How to structure work from home days [Web log post]. Retrieved from: https://www.rmit.edu.au/study-with-us/levels-of-study/postgraduate-study/why-rmit/how-to-structure-work-from-home-days

Paquette, C. (1979). Quelques fondements d'une pédagogie ouverte. *Québec français* 36, 20–21 (T. Morgan, Trans.) Retrieved from: https://homonym.ca/?s=paquette

Paquette, C. (2005). La pédagogie ouverte et interactive: une brève histoire. Retrieved from: http://arc-en-ciel.csdm.ca/files/Pedagogie-ouverte-et-interactive.pdf

Poellhuber, B., Anderson, T., Racette, N., and Upton, L. (2013). Distance students' readiness for and interest in collaboration and social media. *Interactive Technology and Smart Education*.

Richards, G., Marshall, S., Elias, T., Quirk, D., Ives, C., and Siemens, G. (2010, June). Developing university courses with OERs. *EdMedia+ Innovate Learning* (pp. 1069-1073). Association for the Advancement of Computing in Education (AACE).

Stracke, C. M., Downes, S., Conole, G., Burgos, D., & Nascimbeni, F. (2019). Are MOOCs open educational resources?: A literature review on history, definitions and typologies of OER and MOOCs. *Open Praxis*, 11(4), 331.

Todd, Z. (2016). An indigenous feminist's take on the ontological turn:'Ontology'is just another word for colonialism. *Journal of historical sociology*, 29(1), 4-22.Weller, M. (2020, April 22). Digital resilience in the time of pandemic [Web log post]. Retrieved from: http://blog.edtechie.net/resilience/digital-resilience-in-the-time-of-pandemic/Zimmerman, J. (2020, April 24). Video Kills the Teaching Star: Remote learning and the death of charisma [Web log post]. Retrieved from: https://www.chronicle.com/article/Video-Kills-the-Teaching-Star/248631

Different Hats, Different Voices, Different Jobs: The Pracademic Experience

Keith Heggert

A late, stop-start entry to academia

Like many other academics currently in the field of Education, I came to academia quite late. However, unlike my colleagues, my journey was considerably more meandering and varied than the traditional teacher-to-academia pathway. While I had a decade-long career as a high school teacher and school leader, working in government and non-government schools in Australia and the United Kingdom, I also worked as a professional trainer and Organiser for one of Australia's largest education unions. I also did freelance work as a learning designer for higher education institutions and corporations. There was nothing seamless about my transitions between these roles; in fact, there were numerous times when I was working across all three industries, in a range of different classifications, and often in precarious circumstances. And, at the same time, I was pursuing doctoral studies in civics and citizenship education, and also working as a lecturer and tutor in initial teacher education at two different Australian universities.

This experience—while fraught at times—has provided me with a unique insight into some of the challenges that face practitioners entering the academy, especially within the field of teacher education, and my experience taught me a great deal about how best to navigate the minefield of being both and insider and outsider, often at the same time.

A voice for teachers

Specifically, my role as an insider and outsider, that is, as a pracademic (Susskind 2013), meant that I had both the authenticity and the authority to encourage teachers to act collectively in order to promote the importance of the role and the respect in which they were held by wider society.

As a teacher and a union Organiser, I was anxious about the way narratives related to failing schools, failing education systems and most concerning, failing teachers were becoming common in media discourse (for example, see Barnes and Cross 2018). Teachers were constantly being framed as lazy, apathetic and unintelligent. Australia's declining results in standardised testing were blamed on ignorant, poorly trained teachers who lacked the desire or ambition to improve student outcomes (Wilson, Dalton and Baumann 2015). It seemed like every politician, think tank and radio shock-jock had a solution that was going to reverse Australia's decline—all of which they had arrived at without speaking to a single teacher.

What was apparent to me was that the voices of teachers were far too often absent from these debates. In fact, nobody working in policy or the media seemed to be speaking to teachers about their concerns; they were not being consulted about the pressures they were experiencing nor about the raft of changes that had become common in schools and sectors across Australia. This reflected debates about education about which I was passionate. Just as I believed that civics education should be done with students, not to students, so too did I feel that education reform should be done *with* teachers, not *to* teachers. And if teachers were going to be part of any kind of reform, then they needed to be empowered in order to have their voices heard. They needed to develop a collective identity and a shared professional identity. The place for that to happen was in initial teacher education programs, and my role, as I came to see it, was to encourage this development.

Narrowing the practice gap in academia

The gap between education academics working in initial teacher education and practicing teachers is well known (see, for example, Vanderlinde and van Braak 2010, or Zeichner 1995). Teachers are often dismissed as being conceptually confused about learning, or unwilling to embrace recent research (Hayes 2014), using debunked theories for little gain. The debacle about learning styles is one example of this: despite limited empirical evidence for visual, auditory and kinaesthetic learners and the validity of these as 'learning styles', many teachers rushed to embrace approaches based on these ideas, and now are unwilling to change their practice to fit with more current understandings of how students learn. Alternatively, academics are quickly labelled out of touch, and the findings of their research of little practical use 'at the chalkface' (Murray 2002), and hence they are dismissed by teachers who 'know what they are doing'.

While both parties acknowledge the presence of the gap between research and practice and the need to work together more closely to reduce its size and improve educational outcomes for pre-service teachers and ultimately students, this gap has so far proved intractable. This is likely due to the complex, diverse, and constantly changing phenomena that influence the different understandings of teachers and academics; any approach aimed at resolving this issue will need to be flexible, localised, and based on individual contexts.

As I began teaching pre-service teachers as an academic, I harboured my doubts about the distance between many of the other academics in the initial teacher education program and the current state of the teaching profession. Some academics had been teachers, but for many this was some considerable time ago. Others had never been teachers at all. While I acknowledge that there is a place for subject matter expertise, I was concerned that the situated aspects of learning to be a teacher were too often ignored in favour of the cognitive ones. I think—and I would argue there is plenty to support this—that one doesn't simply become an English teacher, for example, by knowing all the works of Shakespeare and having developed a lesson plan or a program of study to teach them. Instead, one learns to be a teacher through the practice of being a teacher: there is something of the experiential model here, and also the apprenticeship idea, but I think it's perhaps even more complex than that.

Teaching, as a profession, is a dense nexus of knowledge, wisdom and experience—and the best way to get that experience is through actually working as a teacher. Of course, such experiences need to be carefully managed—I'm not advocating for simply throwing students into the classroom—and I also acknowledge the role of the practicum or professional experience is important here; but I think that there was, and is, still too much of a gulf between the theory and the practice of what we as teachers do and how we teach young teachers that.

The solution, of course, is to have more pracademics, like myself, within teacher education programs, not just in specific subject areas, but across the whole program. In this instance, the pracademics serve as a bridge between theory and practice; they can ground academic research in their lived experiences and serve to contextualise the research into teacher's lives.

Speaking back to the individualist agendas within ITE

I left teaching and joined the Independent Education Union as an Organiser because I believed that teachers needed to work together if they were to restore their profession. It was a decision not without some risk; I was told that it was likely to be the end of my teaching career ("you can't go back!") and I must admit it was disconcerting being away from the classroom; but I soon had my teaching 'itch' scratched because, almost at the same time I started work for the union, I also started working casually as a lecturer in an initial teacher education program at university.

I was immediately conscious of the differences between my own experiences as a teacher, and more recently as an Organiser, and what was being taught within this teacher education program. This placed me in something of an ethical quandary: how could I communicate to my students the reality of what it meant to be a teacher in New South Wales, while at the same time ensuring that they had the best experience in their teacher training? In a strange contradiction, I felt that I was almost the outsider in this case. Despite having only very recently come from teaching, and still working with teachers on a daily basis, my experiences—which I felt could be of real value to teachers—seemed to be held in little regard by the structure of the course I was teaching.

I also found that I had some serious concerns about the nature of that course. Initial Teacher Education (ITE) in Australia is becoming increasingly regulated; there is a great deal of emphasis on testing and assessment and ensuring that teachers are 'classroom-ready' from the moment they graduate. I find this hard to reconcile with my own experience as a teacher and a school leader: no teacher is really 'classroom-ready'—rather, teaching is something that, for a lot of it, you learn by doing. No training program can cover all of the complex and multi-levelled decisions even the most junior teacher makes on a day to day basis. Good schools and systems recognise this, and provide a range of mentoring opportunities for new teachers to grow into the role. In some ways, the government's insistence on 'classroom-ready' was, I felt, counterproductive.

Such an approach was coupled with an increased emphasis on the Australian Professional Standards for Teaching (APSTs). These were reasonably new, and everything that student teachers did was centred around the notion of meeting these standards at the graduate level. While in and of itself, I don't necessarily think the standards were that bad an idea, the way pre-service teachers (and indeed, teachers as a profession) are positioned in relation to the standards was another aspect that I found troubling. Within the standards, teachers were framed as autonomous, individual practitioners. It was almost like the developers of the standards expected teachers to work individually. There was no focus on teaching being a collective endeavour, nor about the responsibility of schools to teachers. Instead, there was an emphasis on individual practice, individual content knowledge, and individual solutions to challenging students. This was diametrically opposed to the reality of the profession that I had seen, too. I'd never worked in a school where teachers weren't willing and determined to work together—from sharing resources to assisting when dealing with challenging students. And my work with the teaching union had only further heightened my understanding that, if teachers are going to gain control of their profession, then the only means they have to do it is via their collective will and shared advocacy. This conversation—and the importance of it—was entirely absent from the initial teacher education programs I participated in, much to my frustration.

I developed a role as a pracademic in this situation, where I sought to problematize the teaching standards. By drawing on my own experiences as a teacher, school leader and Organizer, I presented students with scenarios that tested the APSTs against each other, or other legislation. I introduced students to the notions of work health and safety legislation, and especially the responsibilities of the employer to teachers. And I emphasised—through guest speakers, examples, scenarios and repetition, the idea that teaching is a team sport, and good teachers support others. In this way I felt that part of my role as a pracademic was to resist the imposition of 'teacher-eat-teacher' standards and accountability frameworks within the profession.

Problematizing the ethics of teaching

I had become more and more of an advocate for teachers and the role that they played in society; this was motivated by my concern about the

Global Education Reform Movement (GERM), the increasingly privatised education system, and the general dismantling of the teaching profession from both governmental and corporate sources (Sahlberg 2016). My commitment to these issues expressed itself in my role as an advocate, Organiser, speaker and writer, as well as an academic. I was clear about my subjectivity to my students, and took every opportunity to speak to them about my concerns in this area. However, as I was doing so, I was conscious that I might not be best preparing them to survive in their chosen career.

Teaching, especially for early career teachers, is a difficult and demanding profession. Indeed, that is part of the reason why I speak so forcefully about these topics—in the hope of engendering some change. However, not all teachers share my point of view about either the necessity of that change, or the means to encourage it. This difference of opinion forced me to consider whether I was acting in the best interests of my students.

As someone coming from the profession, I had a stake in the teaching profession and its future—unlike some of my academic colleagues. As someone who was precariously employed, I also knew that I might return to teaching. However, I also needed to be mindful of whether I was providing the best possible experience for my students by discussing these ideas and advocating for them to take action as a collective. While I felt that such advocacy to pre-service teachers was an important part of learning about teaching (and one, as I describe earlier, that I felt had been absent from much of their education), I was also aware that I might be setting up the students for failure and perhaps even reducing their possibility of being an employer. In some ways, it was okay for me to speak about being a rabble-rouser and activist; but for new teachers seeking employment in their first schools, such an approach might actually prevent them from gaining permanent employment, and if that was even a risk, could I ethically engage in such behaviour? Of course, there is also the question of whether I could ethically not encourage them to act like this, too.

While this did cause me some concerns, I realised that my position as a pracademic would allow me to satisfy my doubts and also use it as a learning opportunity for the students: much of my teaching was very much based in the lived experience of teachers. The concerns and questions that this issue raised were part of what teachers were grappling with—and seeking to take action about, in many cases—throughout their working lives. If I wanted to raise the status of the teaching profession and promote the voices of teachers, then I needed to foreground the discussion of these issues—and the knowledge that developed out of them—as a central part in my work in initial teacher education. This discussion itself was a learning opportunity, and I would use it as such.

Conclusion: Finding a space for the pracademic

The three themes that I have outlined above have a degree of commonality. Taken together, they chart some of the learnings that I, as a professional entering academia via the route of precarious employment, have come to understand. They also describe my position as neither insider or outsider within academia—and indeed, I am no longer an insider, nor quite an outsider yet, within the teaching profession. I have tried to outline some of the challenges that I faced as I entered the academy; of course, these challenges are particularly contextual, related both to the Australian education system as a whole and my own personal and professional experience, and I think there is an need for the solution, such as it is, to be contextual as well.

I suggest that rather than arguing about being 'inside' or 'outside', we use the term 'pracademic' as a way to create an entirely new space. Inside and outside are often seen as being mutually exclusive. I would argue that an 'insider-outsider' approach weakens both the knowledge of insiders and that of outsiders, and instead I suggest that pracademics (that is, practitioner academics, in the sense that they are still intimately involved and working with the industry from which they are drawn) are a bridge between the two. Indeed, they are capable of providing valuable expertise within specific contexts in a way that is available to neither insiders, nor outsiders.

References

Barnes, M., & Cross, R. (2018). 'Quality' at a cost: the politics of teacher education policy in Australia. *Critical Studies in Education*, 1-16. DOI: 10.1080/17508487.2018.1558410

Hayes, D. (2014). Why important education research often gets ignored. *The Conversation*. https://theconversation.com/why-important-education-research-often-gets-ignored-33040

Murray, J. (2002). Between the chalkface and the ivory towers?: A study of the professionalism of teacher educators working on primary initial teacher education courses in the English university sector (Doctoral dissertation, Institute of Education, University of London).

Sahlberg, P. (2016). The global educational reform movement and its impact on schooling. *The handbook of global education policy*, 128-144.

Susskind, L. (2013). Confessions of a pracademic: Searching for a virtuous cycle of theory building, teaching, and action research. *Negotiation Journal*, 29(2), 225-237.

Vanderlinde, R., & van Braak, J. (2010). The gap between educational research and practice: Views of teachers, school leaders, intermediaries and researchers. *British educational research journal*, 36(2), 299-316.

Wilson, R., Dalton, B., & Baumann, C. (2015). Six ways Australia's education system is failing our kids. *The Conversation*.

Zeichner, K. M. (1995). Beyond the divide of teacher research and academic research. *Teachers and teaching*, 1(2), 153-172.

The stories we tell and hear: how we can learn from carefully crafting in uncertainty

Sarah Yardley

A wise friend once said to me 'When you face uncertainty, look back, and tell yourself the stories of your past, how you have learned and gained from them, and how those you believe in and who believe in you have stood the test of time.' I was a medical student, suffering from imposter syndrome, and had much to learn about the importance of stories in healthcare, as well as my own life.

Sometime later, as a new PhD graduate, I was questioned about my evolving career: 'what links your work?' Although I could give it academic labels, (socio-cultural, interpersonal interactions and relationships, complexity and unintended consequences), it could be summed up in a less fancy way—I was fascinated by the stories people tell and trying to see how to answer the challenge of 'but that's not how it works in the real world' as a riposte to theory and research from frontline clinical practice. I wanted, and still want my work to lead healthcare professionals to seeing things differently, prompting improvement through different thinking and actions.

These experiences came back to me when someone suggested a helpful exercise for developing my career might be to consider what I would want people to say at my funeral. I now think that if the practitioners think I'm a bit too keen on theory, and the theorists think I'm a bit too pragmatic then I might have the boundary tensions—living in the gap—about right. I hope what people would say about me come down to two essentials: time for others and an interest in improving the consequences of 'what happens in the in-betweens'—that is actions and reactions between people and artefacts within the 'system(s)' (also known as life!).

This is because I believe the stories we tell about ourselves and others matter. Stories, told and untold, are how we create meaning, make sense and live with uncertainty. Stories create and limit our imagined futures. Arthur Frank (2010) describes humans as being the "sum of perpetually accumulating stories" with each of us embodying an inner library of stories that work with, for and on us:

> "To be human is to confront a sequence of questions throughout a life, of which boundaries to respect, which to cross, and how to know the rules of crossing. Stories create boundaries, yet they are also the humans' companion in living with—though not necessarily within—these boundaries." (p. 1)

In this way we understand 'how things work in the real world'. Yet another aspect of being human is to live with uncertainty. The uncertainties described in medical students by Renee Fox (1957) apply to us all. These come from:

- "incomplete or imperfect mastery of available knowledge"
- "Limitations in current medical [or other] knowledge"
- And, perhaps most importantly: "difficulty in distinguishing between personal ignorance or ineptitude and the limitations of present medical [or other] knowledge"(p. 2).

Our stories provide ways to attempt an untangling of which sort of uncertainty we are facing and how to live with it.

Stories are both personal and collective. When I meet people in my professional roles—clinician, researcher, educator—I'm interested in how our stories will interweave. If we engage meaningfully we will also leave each encounter a little changed, hopefully for the better. Yet care needs to be taken; the stories we tell have potential for unravelling if an interaction causes a thread to snag. Most of the people I meet in my professional work don't have very tidy or certain stories: sometimes that's because they have a serious illness but mostly it's because life just isn't tidy or certain, and none of us know quite how near the beginning, middle or end of each story thread we might be.

When I was growing up my mother would encourage us to take care of our best clothes by turning them inside out, and carefully folding or hanging to avoid snagging. We would see the messiness of the construction and had to resist the temptation of pulling randomly at loose threads. Instead my mother would decide if a loose thread needed attention or not, and if so variously thread these back in, add new stitches or cut away redundant material—according to what was needed to keep the clothes 'best'.

I find this craft-based metaphor in keeping with my experiences in practice and the ideas I research with the goal of improving what happens in the in-betweens and the workings of the real world. In Palliative Care, patients and those close to them are often trusting us with what is on the inside as much as with the messiness of their stories. When we engage with them, a key question is how do we identify which stories it is helpful to attend to and how. Thoughtlessly pulling threads might do much damage, but 'doing nothing' may equally have untoward consequences. An active decision process is needed to maintain the 'best'. This may require turning things inside out, but should be done so without wilful snagging or unthinking pulling of threads. Instead we should delicately explore what needs to be woven back in, or cut out, to allow each person to live their best possible story despite the questions and boundaries faced.

I was recently asked to collaborate and participate, along with colleagues, in Forms of Care, a study of 'actively-not-intervening' as a key feature of palliative care practice.(3). This brought my ideas of stories and craft metaphors to a professional learning experience through collaborative research work.

As a clinical team we hoped participation in the research would help us develop our reflective and reflexive practices in meaningful ways. I am using reflective here to mean thinking after the event about decisions from different perspectives including what one might repeat or do differently in the future. Reflexive refers to the more intuitive but essential acting on reflections on the spot based on what is happening in my interactions with other people 'live'. Of course, the former is needed to inform the latter (and vice versa) as our capacity to act and learn depends on past experiences.

Anthropologists can help healthcare teams reclaim a broad perspective on what reflexivity and reflective practice is, at its best, by providing evidence to support how teams draw on a spectrum of creative and timely ways to thoughtfully engage in daily work. If we as healthcare professionals are to to play our roles well (metaphorically dressing for different occasions and purposes so we are well equipped to complete each activity well) we need to practice layering (what is needed for a particular time or place, neither too much or too little) and crafting an overall construction (different items that complement into integrated whole 'outfits').

To express that more practically, our purpose in palliative care might be to work alongside someone who asks 'how long do I have to live?' when we meet them. There are many possible layers to this question and first we need to understand why it is being asked. Just as when different people look at the weather forecast to decide how to dress it depends on the activity they intend to carry out, so the content and detail of our layered answer will only be helpful if we have unpicked what is underlying and driving this question of time left. Doing our work well is to find a combination of layers that when crafted together will construct a helpful framework to support the person asking – and hence successfully achieving this for them means finding something that matches their individual concerns and priorities.

Participant-collaboration in ethnographic research creates an opportunity for mutual learning through layering the perspectives of healthcare teams and anthropologists to construct new stories. In this way there is potential for local impact as well as wider transferable findings.

When healthcare professionals undertake reflection and seek to be reflexive this is because we want to take care rather than to snag, to be deliberate and informed in weaving together our conscious and active decision-making even if the decision is to simply be alongside or to help hold uncertainties in our therapeutic and collegiate relationships. In a speciality such as palliative care it is rare to find someone who is not genuinely and meaningfully attempting this. Yet, in contrast, mandated 'official' reflections commonly demanded by regulators and employers in pre-prescribed formats, for summative purposes, are a negative experience. The pervasive sense that written evidence is required to prove reflection is happening frustrates many. Dissociation from, or devaluing of, the process because of 'what counts' to officialdom can paradoxically lead to loss of learning—hiding the clothes at the bottom of the wardrobe when instead loose threads should be woven back in, repaired with new stitches or cut away.

The ethnographic gaze offered to us as part of our collaboration prompted for me a much more constructive approach to taking another look at what is on the inside, personally and professionally. We were encouraged to look at 'place' differently and think more deeply about 'home' and our role in making it. Place is a key theme within the Forms of Care project, shown to intimately interrelate with changes in condition or personal factors. The idea of 'placing' (4), both people and things, in the sense of situating or contextualising is an ongoing process. This, rather than gatekeeping places as appropriate or not for people to be in, or access, is coming to the fore. The real life experience in palliative care for patients, informal carers and professionals is that needs are relational within places. How place helps or hinders meeting needs varies by a wider range of characteristics than simple fixed physical location. We have been encouraged to recognise that where people live may fall short of cultural ideas of 'home' as a 'familiar, safe place' when uncertainty, messiness and disorder are defining characteristics of illness. The idea of placing as an ongoing concern gives us a framework to think more carefully about how to provide a sense of safety, order and care in emotional and symbolic realms as well as clinical and practical.

As a result of this we have been strengthened in our ability to think differently and deeply about how to articulate what it is to care and to hold situations where success needs to be defined by something other than cure. I have gained a greater awareness of the nuances and subtle shifts in the choices I make and how the challenges to oneself as well as to others of a fluid, mixed yet integrated identity can be used to deepen reflection and reflexivity. In these situations I am actively and deliberately doing things that equally mean not doing other things but are most certainly not 'nothing'. It is not 'just doing' but choosing to 'do differently' not being under-dressed, or even undressed, instead being dressed differently for different goals.

An example of this awareness is making more deliberate and conscious efforts to be explicit with people about my willingness to 'co-....'—sometimes this is co-llaborate, co-produce, co-construct, or co- something else. I've always tried to practice with an emphasis on empowering and respecting autonomy and choice. Often this means discussing the pros and cons of various options with people. I had not previously thought so much about making explicit my approach as well as carrying it out so we are jointly working in the same framework—and if necessary modifying my approach to a framework that better suits others. I have a new inner question—'what is the pattern this person wants to weave?' Knowing this will help me offer new threads of thought or action that they might choose to interweave into their current and future stories of health and care.

A further example is expanding the range of conversational approaches I might take—a conscious tentativeness (taking care not to snag threads)—to allow people to explore preferences for care and weigh up difficult choices from the available options by actively reflecting and working reflexively with them—often reframing non-intervening as an active rather than passive approach. I have only anecdotal data (stories!) but it seems to help by emphasising a willingness to listen, seek to understand a person and ultimately convey a sense of care.

Inviting ethnographers into our working lives is enriching our practice. Many threads need to come together to capture the complexity of what we do. We all need critical friends (in research and in practice) and to engage in joint enterprises to develop our thinking and abilities to do so and I'd encourage anyone considering having an ethnographic team to include one to enrich their practice. I've gained much from the process to help me in my motivation to be as well-equipped as possible in my approach to therapeutic and collegiate relationships at work.

Before finishing on a personal note, my plea to anthropologists and others in related fields is please do help the frontline practitioners of healthcare reclaim what reflexivity and reflective practice can look like with evidence to support diversity in addressing the mandate to prove that we are thoughtfully engaged in our work. Recapturing the value of creativity and drawing on different paradigms to help us make the familiar unfamiliar as well as helping develop a wider understanding of 'what counts' could greatly help us as we seek to use our reflections to expand our individual and collectively capabilities to ensure care when cure is not possible is delivered well. Joint endeavors using these principles can be equally beneficial to practice and research.

Perhaps inevitably, writing a piece like this, raises as many new ideas and questions for me to explore in my own personal narrative as much as it helps me make sense of where I have come from. Some of my learning is perhaps only new to me, after all medicine has long been considered an art as well as a science. Even so, I hope this contribution will be useful even if only by prompting others to consider what works for them metaphorically to develop their practice.

When researching professionalism I was told by a medical student that what it meant was 'you were not a person anymore'—she perceived the requirement as suppression of all individual identity to become something homogenous and nondescript. Her early experiences of practice were that to stand out in any way was wrong, and that to do more for a patient than senior colleagues thought was appropriate would be deemed as unprofessional as doing less than expected. Boundaries are helpful, and often how we get through the day, but there is great danger in defining unprofessional as anything someone more powerful does not like. I hope stories, scholarship and practice such as mine will challenge these ideas. Healthcare is people not just about people. The in-betweens, stitches if you will, are what will almost always make or break it in the boundary-crossing work needed if we are to construct the best tools (clothes) for ourselves and our patients suitable for each occasion. Respectfully and consciously interweaving our stories may be one way to do so.

Acknowledgements

With thanks to the Forms of Care Team: Simon Cohn, Erica Borgestrom & Annelieke Driessen for their helpful comments on earlier drafts and enthusiastic collaborative engagement with our clinical service during the course of their research.

References

Frank A. (2010). *Letting stories breath: a socio=narratology*. London, University of Chicago Press, pp. 3, 60,70.

Fox, R.C. (1957). Training for Uncertainty. *The Student-Physician*, Merton, R.K., Reader, G., and Kendall, P.L., eds., Cambridge, Mass.: Harvard University Press, pp. 207-241.

Cohn S, Borgstrom E & Driessen A. Forms of Care study website https://www.lshtm.ac.uk/research/centres-projects-groups/forms-of-care#welcome [accessed 10.07.2020]

Driessen A, Borgstrom E, Cohn S (2020). 55 Placing death and dying: on the work of making place at the end of life. *BMJ Supportive & Palliative Care*, 10:A28.

Examining Practice Wisdom

Justin Dunne

"There is a 50/50 chance she will try and kill herself today," the psychologist reported. I was the Manager of a National Health Service (NHS) programme working with young people with substance misuse issues, and this colleague had reported back to me on an appointment that had just taken place between a 15-year-old female heroin user and a Consultant Psychiatrist who was responsible for prescribing. The Consultant had not read the client notes and had conducted the meeting in such a way that the client fled the room in a state of distress. This client was highly unstable emotionally and had a history of suicide attempts. She was homeless but would stay with her 23-year-old boyfriend who was also an injecting heroin user. Her life was extremely chaotic.

When my colleague spoke to me about what had happened, I remember feeling frustrated and alarmed. Here was a highly trained and well-paid Consultant taking short cuts. This client had a history of difficulties working with 'professionals' and understanding this backstory and her general emotional state was important for working with her effectively. To make matters worse, I had previously expressed my concerns to the Commissioners of the service that parachuting somebody in once a week to do prescribing may not be the best approach when working with these vulnerable young people where building a trusting therapeutic relationship seemed so important. Even though many of my team were support workers who were not highly qualified or well-paid, they had excellent engagement skills and built good alliances with these young people that allowed them to work through the difficulties that had led to their drug use. They cared deeply about these individuals and it showed me that being highly qualified did not equate to being highly effective.

That day caused many of us in the service a great deal of anxiety. The psychologist who had brought me the news spent all day trying to locate her and eventually managed to contact her and calm her down that evening. Fortunately, she did not take her life but it was a genuine possibility that day knowing her fragile state. It was a critical incident that made me reflect very deeply about our practice as a service.

For these vulnerable young people our intervention literally could be a matter of life and death. As a consequence, I started a review of the service with my team and reported my concerns to Commissioners about what had happened. I asked the fundamental question, 'Why do we do what we do?' I thought about what would have happened had this young person taken her life and imagined myself being in a legal hearing answering questions about why we did what we did as a service. In truth, I'm not sure I had an answer at that time.

We operated by modelling ourselves on adult drug treatment services and Child and Adolescent Mental Health Services. We paid attention to the guidance and policy in our practice area although this was patchy at that time. Mostly we operated somewhat intuitively based on the experience and skills held by the team. Two were nurses, one of which was trained in Family Therapy. Four other staff were outreach support workers who used a variety of general support approaches with some motivational interviewing and cognitive behavioural therapy techniques. One of these support workers was a qualified psychologist. Our monitoring suggested that we helped a lot of young people and we even won a prestigious Government Home Office award as the best drugs team in our region. We were invited to a national awards ceremony in Westminster with celebrities and Members of Parliament where we watched a video presentation the Home Office made about our service.

I remember sitting there thinking, 'Wow, we seem amazing!' but also thinking about the weaknesses and stresses our service faced daily. The video was not a true depiction of the service, just a glossy snapshot of when we got it right. I have no doubt we did some excellent work and truly helped a lot of young people, but I could not stop thinking that how we operated seemed to happen more by chance rather than deliberate design.

I also became concerned about those who did not successfully move through the service. There were some who would engage for a few weeks and then drop out. There seemed to be a belief amongst staff that when clients did this that it was because the client was not ready to engage in treatment. Readiness for change is an important factor in addiction treatment (Prochaska and Velicer 1997; DiClemente et al. 2004) so this is a reasonable assumption for staff. But in such circumstances, we always assumed that the outcome for such a client was neutral, we never considered that the outcome of our contact could be negative.

What I learned from the story of the girl storming out the service was that it was possible for these vulnerable people to end up worse off because of our intervention. As a team we were well-meaning, committed, had a level of skill and were genuinely trying to help, but that did not mean that we couldn't unwittingly contribute to decline in a client's well-being if something about our practice and approach was poor. This was a lightbulb moment for me and has shaped me as a practitioner and academic ever since.

At that time, I was doing my first ever postgraduate study, a diploma in addictive behaviour with a prestigious University Hospital in London. I had time to think and reflect about what we did as a service during this course. I had access to research that was rarely available to practitioners due to costs and was introduced to a repository of useful journal articles discussing the issues I had become concerned about. It was the first time as a practitioner I had thought about what I do using genuine critical reflection.

Journey into Academia

My experience in practice and the study I engaged in started a journey that led me to work for a University and complete a PhD that looked at evidence-based practice with vulnerable young people. A journey that was a complete surprise to me because I certainly never thought of myself as an academic or academically inclined. I very much view myself as a practice-focused academic. It is the thought of trying to improve practice for the kind of people I used to work with which provides the main motivation for the work I now do.

If I'm really honest though, even now after thirteen years in higher education where I obtained a doctorate and became a Senior Fellow in the Higher Education Academy, I often feel like I don't belong. I feel like an imposter especially when I come across highly intelligent colleagues writing for prestigious journals with consummate ease. Despite my achievements, academic work does not come naturally to me apart from my ability to present to audiences which I absolutely love doing. Study and writing is a challenge. I did okay at school but not great.

Difficult beginnings

My father passed away when I was 12 and school didn't seem important. I remember vividly my first day back after a period away as I grieved. A French teacher shouted at me because I did not know what a particular verb was in a particular tense. I remember him saying, "Why don't you know this?" He had a scowl on his face and real venom in this tone. I remember little bits of spit coming out of his mouth as he raged at me. I looked at him, a bit choked up, and replied, "This is my first day back after my dad died." He had failed to notice that I had not been present in class for six weeks! I could not answer his question as I had not done any of the study that would allow me to know what he was talking about. I felt humiliated and angry and from that point on I disengaged from school.

I spent the next four years messing around and doing as little as possible. This resulted in poor grades and report cards that were less than complimentary about my effort. Over time I started to believe them. I started to think, 'I'm rubbish at this school stuff'. I forgot all the comments I had as a boy saying how bright and engaged I was. Now I was the stupid one who didn't try. In my final year, having already significantly narrowed down my qualification possibilities, I did miserably in my mock exams. It was a wake-up call for me as I still needed to leave this horrible school and find employment and for three months, I got my head down and worked hard.

I sought support from a youth worker with a First-Class Honours Degree in engineering. He taught me, in a handful of sessions, all the Mathematics skills I should have learned in five years. This was one of several qualifications that turned from a failure into a pass. Despite this effort, the overall outcome of my schooling was a very modest set of results. I think it's that experience that even now means, as a writer and researcher, I feel like a fraud. I left school at 16 feeling glad it was all over with. I did not feel intelligent in any kind of academic way and I certainly was not interested in any more study. Instead, I went to work for insurance companies for three years, something that I did not enjoy. Then my career took a different path. Inspired by the person who helped me through my exams, I started doing voluntary youth work. This led to a series of jobs working with young people and the wider community and eventually resulted in specialising in substance misuse work and my job in the NHS.

I discovered something I was good at and enjoyed. I was determined to help these young people navigate the difficulties of their teenage years successfully and realise their potential. I was passionate, I related well to these young people and I was highly creative in the programmes I delivered. What was interesting though was I was not qualified and never undertook any formal youth work training. I was someone who learnt from experience. If I studied, it was informally as I looked to learn lessons from those who seemed good at their job. I observed closely how they did things and what it was that generated positive responses. I was always trying to work out how I could do things better and always looking for new and creative ways for engaging young people effectively.

In truth, I was a little cynical of those who were qualified. I was often extremely underwhelmed by their practice and imagination. I found many a bit snobbish because they had some status that I did not and as I developed my career into substance misuse treatment, I found some social workers particularly (as what I would describe as) a bit up their own backsides!

As someone who is now involved in the journey of nurses and social workers becoming qualified it is an interesting journey to reflect upon. The label, status or qualification has never interested me, even as an academic helping people to attain such things. What drives me is a desire to improve practice with the vulnerable people I used to work with and perhaps once was.

I have moved from being a cynic to an advocate for education and training. My academic journey has given me a better sense of how to find useful evidence that informs and improves practice. I often think that I would be a significantly better manager and practitioner now than I was before my academic career and having done a great deal of study. I have learned so much that I wish I knew back then and would like to share some of these lessons. Nevertheless, one of these lessons is something I discovered long before my academic career. *Experienced practitioners often have considerable wisdom.* They understand the subtleties of effective practice and are an excellent repository of knowledge. Reflecting on my practice and academic journey, here are some things I've discovered that I think are important for practitioners to consider.

Harm that is induced by treatment itself

When studying my first postgraduate qualification and whilst still working as a service manager, I first came across the idea of iatrogenic effects.

An iatrogenic effect in medicine is when a planned treatment inadvertently causes a negative or poor outcome (Huefner et al. 2009). The term literally means "physician caused" (Bootzin and Bailey 2005, p. 872) but is often more broadly considered as "harm that is induced by treatment itself" (Moos 2012, p. 1592). Rhule (2005) points out that it is accepted that a treatment is designed to cause change and it is therefore reasonable to assume that deterioration is a possibility as well as improvement even if harmful consequences were unintended. An iatrogenic effect is differentiated to a negative effect (Weiss et al. 2005). A negative effect may still occur within a programme due to wider factors but not as a direct result of a specific intervention itself. Moos (2012) show that wider personal and environmental factors of the client can cause deterioration effects within the context of a programme of care but are not directly caused by the intervention itself.

Understanding this made sense of my experiences as a practitioner, especially in light of the critical incident with which I opened this chapter. Without a doubt, there were reasons beyond the programme we offered for why a client may not pass through the service as we hoped—but it was also possible that we could be part of the problem. Learning about iatrogenic effects highlighted the importance for me that we had an ethical responsibility as practitioners to really understand our craft and do no harm. It drove me to want to know what worked and perhaps more importantly, why? It got me asking questions as to why one client seemed to respond well within a programme and why another seemed to struggle even though they were receiving the same care? Without doubt, these questions have driven my academic career.

Evidence-based practice

As my academic career developed, I conducted a PhD looking at evidence-based practice with vulnerable young people. The study was conducted with a charity that had successfully worked with vulnerable young people for many years. I was keen to explore the subtleties of practice that led to success or failure and to try and make sense practically and theoretically of why particular approaches worked or not. It was a study designed to help the kind of Service Managers that I had been, to have the opportunity to shape their programmes for maximum effect whilst minimising harm. It encouraged me to think about what we mean when we talk about evidence-based practice (EBP), how the wisdom of experienced practitioners could be a valuable source of knowledge for improving practice and how the variants in programmes might determine success or failure.

When considering the notion of EBP, I read Kazdin (2008) who argues that evidence must come from more than what is studied scientifically, and he is critical of the lack of evidence produced in practice contexts. As a practitioner who has seen the benefits of learning from the observation of others this has appeal. Those of us who work in practice are aware of the need to tailor interventions to individuals as they come with different needs, psychological states, support networks, cultural backgrounds, etc. Understanding how interventions—developed in a highly controlled setting—can adapt in practice is necessary. In this way I find myself in agreement with McCormack et al. (2002) who suggest that EBP should be based on three considerations: evidence, context and facilitation. Evidence is arrived at through research and experience, context is to do with culture and leadership, facilitation is about ensuring the right roles, and skills are in place to deliver practice (André et al. 2016).

This highlights the need for more practice focused academics like myself, to be working closely with practitioners to get greater insights into EBP. Although I am no longer a practitioner, my desire as an academic is to work with practitioners in such ways to help improve practice and expand knowledge.

Practice wisdom

One way that the active ingredients for effective practice can be discovered is through examining practice wisdom (PW). As Chu and Tsiu (2016) state:

> Experienced frontline practitioners are repositories of knowledge that is highly personal and often unarticulated ... conceptual tools and resources [should be provided] that allow practitioners to use their ability to make professional judgements, grasp scenarios accurately, mobilize knowledge and learn from both their successes and failures. There has never been a better opportunity for [researchers] ... and frontline practitioners to work together in order to discover and create knowledge through action, to pass age-old wisdom and to make context specific knowledge generally accessible. (p. 52)

As a concept, PW has received little academic attention perhaps because it focuses on the inductive and sometimes intangible creation of knowledge which is difficult to articulate using objective scientific language (Samson 2015; Chu and Tsui 2016). Definitions vary as to what PW means but the idea of knowledge arising out of practical experience is a common feature of these definitions[1]. Mitchell (2011) describes PW, "... as practice-based knowledge that has emerged and evolved primarily on the basis of practical experience rather than from empirical research" (p. 208). In this way, PW provides an opportunity to learn from experience.

Dewane (2006) suggests that skilled practice should bring together knowledge obtained through education and training as well as that arrived at through life experiences and belief systems. What might seem like intuitive practice has a basis in experience, reflection and learning from academic sources, colleagues, and clients. In this view, PW knowledge is gained through embodied reasoning (Chu and Tsui, 2016). Samson (2015) argues that for PW knowledge to emerge, two concepts should be considered. Firstly, there is the idea of tacit knowledge or "knowing-in-action" and secondly, the idea of evaluating the work a practitioner engages in or "reflecting-in practice" (p. 123). PW is based on both intuitive and analytical reasoning (O'Sullivan 2005) and therefore can be thought of as a process via which to arrive at new knowledge. Once PW is discovered, it should be scrutinised and understood in terms of how both theory and experience explains 'why' something works to ensure theoretical fidelity. This is where practice-focused academics are important. We can play a significant role in the critical analysis of PW.

***

As an academic I still feel like a novice but at the same time I believe I am pursuing something that I believe is important. Sometimes, I feel I don't belong in this academic world but perhaps that is because a new kind of practice-focused academic is needed. I have no desire to be a renowned academic, I simply want to continue to ask important questions about practice and offer suggestions as to how we might work more effectively with vulnerable people. This is what excites me, and I know my background as a practitioner brings a perspective that is helpful in exploring emerging ideas in research regarding EBP and Programme Theory. I am more interested in finding ways for such knowledge to be shared and considered as widely as possible then finding my name in highly ranked journals as much as this might help the institution I work for with its contributions to the Research Excellence Framework (REF). (I realise this is important for funding but cannot pretend it particularly motivates me. Improving practice is the most important thing for me as an academic. Sharing knowledge that may prevent critical incidents in

1. Further discussion on Practice Wisdom definitions can be found in DeRoos(1990), Litchfield (1999) and Klein and Bloom, (1995).

what can be life and death situations with vulnerable people should be of paramount importance and therefore making research and knowledge widely available and accessible is critical. I am not sure REF helps in this way.)

I am surprised to find myself where I am in my career, but it presents an opportunity and—although I sometimes feel I don't belong—it is an opportunity I must embrace and am excited by future research and writing possibilities. Something I never imagined saying as a disenfranchised 16-year-old who left school feeling stupid.

References

André, B., Aune, A. G. and Brænd, J. A. (2016). Embedding evidence-based practice among nursing undergraduates: Results from a pilot study. *Nurse Education in Practice*, 18, pp. 30-35.

Bootzin, R. R. and Bailey, E. T. (2005). Understanding placebo, nocebo, and iatrogenic treatment effects. *Journal of Clinical Psychology*, 61(7), pp. 871-880.

Chu, W. and Tsui, M. (2008). The nature of PW in social work revisited. *International Social Work*, 51(1), pp. 47-125.

DeRoos, Y. S. (1990). The Development of PW through Human Problem-solving Processes. *Social Service Review*, 64 (2), pp. 276-287.

DiClemente, C. C., Schlundt, D., & Gemmell, L. (2004). Readiness and Stages of Change in Addiction Treatment. *American Journal on Addictions*, 13(2), 103-119. doi:10.1080/10550490490435777

Dewane, C. J. (2006). Use of self: A primer revisited. *Clinical Social Work Journal*, 34(4), pp. 543-558.

Kazdin, A. E. (2008). Evidence-based treatment and practice: New opportunities to bridge clinical research and practice, enhance the knowledge base, and improve patient care. *American Psychologist*, 63(3), pp. 146-159.

Klein, W. and Bloom, M. (1995). Practice Wisdom. *Social Work*, 40(6), pp. 799-807.

Litchfield, M. (1999). PW. *Advances in Nursing Science*, 22(2), pp. 62-72.

McCormack, B., Kitson, A., Harvey, G., Rycroft-Malone, J., Titchen, A. and Seers, K. (2002). Getting evidence into practice: the meaning of 'context'. *Journal of Advanced Nursing*, 38(1), pp. 94-104.

Mitchell, P.F. (2011). Evidence-based practice in real-world services for young people with complex needs: New opportunities suggested by recent implementation science. *Children and Youth Services Review*, 33, pp.207-216.

Moos, R. H. (2012). Iatrogenic Effects of Psychosocial Interventions: Treatment, Life Context, and Personal Risk Factors. *Substance Use & Misuse*, 47(13/14), pp. 1592-1598.

O'Sullivan, T. (2005). Some theoretical propositions on the nature of PW. *Journal of Social Work*, 5(2), pp. 221-242.

Prochaska, J. O., & Velicer, W. F. (1997). The Transtheoretical Model of Health Behavior Change. American Journal of Health Promotion, 12(1), 38-48.

Rhule, D. M. (2005). Take Care to Do No Harm: Harmful Interventions for Youth Problem Behavior. *Professional Psychology: Research and Practice*, 36(6), pp. 618-625.

Samson, P. L. (2015). Practice Wisdom: the art and science of social work. *Journal of Social Work Practice*, 29(2), pp. 119-131.

Weiss, B., Caron, A., Ball, S., Tapp, J., Johnson, M. & Weisz, J. R. (2005). Iatrogenic Effects of Group Treatment for Antisocial Youths. *Journal of Consulting and Clinical Psychology*, 73(6), pp. 1036-1044.

Street Praxis

Fay Akindes

> The trouble is that once you see it, you can't unsee it. And once you've seen it, keeping quiet, saying nothing, becomes as political an act as speaking out. There's no innocence. Either way you're accountable. ~ Arundhati Roy

There is an unspoken rule in academe that you don't "rock the boat" before tenure—before you have permanent employment and job security—that it's too risky. Some faculty of color, for example, are advised not to attend affinity group meetings or teach Ethnic Studies classes to avoid jeopardizing their tenure and promotion. This deterrence away from the very communities that uplift faculty of color suggests how those in power, such as tenured faculty and department chairs, control out of and through fear. Why is acknowledging one's racialized ethnicity and teaching diversity courses threatening and subject to policing? Why must one wait for tenure to speak? If a university doesn't accept one's voice, does it warrant one's presence? If faculty store in reserve what they are afraid to say today, will it matter in the future?

My Beninois husband Simon and I were non-tenured in different departments at the same university and chose to speak up/out about injustices in the university. These injustices typically centered on racism. We were part of a small group of faculty of color that shared our concerns with the chancellor—we wrote a letter that opened the door to meetings around a conference table. The injustices we addressed were related to the hiring and firing of faculty and instructors of color.

In time, our small group of five faculty grew into a recognized affinity group for the university's faculty and staff of color. An Ojibwe elder visited, naming us *Manitoulin*—an Ojibwe word for "island" or safe haven. As I write this, I'm wondering if we could've done more to protect our colleagues, especially international faculty who lost face, and/or their jobs.

The most troubling case in my memory was a Chinese professor who, after more than 10 years, requested a break from teaching Saturday classes. He was missing his young son's sporting events, among other things. I empathized with him. My son played soccer and I knew the impact of Saturday teaching—it shortened the weekend and extended the work week. One semester, after his many requests were ignored, this tenured, associate professor was assigned a Saturday class and he walked out. After a public hearing with a faculty governance committee, the chancellor demoted him to assistant professor with a $5,000 salary cut. Conversely my Black students talked of a white faculty member who missed classes and was quietly dealt with after students complained. The respect extended to this white faculty contrasted sharply with our Chinese colleague who was publicly disciplined.

There were other dismissals of faculty of color, including international faculty. Remembering these cases is troubling when thinking about the ease with which some white faculty were granted tenure and promotion with minimal scholarship. Discrepancies exist and persist, in part, because departments have autonomy in maintaining vague and arbitrary tenure and promotion guidelines, but also because systemic racism and white supremacy sometimes reward mediocrity.

Students were not immune from racial injustices. In 2003, Black students on campus were traumatized by racist graffiti scribbled next to a promotional poster for *Ghosts of Mississippi*, a film about civil rights activist Medgar Evers. When Black students reported the graffiti to the administration, it was quickly removed, what students interpreted as white-washing.

Black students in my class were frightened and confused. Someone on campus was communicating violence against Black students. Why didn't the administration respond by acknowledging the graffiti as unacceptable? Why did it ignore the incident? In response to the administration's indifference, the Black Student Union (BSU) organized a silent march and invited the media, including Milwaukee TV news. Walking quietly from the Student Union to Main Place was one of the most chilling moments I've experienced. I marched behind the students and witnessed the group balloon to hundreds of supporters before reaching Main Place. BSU President Dannie Moore, my student and advisee, asked me to speak. I said it would have been easy to pretend that racists do not walk the corridors of our university, but they do. The racist graffiti was a symbolic lynching and we all deserved to feel safe on campus.

Lessons were embedded in this silent march. When a traumatizing event occurs, people have a need to congregate and witness leaders publicly denounce racism. Meaning is historically contextualized; two words carry the weight of a history of racism. Dannie learned the power of agency. He continued on to graduate school and today is Vice President of Strategic Initiatives and Chief Diversity, Equity, and Inclusion Officer at Eastern Kentucky University.

Years later, after the chancellor retired and his cabinet moved on to other positions, a similar racist incident happened and the new administration's response was quick, well-coordinated, and clear: racism is not welcome here. The administration organized public forums in the theatre attracting more people than available seats. Students expressed fear and trauma, and the entire university provided comfort and solidarity. This incident involved a noose in one of the resident halls.

I remember this incident vividly. It occurred at the start of February—Black History Month—and coincided with Simon's encounter with the Kenosha Police. He was stopped for wwB—walking while Black—in our predominantly white neighborhood less than two miles from the university. He was driving home from a doctor's appointment and his illness and fatigue led his car to swerve into a shallow depression on the side of the road. He didn't have his AAA card for roadside assistance so he started to walk home when several police cars arrived in response to a 911 call reporting a "drunk Black man." Simon was handcuffed and sat in the patrol vehicle for some 45 minutes while police officers searched his Subaru Outback. Would he have been treated differently had his skin been white, particularly since he was ill and not drunk? We later filed a complaint with the police department and was told that the officer in charge was in training and should've been supervised more diligently.

The noose incident is also memorable because the Center for Ethnic Studies, which I directed at the time, organized a teach-in with nearly a thousand students attending the day-long program. A day before the teach-in, a colleague and I received an anonymous letter in our mailbox mocking us for the teach-in. References in the letter suggested that the writer (or writers) was affiliated with a certain committee of administrative mid-managers. It was an act of cowardice—what bullies do in middle school.

Years later, after I received tenure and had witnessed a string of racist micro-aggressions toward faculty of color, I was elected to serve on the Personnel Review Committee (PRC)—the faculty governance committee that reviewed dossiers for tenure and promotion. Serving on this committee exposed the hidden racial politics in academe. I saw discrepancies among departments surrounding the unspoken, invisible, yet omnipresence of race.

One year there was an unanimous recommendation to deny tenure to a faculty who had underperformed in research. This person's department contested the PRC's decision and requested a reconsideration. The PRC again voted unanimously not to recommend tenure. Unbeknownst to me, a white tenured faculty (someone who was not on the PRC or the faculty member's department) was collecting signatures in a petition that was presented to the chancellor. The faculty member—who had not gained a single vote of support by PRC members who had scrutinized evidence, dossiers, files, and records—was awarded tenure and promotion. The PRC was chaired at the time by a South Asian woman with a majority of the committee comprised of faculty of color.

This situation sent a disturbing message to faculty of color. Our collective decision based on evidence (or lack of it) was meaningless. Ironically the faculty who gained tenure and promotion through intervention by white faculty resigned. The petition, created as a sympathetic favor, made public the faculty's deficiency which, I imagine, was a heavy burden to prove false. Petitions connote an act to right an injustice, yet the faculty was not discriminated against. The rules were clear: there was a lack of scholarly evidence to justify tenure. Black faculty with active scholarship had lost their jobs for reasons ambiguous, questionable, and contested in public hearings. Rules are malleable.

Early in my teaching career, I found safety in calling myself an "accidental professor." If it wasn't my intention to teach then, perhaps, I couldn't be judged harshly if I failed. Over time I realized that nothing is accidental. All of my life experiences contribute to my understanding of academe: public K-12 schooling, undergraduate studies, broadcast marketing and promotion, graduate school, university teaching, and now, administrative work. Collectively my life experiences inform my recent encounters with anti-racism in the streets.

***

2020 was the year when the "quiet racism" of Kenosha, Wisconsin, my home since 1997, moved from the back to the front stage. It awakened with amplified fury in social and corporate media, then spilled into the streets. It happened on the last Sunday afternoon in August: white Kenosha police officer Rusten Sheskey stood behind a Black man, Jacob Blake, and pulled the trigger seven times with Jacob's three young sons sitting inches away, witnessing. Some of us were shocked, caught off-kilter, while my daughter and her circle of activist friends were *on call*. When she failed to join us for dinner I imagined her at the crime scene protesting police brutality against Black people. This was an issue that fueled the Coalition to March on the Democratic National Convention, a march that had occupied her activism for a year and had taken place in Milwaukee just three days before the Blake shooting. The last week in August unfolded, fixing Kenosha in the international media's eye—in corporate and independent social media—raising questions that could not be ignored or muted. Latent racism was exposed on center-front-stage.

On the first night of curfew, a wall of Kenosha police, sheriff, and National Guard soldiers dressed in war-gear directed protestors to move south on Sheridan Road. Where are they heading, Seattle independent video-journalist C.J. Halliburton wondered, what's down there? As it turns out, the police and soldiers were pushing protestors toward a petrol station where armed white civilian men were waiting. Some of them were militia answering a Facebook call-to-arms posted by former Kenosha Alderman Kevin Mathewson. In the melee that followed, 17-year-old Kyle Rittenhouse killed two white protestors and injured a medic with his illegally purchased rifle. He was not arrested but returned home to Antioch, Illinois 20 miles southwest of Kenosha. In ensuing news, video taken hours earlier showed an officer in a military tank welcoming Kyle to Kenosha with a bottle of drinking water.

The following night while walking to join a peaceful protest, our daughter and two friends, one a medic, were "disappeared" by officers in an unmarked pick-up truck—a tactic used in Portland, Oregon to terrorize protestors in scenes reminiscent of college students and freedom fighters disappeared in Latin American countries. Our home was disrupted by a phone call from a friend: "I think Adelana was picked up by the Feds."

I made several calls to the Kenosha Sheriff's Department and later learned that what I was told were lies.

Adelana spent 24 hours imprisoned with no phone call, drinking water, and, for several hours, no protective mask against Covid-19. She was in a cell the size of our livingroom rug with five other women and three non-binary people. Their requests for phone calls and medical help went unanswered, though they eventually received masks. Their access to water was a little sink attached to the toilet; no one drank water that night. They communicated resistance through street chanting and found solace in singing songs, such as Bill Withers' *Ain't no sunshine when she's gone.*

The following morning when they were transported six miles from the Kenosha County Detention Center to the Kenosha County Jail, Adelana observed one of the strongest women in the group break down and cry when shackles were attached to her ankles. That, combined with hand-cuffs, the orange jumpsuit, and lack of sleep and water had taken their toll. The system was criminalizing peaceful protestors for exercising their constitutional rights. Conversely on the first night of curfew, 17-year-old Kyle Rittenhouse was allowed to walk away unfettered in the midst of Kenosha police, sheriff, and the National Guard after killing two men and injuring a medic. This disturbing display of white male privilege contrasted sharply with how anti-racist activists of color were treated by law enforcement workers.

Less than 24 hours after being released, Adelana spoke at a news conference organized by the Milwaukee Alliance Against Racism and Political Repression. Buoyed by the supportive crowd, she spoke in the moment, seething with anger against a system of racist injustice. While my former students (wearing *Latinos for Black Lives Matter* t-shirts) and I joined the march, chanting in unison, Adelana was interviewed by national and international news reporters, including the Associated Press whose article was syndicated around the world.

The following morning she was interviewed by the Canadian Broadcasting Corporation in a live TV interview. The news anchor spoke for many viewers when she said that Adelana chose to violate curfew and, therefore, was detained. Adelana answered that she didn't think the treatment she and her cell-mates received was justified—that it was devisive. She shared a quote from Adwoa Asentu: *Curfew is just another way of saying Sundown Town.* Adelana had shared a cell with four other Black people and one Native American, Latina, Asian, and White person (from Norway). The identities of those those disappeared spun a worn, familiar narrative that reified systemic racism.

Weeks later, Adelana and I marched with Jacob Blake's family and members of Kenosha's recently formed BLAK—Black Lives Activists of Kenosha—including co-founder Porche Bennett-Bey, named 2020 Guardian of the Year by *Time* Magazine. Also present was the Rev. Jesse Jackson of Chicago who spiraled me back to the 1980s and a Broadcast Promotion & Marketing Executives Conference in Las Vegas. Rev. Jackson stood at the lectern, looked around the ballroom, and expressed his disappointment that among this influential group he could see only a handful of people of color. Until he said that, I had repressed the fact that my Hawaii Public TV colleague and I were racial minorities, atleast on the "mainland." Rev. Jackson pointed out the power of broadcasting and our responsibility to diversify racial representations on television. Years later, when I applied to graduate school, Rev. Jackson appeared in my essay explaining why I needed to study multicultural broadcasting. During the 2020 Kenosha march, I stole a quick handshake from the Reverend and silently thanked him.

***

Awe and wonder. This is what I feel for Adelana and her generation, young people who are politically informed and committed to making a difference—challenging obsolete systems of racism that divide and exploit. While waiting for our daughter's release from the Kenosha Sheriff's Jail, I mingled with alumni, college students, and professors from Green Bay, Milwaukee, Madison, Stevens Point, Racine, and Kenosha. What is our responsibility as educators? Our students were in the streets leading marches with megaphones and handwritten signs condemning police brutality and systemic racism. How did public displays of protest intersect with students' learning experiences in our classrooms? Critical thinking and democratic citizenship are often listed as learning outcomes in our intentionally constructed syllabi and university websites. How do we acknowledge racial unrest in our streets as informing our students and their lives? How do we contextualize our teaching and learning practices in street praxis? In what ways do we invite the world to enter our learning environments? As my colleague Jordan Landry at UW-Oshkosh asks, how do our intersectional pandemics inform our intersectional pedagogies?

One of my Black African colleagues says that the Covid-19 pandemic will soon end with vaccinations now in circulation. Racism, however, will not end. I now see that the momentary blindness that we sometimes experience may not apply to this particular moment. Racism produces and reproduces a persistent blindness—a refusal to see.

***

My thanks to Professors Adetona Akindes, University of Wisconsin-Parkside, and Farida Khan, University of Colorado-Colorado Springs, for reading and commenting on early drafts.

Author Biographies

Fay Yokomizo Akindes produces educator development programs at the University of Wisconsin System. Formerly she taught communication at the University of Wisconsin-Parkside for 20 years. She was a 2005-06 Fulbright Teaching Scholar at the University of Abomey-Calavi in Benin, West Africa, and taught at Dalkeith House, Midlothian, Scotland in Spring, 2017. Prior to earning her Ph.D. and M.A. Degree at Ohio University, she worked in broadcast promotion and marketing in San Diego (KPBS-FM) and Honolulu (KGMB-TV and KHET/Hawaii Public TV). She was born, raised, and public-schooled on Molokai.

Maha Bali / مها بالي, PhD is an Associate Professor of Practice at the Center for Learning and Teaching at the American University in Cairo, where she has been a faculty developer since 2003. She holds a PhD in Education from the University of Sheffield, UK. She is the co-director of Virtually Connecting and co-founder of Equity Unbound (links below), and is an advisory board member of OneHE and the Erasmus+ Virtual Exchange project. She tweets @bali_maha and blogs at https://blog.mahabali.me https://www.virtuallyconnecting.org/ https://unboundeq.creativitycourse.org/

Dr. Bryony Black is Director of Initial Teacher Education at the University of Sheffield. She joined the university in September 2010, having spent the first 12 years of her career teaching mathematics in secondary schools. Bryony completed her Doctorate in May 2020, focusing on the retention of mathematics leaders in secondary schools in England, and has been working on ways to engage with research into Initial Teacher Education since coming to work at the university.

Gareth Bramley is a Senior Tutor at the University of Law, specialising in the teaching of students for legal practice. He was previously employed as a University Teacher at the University of Sheffield for 9 years, and before that was employed as a Commercial Litigation Solicitor in an International law firm. Gareth is currently undertaking doctoral studies in Education at the University of Sheffield, having previously been awarded with the PGCert in Learning and Teaching and gaining Senior Fellow status with AdvanceHE (formerly the HEA) in 2015. Gareth is currently focusing his pedagogical research on philosophy and education, and is passionate about emotional engagement in learning and teaching.

Anne Butterworth is a senior lecturer in advanced clinical practice (part-time) and a PhD researcher (part-time), funded through the ESRC Grand Union DTP health and wellbeing pathway. Anne is a registered nurse (adult) with a background in community nursing and higher education. Her clinical roles have included working across different regions of England as a district nurse, and in specialist palliative care as a community Macmillan nurse, having qualified as a non-medical prescriber in 2009. She still practices as an RCN accredited Advanced Level Nurse Practitioner in Out-of-Hours/Urgent Care, but also took pandemic public commitments leave in 2020 to work back in the NHS (and is currently helping with the Covid19 vaccination programme).

Anne's PhD study builds on work completed in her Master's degree in applied social research at Manchester University, and it explores the nature of psychological support as part of district nurse provision of palliative care for patients and their families. Through a practitioner-ethnographer approach, informed through engagement with patients, families and practitioners, unique methods will be used to observe care in context and increase understanding of these less visible aspects of care delivered at home. Anne's research interests include palliative and end of life care; community nursing; advanced clinical practice and video-reflexive ethnography.

Dr. Sara Clayson is a Staff Tutor in the School of Education, Childhood, Youth and Sports at the Open University. Sara's teaching career started in the Primary School classroom before moving into Adult Education and Further Education, where she taught literacy skills to long-term unemployed adults aiming to return to work. Her career in Higher Education started when she became an Associate Lecturer in the Arts and Humanities with the Open University. She maintains an Associate Lecturer post as well as her current role as Staff Tutor in Childhood and Youth Studies, teaching a multidisciplinary Arts module and an introduction to Childhood Studies and Child Psychology module. Sara has

Masters degrees from the Open University in English Literature and in Education, a PhD in English Literature from the University of Birmingham and has published on images of androgyny in Victorian popular fiction. Her current research interests on young people's fanfiction writing draws on both English Literature and Childhood and Youth Studies. Her professional interests focus on teacher identity in Higher Education and the use of personal narratives in reflective practice.

Dr. Teresa Cremin is Professor of Education (Literacy) at The Open University. An ex-teacher and ITE tutor, Teresa now undertakes research and consultancy in the UK and abroad. Her socio-cultural research focuses mainly on volitional reading and writing, teachers' literate identities and practices and creative pedagogies. Her recent books include *Children Reading for Pleasure in the Digital Age* (with N. Kucirkova, Sage, 2019), *Writer Identity and the Teaching and Learning of Writing; Storytelling in Early Childhood: Enriching Language, Literacy and Culture*, (Routledge, 2017, edited collections). A Fellow of the English Association, the Academy of Social Sciences, and the Royal Society of the Arts, Teresa is a currently a Trustee of the UK Literacy Association and chair of DfE Reading for pleasure sub-committee. Teresa is passionate about developing readers for life and leads a professional user-community website and wider movement to support the development of children's and teachers' reading for pleasure https://researchrichpedagogies.org/research/reading-for-pleasure.

Arley Cruthers, MFA is a Paralympic medalist, novelist, and writing instructor. As a member of the Canadian women's wheelchair basketball national team, she won two World Championship gold medals and a bronze at the Athens 2004 Paralympic Games. Her first novel, *Post,* was shortlisted for the Commonwealth Writer's Prize in the Best First Novel category and her second novel, *The Time We All Went Marching,* was named to the Globe and Mail's Best 100 Books of 2011 list. She teaches Applied Communications at Kwantlen Polytechnic University, where she also currently serves as the Open Education Teaching Fellow. She's also the author of the OER textbook *Business Writing For Everyone: An Inclusive Guide To Writing in the Workplace.* Arley is passionate about open education, open pedagogy, ungrading, Universal Design for Learning and disability justice. She holds an MFA from the University of Illinois at Urbana-Champaign.

Dr. Justin Dunne is a Staff Tutor at the Open University in the School of Health, Wellbeing and Social Care. Having found his own teenage years somewhat challenging, Justin spent the first half of his career working in youth, community and care settings eventually specialising in treatment for young people with substance misuse problems. His academic career has seen him lead on several health and social care programmes and develop research interests in evidence-based practice with vulnerable young people. This research culminated in a PhD in 2017. Justin has a passion for developing highly reflective health and social care practitioners who are equipped to support the most vulnerable in society.

Tanya Elias is a long-time distance education student who currently lives with her three teenagers in Vancouver, BC. She spends her days working as an occupational training manager for a private company. In her spare time, she continues to study and ask critical questions related to open, distance and digital education. One day, she hopes to be able to go for coffee with another adult. In the meantime, she is researching the implications of scale within the field of open education as an EdD Candidate at the University of Calgary from the comfort of her bedroom office and kitchen table.

Louise Glover is Director of Civic Engagement for the School of Law, having joined the University of Sheffield in September 2010. She convenes Property Law (Land Law and Equity and Trust Law) and a project module titled 'A Practical Perspective on Commercial Property Development'. She directs the Commercial Law student pro bono clinic at University of Sheffield and leads the School's employability provision. She has recently co-authored an article on clinical legal education published in the European Legal Education Journal. Prior to joining the Law School, Louise trained and worked as a solicitor in the City of London, before becoming partner at a law firm in the south of England. She has also acted as a consultant for the London Real Estate group of an international commercial law firm. Louise is currently collaborating on the second edition of a Land Law textbook.

Dr. Kathleen Harris is Dean of the School of Education and Applied Social Sciences, Associate Professor, at Seton Hill University in Greensburg, Pennsylvania. She teaches early childhood and special education. Kathleen received her doctoral degree in Special Education and master's degree in Early Childhood Education at Kent State University and her undergraduate degree in Early Childhood Education and Psychology at Notre Dame College of Ohio. Kathleen's research interests include: children's spirituality, peer interventions, strengths-based leadership, and contemplative practices for young children. Kathleen has taught toddlers to pre-kindergarten, directed early childhood programs, and does professional development trainings for early childhood professionals and families. Kathleen served on the board for Pi Lambda Theta Honor Society, the Pittsburgh Association for the Education of Young Children (PAEYC), and the American Educational Research Association (AERA). Kathleen has published articles in *Young Children, Young Exceptional Children, Childhood Education, International Journal of Children's Spirituality, International Journal of Early Years, International Journal of Holistic Early Learning and Development, Journal of Integrative Pediatrics and Environmental Medicine, Association of Child Life Professionals Bulletin,* and *Early Childhood Education Journal.* She serves on the Parent Council Policy Board for Seton Hill Child Services Head Start in Greensburg, Pennsylvania, the Editorial Board for the *International Journal of Children's Spirituality* and is a Consulting Editor for *Young Children* and Co-Facilitator for Young Children's Spirituality Interest Forum.

Dr. Keith Heggart is an early career researcher with a focus on learning and instructional design, educational technology and civics and citizenship education. He is currently exploring the way that online learning platforms can assist in the formation of active citizenship amongst Australian youth social movements. Keith is a former high school teacher, having worked as a school leader in Australia and overseas, in government and non-government sectors. In addition, he has worked as an Organiser for the Independent Education Union of Australia, and as an independent Learning Designer for a range of organisations.

Karen Littleton (editor) is a coach, poet and Professor of Education at the Open University, UK. She is currently responsible for academic capacity-building within the Faculty of Wellbeing, Education and Language Studies. Karen has research expertise in the psychology of education and collaborative creativity. She has held Professorships in the Psychology of Education at The Open University, UK and at the University of Jyväskylä, Finland. She has also worked as a visiting professor at the University of Helsinki, Finland and Coventry University, UK and held visiting scholarships at: UNAM, Mexico; University of Oulu, Finland; University of Tampere, Finland and the University of Cambridge, UK. Karen is a member of the 'Hornet Press Poetry Collective' and reads her poems at venues in London and across the South East of England. A former writer-in-residence, at Westbury Arts Centre, she founded the community-based 'Poetry Café' and *'Time to Write'* – where writers gather to share, develop their craft and, crucially, write.

Dr. Jeanette Maritz is a Professor in the Department of Health Studies at the University of South Africa (Unisa). She is also a Professor Extraordinary at the University of Stellenbosch, South Africa. Jeanette is a

C rated established researcher and a nurse by profession. Her research interests include qualitative research, coaching, mentoring, postgraduate supervision and identity. Jeanette explores scholarship and professional development from the margins for both faculty and students through different lenses and geographical contexts. Her collaboration with Paul Prinsloo (Unisa) focusses on faculty identity and politics though a Bourdieusian lens. Their more recent exploration includes new materialism allowing for different ontological questions in mapping the diversities of being faculty.

Sean Michael Morris (editor) is Senior Instructor of Learning Design and Technology in the School of Education and Human Development at the University of Colorado Denver. He is the Director of Digital Pedagogy Lab, an international professional development gathering for educators committed to issues of diversity, equity, inclusion, critical digital pedagogy, and imagining a new future for education. Sean also serves as the Director of Educational Partnerships for *Hybrid Pedagogy*, the journal of critical digital pedagogy. He co-authored *An Urgency of Teachers: the Work of Critical Digital Pedagogy*, and co-edited *Critical Digital Pedagogy: A Collection* as well as the forthcoming *The Critical Instructional Design Reader*. Sean has contributed to *Disrupting Digital Humanities, Digital Pedagogy in the Humanities*; *MOOCs and their Afterlives: Experiments in Scale and Access in Higher Education*; *Applied Pedagogies: Strategies for Online Writing Instruction*; and *Critical Examinations of Distance Education Transformation Across Disciplines*.

Dr. Ed Nagelhout is a Professor of Writing and Rhetoric at the University of Nevada, Las Vegas. He received his PhD from Purdue University in 1996. He has co-edited three collections, published more than thirty peer-reviewed articles or book chapters, along with two open-access electronic textbooks, and presented more than one hundred papers on a variety of topics at a wide range of disciplinary, interdisciplinary, and multidisciplinary venues. His research focuses on writing program administration, teaching in digital environments, digital composing, writing in the disciplines, and open-access literacy and learning. Recent publications include "Game design as literacy-first activity: Digital tools with/in literacy instruction" with Fawn Canady for the collection, *Handbook of Research on Integrating Digital Technology with Literacy Pedagogies*; "Linguistic and rhetorical analysis in interdisciplinary health information research" with Barbara St. Pierre Schneider for the *Sage Research Methods Cases: Medicine and Health*; and "To work: Naming, acting on, and modifying in the college literacy 'classroom'" for the *Journal of College*

Literacy and Learning. He plans to play for an over-65 softball travel team when he retires.

Zoe Ollerenshaw, MEd is a former senior lecturer at the School of Law at the University of Sheffield. Zoe worked in practice for 15 years before joining the School of Law, and was recognised by Chambers and Partners' UK Practice Guide as a leader in her field. In 2000 Zoe joined the School of Law, initially to teach upon the Legal Practice Course, but in 2008 moved to lecture on its academic programmes and worked in a number of senior roles in the department to advance student academic development, student welfare, and teaching quality. She successfully completed her MEd in 2013 with her dissertation focussing on student perceptions of effective feedback. Zoe is passionate about the learning, development and support of students academically and for their well being. She was recognised for her enduring commitment to the diverse needs and interests of students successfully serving as the inaugural Faculty of Social Sciences' Faculty Learning and Teaching Director of Widening Participation, and altering or influencing Faculty and University policies in this area. In 2018 Zoe was awarded a University Senate award for Sustained Teaching Excellence. She has contributed to the development of teaching and learning policy, methods and practices and debate locally, nationally and internationally through various conference presentations.

John Parry is a Senior Lecturer in Early Childhood at The Open University, UK. His research interests focus on inclusion, disabled children's experiences of learning situations particularly in early years and primary settings, the development of friendships and early intervention. He has led and co-led several research projects in these areas and has published subsequent papers in the *Journal of Early Childhood Research, Early Years: International Research Journal, International Journal of Early Years Education* and *British Journal of Educational Studies.* He is also co-author of the book *Special Needs in the Early Years* with Sue Roffey and has co-edited four different collections exploring Early Childhood and Inclusion issues for The Open University Press. His most recent work has been with Professor Jonathon Rix developing 'In the Picture', an approach to observing young children at play and engaging with their perspectives. Before moving into Higher Education in 2010, John had been a practitioner in the early childhood sector for over 25 years, firstly as a teacher and then as a co-ordinator of educational support services for pre-school children.

Laurence Pattacini is a University Teacher in the department of Landscape Architecture at the University of Sheffield. She qualified as an architect in Versailles and completed her Master in Urban Design at Oxford Brookes University. She practiced as a designer before joining Higher Education. She has worked in several European countries and has extensive experience in landscape architecture practice. She has been teaching for over twenty years and is now a Senior Fellow of the Higher Education Academy. She has also been involved in several fixed term academic research projects in the UK related to the built environment and the sustainability agenda. She only recently started to engage with pedagogic research. She is particularly interested in issues related to students' engagement and links between studies and practice.

Kate Campbell Pilling qualified as a solicitor in 1999 specialising in commercial property. She joined the School of Law at the University of Sheffield in 2004 where she taught and convened various modules including Property Law, Land Law, Commercial Property Law and legal skills modules in the Centre for Professional Legal Education. She was also Programme Director for the Graduate Diploma in Law. Kate embeds her innovative teaching methods and practices into these modules and has extensive experience in the use of audio feedback and preparing students for assessment having been Director of Assessments for the School and an external examiner and moderator. In 2020 Kate moved roles within the School to teach Land and Equity modules on the LLB and MA Programmes. She is a Senior Fellow of the Higher Education Academy and a co-author of a textbook on Land Law, currently collaborating on the second edition..

Dr. Paul Prinsloo is a Research Professor in Open and Distance Learning (ODL) in the Department of Business Management, College of Economic and Management Sciences, University of South Africa (Unisa). He is a Visiting Professor at the Carl von Ossietzky University of Oldenburg, Germany, a Research Associate for Contact North I Contact Nord (Canada) and a Fellow of the European Distance and E-Learning Network (EDEN) and serves on several editorial boards. In the South African context. Paul has a B3 research rating confirming his considerable international reputation for the high quality and impact of his research outputs. His academic background includes fields as diverse as theology, art history, business management, online learning, and religious studies. Paul is an internationally recognised speaker, scholar and researcher and has published numerous articles in the fields of teaching and learning, student success in distance education contexts, the ethical collection, analysis and use of student data in learning analytics, and (digital) identities. In his collaborative research with Jeanette Maritz (Unisa) on faculty identity in higher education they extensively used and applied Bourdieusian theory and more recently, new materialism in mapping the multiplicities of being and becoming faculty.

Dr. Lucy Rai (editor) qualified and began her career as a child protection social worker in Bristol, UK. She began teaching social work in higher education in 1995, initially in a Further Education College (FE) and since 2001 with the Open University. A common thread across her teaching and scholarship has been on supporting non traditional students to progress in their careers through higher education. Both in FE and in at the Open University, many students come to study with patchy or distant educational preparation, but a wealth of personal and employment based experience. Lucy has retained her close connections between practice, education and scholarship with her research and publications have primarily focused on academic and professional writing in in social work, with a particular interest in reflective writing, identity and emotion. Lucy was the founding director of PRAXIS, the scholarship and innovation centre for the Faculty of Wellbeing, Education and Language Studies at The Open University. PRAXIS has worked closely with the Digital Pedagogy Lab to raise the profile of critical digital pedagogy in the Open University UK. Lucy's current teaching and scholarship focuses on innovating digital pedagogies to support the learning of foundation level learning in health and social care. She also still publishes and supports learning in practice relating to social work writing.

Chloe de los Reyes was born in the Philippines but moved to the United States three months shy of her 13th birthday. Even though she originally wanted to earn a degree in the food industry or related field, she found herself taking more and more English classes during her time at CSUSB. When she received her Bachelor's degree in English Literature, she applied and was accepted to the M.A. in English Composition program at the same university. The program and her work as a writing tutor and an international exchange tutor in Germany allowed her to talk about, as well as piece together, all of the things she was interested in about writing as well as her personal experiences as a multilingual. Upon receiving her M.A., she continued to teach as an adjunct in several departments at CSUSB: in the English Department's First-Year Writing Program, the International Extension Programs, and the Educational Opportunity Program. She also briefly taught at University of La Verne's writing program. All of these sites have allowed her to work with students who have similar backgrounds to hers. In Fall 2019, Chloe de los started a full-time, tenure-track position at Crafton Hills College, where she mostly teaches composition. Much of her work currently is focused on initiatives centered on equity and diversity. Her scholarly interests include academic status, collaboration, multilingual writing, and the intersections of language, identity, and culture.

Sean Robinson, MFA is an educator from the White Mountains of New Hampshire. He holds an MFA from the University of Southern Maine's Stonecoast program, and a Certificate of Advanced Graduate Study from Plymouth State University in Educational Leadership His academic work has been presented at Dartmouth College, UC Berkeley, and at conferences abroad, focusing on the representation of minorities in popular fiction. His research interests also include the idea of place in writing and pedagogy, which has led him on research trips with the support of Plymouth State University, the University of Washington, and the Marion and Jasper Whiting Foundation to the American Pacific Northwest, Ireland, and Italy.

Joe Stommel has been a mental health professional and instructor since 1974 and was Colorado Department of Corrections Administrator of Alcohol and Drug Services from 1990-2008. He has done extensive training and authored numerous publications. He retired in 2008 and is now a consultant and online college instructor.

Neil Summers is a staff tutor in the Faculty of Wellbeing, Education and Language Studies (WELS) and has 40 years of experience as a practitioner lecturer and researcher. Neil started his career as nurse practitioner and then moved into Nurse Education. He initially worked at the Bath & Swindon College of Health studies and the University of the West of England where he worked as a Senior Lecture and Associate Head of School. He has research and practice interests in supporting people that live with various conditions including mental health and learning disabilities. He has experience of teaching and facilitating mixed groups of professionals, students, carers and users of services.

Neil is also a practising counsellor and offers support to young people, adults and families. He offers different types support, to help people explore greater independence, aiming to help people better cope with current and future issues they may experience.

Joan Upson, MEd is a Senior University Teacher in the School of Law at the University of Sheffield. She is Director of Professional Development (Teaching) and Director of the LLB Programme in the School of Law, as well as being the module convenor for a number of subjects across the Law programmes. During her career she has gained experience at a number of institutions where her work was focused on European and Environmental law, before coming to Sheffield some 15 years ago. At Sheffield her work has been more civil law based and outside of the law, focused upon staff and student development. She is a Senior Fellow of the Higher Education Academy and recently completed the MEd at Sheffield. Her continuing interest in pedagogic research and the student base in particular have led her to embark upon a doctoral programme in education at Sheffield and her work in these areas has led her to present at a number of local, national and international conferences.

Susannah Wilson started her career teaching English at secondary level. She then moved to the further education (FE) sector, where her love of post-it notes and use of sock puppets in the classroom – unremarked upon at secondary level – bewildered and bemused her new students. She is an experienced teacher in both face-to-face and online learning contexts, and has become increasing interested in the ways that technology can be used to enhance dialogue within an online learning context. Her research interests include assessment and feedback literacy. She is increasingly passionate about the role of FE education generally, and the role of technologies in online and blended learning contexts.

Dr. Jim Wolper has AB (Harvard, 1976) and PhD (Brown, 1982) degrees in Mathematics (Algebraic Geometry). He became a flight instructor in 1995, and has since worked part- time as a professional pilot, flying the Beech King Air, a 9-seat turboprop. In addition to many research papers, he wrote Understanding Mathematics for Aircraft Navigation (McGraw–Hiill, 2001). His current research focus areas are the foundations of Mathematics and Mathematical writing.

Dr. Sarah Yardley is a Consultant in Palliative Medicine, Central & North West London NHS Foundation Trust Honorary Clinical Senior Lecturer, Marie Curie Palliative Care Research Department, University College London and THIS Institute Post-doctoral Fellow.

As a clinical academic, Sarah is interested in how patients, families, carers, and healthcare professionals do the work of frontline day-to-day healthcare and make sense of their experiences; hospital-community and specialist-generalist interfaces in care; and patient transitions between hospital and community care, including care in Emergency

Departments and Acute Medical Units. Sarah's research expertise is in qualitative methodologies, applied to health professions education, palliative care, psychiatry and patient safety through study of sociocultural influences, informal learning and 'real world' practices. Her research seeks to understand and improve human-dependent healthcare such as the impact therapeutic and professional collegiate relationships have on current and future care. Sarah is an innovative methodologist whose PhD received the ASME New Researcher Award (2010). She is also on the Editorial Board for the journal *Palliative Medicine* and works clinically in a large palliative care service (hospital and community).

Dr. Xia Zhu is a Lecturer in Marketing at the Open University, UK. Previously, she worked at Keele University and Sheffield Hallam University. Xia obtained her MSc in Marketing from UMIST, and her PhD in Marketing from University of Manchester. Her subject-based research focuses on *services marketing* and *business-to-business marketing*. She has been awarded by British Academy/Leverhulme Small Research Grant to examine social media engagement during museum visits. She has a number of publications and is a peer reviewer for a number of academic journals and funding bodies.

Xia has gained experience of teaching marketing across undergraduate and postgraduate levels at various universities. She has served as External Examiner in the wider academic community. Her externally focused work also includes working with the Open University's Validation Partnership Team and acting as Academic Reviewer for the university's national and international partner institutions. Xia is interested in exploring *online distance learning, student experience, academic professional development, and higher education internationalisation*. She has been working with academics internationally on different projects. Before her academic career, she worked as a business development manager in a British company expanding its business in the Far East. Xia is Fellow of the Higher Education Academy.